THE
GREAT ENIGMA

(1892)

William Samuel Lilly

ISBN 0-7661-0133-9

Request our FREE CATALOG of over 1,000
Rare Esoteric Books
Unavailable Elsewhere

Freemasonry * Akashic * Alchemy * Alternative Health * Ancient Civilizations * Anthroposophy * Astral * Astrology * Astronomy * Aura * Bacon, Francis * Bible Study * Blavatsky * Boehme * Cabalah * Cartomancy * Chakras * Clairvoyance * Comparative Religions * Divination * Druids * Eastern Thought * Egyptology * Esoterism * Essenes * Etheric * Extrasensory Perception * Gnosis * Gnosticism * Golden Dawn * Great White Brotherhood * Hermetics * Kabalah * Karma * Knights Templar * Kundalini * Magic * Meditation * Mediumship * Mesmerism * Metaphysics * Mithraism * Mystery Schools * Mysticism * Mythology * Numerology * Occultism * Palmistry * Pantheism * Paracelsus * Parapsychology * Philosophy * Plotinus * Prosperity & Success * Psychokinesis * Psychology * Pyramids * Qabalah * Reincarnation * Rosicrucian * Sacred Geometry * Secret Rituals * Secret Societies * Spiritism * Symbolism * Tarot * Telepathy * Theosophy * Transcendentalism * Upanishads * Vedanta * Wisdom * Yoga * *Plus Much More!*

KESSINGER PUBLISHING, LLC

http://www.kessingerpub.com

email: books@kessingerpub.com

THE GREAT ENIGMA

By WILLIAM SAMUEL LILLY

> . . . οἱ θεοὶ σθένουσι χᾠ κείνων κρατῶν
> νόμος· νόμῳ γὰρ τοὺς θεοὺς ἡγούμεθα,
> καὶ ζῶμεν, ἄδικα καὶ δίκαι' ὡρισμένοι·
> EURIPIDES

NEW YORK
D. APPLETON AND COMPANY
1892

LONDON:
PRINTED BY WILLIAM CLOWES AND SONS, LIMITED,
STAMFORD STREET AND CHARING CROSS.

TO

THE VISCOUNT HALIFAX.

My dear Lord Halifax,

The book which I now offer to you is of the nature of an *argumentum ad hominem*, addressed to a class of readers practically outside the Christian pale. It is an inquiry, from their point of view, into the tenableness of the religion which for more than a thousand years has supplied the foremost nations of the world with an answer to The Great Enigma of human existence. Unquestionably, a feeling that this answer will no longer suffice is very widely prevalent. The professed teachers of Christianity, from Leo XIII. to "General" Booth, whatever their differences, agree in confessing that its hold over the modern mind is rudely shaken. The question of questions now before mankind is whether "the good Lord Jesus has had His day" and must be numbered among the dead gods, or whether He is, in very truth, alive for evermore, and His life the light of men.

The following pages present, in aid of the solution of that question, certain considerations which have proved helpful to me, with special reference to the religious difficulties peculiar to these times. Possibly, they may be of use to some who find themselves unable to employ the old theological symbols. In dedicating the book to you, by your kind permission, I desire not merely to pay a tribute to a deeply prized friendship, but also to testify my sympathy with much of the work done by the movement within the Anglican Communion associated, in a special way, for many years, with your honoured name: a movement which appears to me to have largely increased the power for good of the National Church as "a serviceable breakwater"—to use Cardinal Newman's happy expression—against the abounding impiety of the age.

Thinking thus of the Church of England, I, although not of it, would say with our revered friend, whose name I have just written, that "I should wish to avoid everything (except, indeed, under the direct call of duty, and this is a material exception) which went to weaken its hold upon the public mind, or to unsettle its establishment, or to embarrass and lessen its maintenance of those great Christian and Catholic principles and doctrines which it has, up to this time, successfully preached." I may add that the movement for its disestablishment seems to me one of the most retrograde and disreputable manœuvres of our party politics. It is the common teaching of the masters of political science, from Plato to Hegel, that to the perfection of the social organism, as of the individuals composing it, religion is necessary. Among English writers no one has more strongly protested against the repudiation of this doctrine than Mr. Gladstone. Thus, in his once famous treatise on *The State in its Relations with the Church*, he denounces " the separation of religion from government, Firstly, because it asserts practical atheism, that is a great and moral human agency, knowingly, deliberately, and permanently divested of regard to God. Secondly, because it asserts that atheism in its most authentic form, namely, by casting out its antagonist, religion, from what are most permanent and authoritative among men, their public politics. Thirdly, because the assertion is made, not by individuals alone, but by masses, invested with political power, and, under the most wretched infatuation, claiming it as a right of freedom thus to banish themselves from the Divine protection and regard." No doubt this view no longer dominates either the general mind, or the mind of the distinguished person who thus expressed it with the copious and vehement rhetoric of which he is a master. But that fact raises no presumption whatever against its validity. And those of us who decline to recognize in ballot-boxes the sole organ of political truth, and in majorities told by head the one test of right and wrong in the public order, are assuredly bound to bear witness to truer conceptions of the social organism than such as now find popular favour. "Things are what they are." Their nature is not in the least changed by the fond wishes of an age which sets up expedience as the unique rule of legislation, and material well-being as the only end of the State.

So much to justify my description of the movement for the disestablishment of the National Church as retrograde. I have also called it disreputable. There can be no question at all that the number of Englishmen, whatever their speculative opinions, who honestly wish to see the Church of England disestablished, is inconsiderable. Equally beyond question is it that the agitation for that end is being forced upon the party now in power by "an insolent and aggressive faction" animated by sectarian hatred. The faction of which I speak is, in truth, an amalgam of two sects: the revolutionary *doctrinaires* who are inspired by a Jacobinical dislike of Christianity, and that baser portion of the Dissenting interest—"most unblest phrase," Coleridge used to call it—whose dominant motive is jealousy of the social superiority of the Anglican clergy. The wanton sacrifice of a venerable institution which, apart from its directly religious claims, is of great secular utility, as a vast organization of charity and a widely effective school of moral culture, might well seem to politicians not wholly given over to majoritymongering, a heavy price to pay for the support of the brotherhood of Chadband and Stiggins, and their strange allies, the English admirers and disciples of Hébert and Chaumette. May we not reasonably hope that the event will justify Mr. Gladstone's words, in the treatise from which I have quoted: "Our country seems to promise, at least, a more organized, tenacious, and determined resistance to the efforts against national religion than any other country which is prominent upon the great stage of the civilized world"?

I am, my dear Lord Halifax,
Most sincerely yours,
W. S. LILLY.

ATHENÆUM CLUB,
October 22, 1892.

Fragments of the present work which have appeared in the Quarterly, Fortnightly, *and* Contemporary Reviews, *and in the* Nineteenth Century, *are here reprinted by permission of the respective editors, whose courtesy I desire to acknowledge, with thanks. And I am indebted to my friend, the Rev. Dr. William Barry, for his great kindness in reading the proof sheets of the book, and in favouring me with various sentences and suggestions scattered up and down it.*

W. S. L.

SUMMARY.

CHAPTER I.

THE TWILIGHT OF THE GODS.

	PAGE
Man alone of all animals wonders at his own existence. "What am I? Whence am I? Why am I? What is my final end? What the means to it?"—that is The Great Enigma with which the generations of mortal men have ever been confronted . .	1
The answers have been sought in philosophies and in religions	2
Causation is, in fact, the great problem both of philosophy and of religion; but they approach it from different sides	2
The common ground and the last explanation of both philosophy and religion are certain great verities, bound together in links of necessary thought, which render a philosophy of religion possible . .	3
Hitherto the great majority of men have sought the solution of The Great Enigma in religions, and in the religion which is behind all religions . .	4

xii SUMMARY.

PAGE

Religions have explained the human by the superhuman. They have contained—even the poorest and lowest of them—an ethical element in virtue of which this life was viewed, more or less clearly, as a period of probation 4

But in Christianity this ethical element assumes a very different character from what it possesses in any other mode of faith. Christianity proclaims that man is made and fashioned by the hands of the Divine Creator; that he is capable of the perfect felicity of the Beatific Vision which is his true end, and that the way to that end is by a right ordering of his will in this state of moral discipline . . . 4

This is the solution of The Great Enigma taught, in the Catechism, to every Catholic child: "Why did God make you?—To know Him, love Him, and serve Him in this world, and to be happy for ever with Him in the next." To incorporate moral culture with religion is among the most important achievements of Christianity 4

In the present day, however, religions—Christianity among them—are widely supposed to have been "found out" 5

They are explained by professors of the science of religion as the accidents of periods: the poems in which man, at sundry times and in divers manners, has enshrined his ideals of the Divine, his aspirations towards the Unseen 6

Nor does this explanation stop short at the Christian Trinity. The Third hypostasis of the Sacred Triad, it will have to be merely the personification of a

SUMMARY.

	PAGE
metaphor. The Second it accounts of as the deification, under Platonic influences, of the Son of Mary. The First is stripped of the ecumenical attributes wherewith He had been invested, and is revealed as the national God of a small tribe of Western Semites	6
The Sacred Books of Christianity are subjected to a criticism which issues in revolutionary views as to their date and origin, and which eliminates the supernatural element from them	7
Moreover, physical science has introduced us to quite other conceptions, both of man and of his place in the universe, than those more or less closely interwoven with the old theological dogmas . .	10
Doubt is in the air. People can no more escape from it than from cholera or influenza . . .	15
Nor is the general doubt merely about this or that dogma. Unquestionable is it that, as the old creeds have lost their hold upon men's minds, the Theistic conception which they more or less worthily enshrined, has become faint. Nor, again, is it confined to the domain of religion. The scepticism of the age extends to all first principles, and is nowhere more signally manifested than in the province of ethics	16
From one point of view, indeed, it is extremely illogical that the decay of religious belief should affect ethical convictions, for the spheres of theology and of moral philosophy are, in themselves, distinct. The very knowledge which we have, by our natural reason, of justice and injustice suffices to give rise to a strict ethical obligation . . . , .	18

But that a rule is conformable with reason is not enough

xiv   *SUMMARY.*

                                                                                          PAGE

to ensure obedience to it. The true principle of duty for the sake of duty is "too bright and good for human nature's daily food." The vast majority of men need the prospect of retributive happiness and suffering to keep them in the right way . . 24

Hence the ideas of moral good and evil, and of rewards and punishments beyond the grave, properly find place in dogmatic religious teaching 25

Christianity is, and cannot keep from being, a vast system of moral discipline. For a thousand years it has taught the foremost nations of the world what "to believe and to do." And its rules of action must share in the discredit cast upon its articles of faith. It is impossible, practically, to view any ethical problem apart from The Great Enigma of the meaning and end of life which fundamentally underlies all morality 25

In the present volume it will first be assumed, for the purpose of the argument, that the solution of that Enigma presented by Theistic belief, and especially by Christianity, is discredited, and the other solutions offered us instead will be considered both in their theoretical and practical aspects. And then the question will be examined whether Theism in general, and the Christian religion in particular, are so utterly untenable as is very generally contended . . 25

The book is of the nature of an *argumentum ad hominem*, and is written for the benefit, not of those who agree with the author, but of those who do not . . 26

There are really, in good logic, only two answers, besides Theism, to the Great Enigma: Atheism and

SUMMARY.

Agnosticism; by Atheism being meant the dogmatic denial of God, and by Agnosticism the mental attitude of doubt, suspension of judgment, nescience concerning Him 27

And of Agnosticism there are two varieties: the merely critical and negative, which maintains that we cannot know whether or no a Divine Noumenon exists; and the scientific or affirmative, which asserts His existence, but denies that He can be known . . 29

CHAPTER II.

ATHEISM.

By an Atheist is meant, in this work, one who dogmatically denies the existence of a First Cause or Creator of all things, "ruling the universe and holding moral relations with mankind" . . . 35

It may be truly objected that such dogmatic denial is not, in itself, worth answering, since "a demonstrative proof of the non-existence of God, assuredly, no one ever has found nor will find" . . . 36

But there is a very practical consideration which invests Atheism with much importance. It is among the masses, who are "as incapable of thinking as they are of flying," and to whom political power has everywhere passed, or is passing, that the propagandists of Atheism are most active and most successful 38

Their methods differ in different countries, but in all worketh one and the selfsame spirit . . .	38
In Germany, Atheism assumes the form of the crassest, coarsest, and most consistent Materialism, and is closely allied with Socialism	38
In England it occupies itself chiefly with attacks upon the Sacred Books of Christianity, the plenary inspiration of which is the corner-stone of the popular religion	39
But France presents the completest view of the Atheistic propaganda; and what Atheism is in France, it is in the Latin races generally	41
The best revelation of it is afforded by certain Catechisms which have been prepared by zealous men as instruments for the atheizing of that country. Notable among these compositions is M. Monteil's *Catéchisme du Libre-Penseur*, which presents an admirably clear account of the dogmas proposed by Atheists in supercession of the old religious and ethical doctrines .	42
The work is divided into three sections, dealing, respectively, with God, Religion, and Morals . .	44
God, it teaches, is "an expression, the exact value of which is the material world, and All is matter" .	45
It continues that "the divine individuality is a lie;" that "we ought not to believe in the existence of the individual named God whom most religions have presented to us," because "such a God has no existence;" and that, "since everything belongs to the material order, the soul does not exist" . . .	48

Religion it pronounces to have "proceeded from the

SUMMARY. xvii

PAGE

foolish deistic hypothesis;" and the Christian religion, in particular, it declares "baneful and deadly; in Jehovah as in Jesus, in the Pentateuch as in the Gospels:" an *exitiabilis superstitio* justly proscribed by the philanthropic pagans of the decadent Roman empire 55

It urges, "Let us abandon religion completely, and take refuge in Philosophy—the product of all reason, and the source of all morality" 62

The "Philosophy" thus commended amounts to this: that man is naturally good: that the passions are the true guides of human life: that their gratification is the true end of human life: and that other life there is none 65

And morality, we are told, is "the sentiment which prescribes to us prudent conduct, and is determined by the reason;" the reason, it would appear, being "nothing but phosphorus" . . . 66

This is the New Gospel that the poor have preached to them as a substitute for a Theism which reasons of righteousness, temperance, and judgment to come . 66

To use the elementary schools as a means for inculcating it, has been the cherished object of the antichristian sectaries who have so largely obtained political power throughout Europe 68

They are training the coming generation to believe that the answer to The Great Enigma is not moral, but material: to put aside faith in the Divine as a senseless and servile superstition; to find the rule of right and wrong in self-interest; to see in ethics only a regulation of police; to acquiesce in physical fatality; and to practise a brutal egoism . . 68

xviii *SUMMARY.*

PAGE

Such are the human animals, with the wild beast unchained in them, which Atheism is rearing as the sovereigns of the democratic future . . . 68

CHAPTER III.

CRITICAL AGNOSTICISM.

Of the merely Sceptical or Critical Agnosticism which is content with professing nescience of God, no better view can be obtained than that which is exhibited by M. Renan's career and writings . . . 71

His spiritual history is the spiritual history of millions writ large. He used his incomparable literary skill to interpret the mind of his generation to itself. And this is the chief cause of his influence . . 72

Another cause is his intellectual opulence. A philologist, a historian, a philosopher, a publicist, he appealed to thoughtful men of every variety of mental character; taking them captive by the breadth of his erudition and the abundance of his ideas, no less than by the magic of his style 74

In order to appreciate M. Renan's influence as a teacher, it will be well to inquire first into the intellectual constituents of his character. And here much help will be derived from his *Souvenirs d'Enfance et de Jeunesse*,—a work, which, as he tells us, he wrote "in order to transmit to others the theory of the universe which he carries in himself;" which we may indeed take as presenting his answer to The Great Enigma 77

SUMMARY.

	PAGE
But all his other writings may, in a true sense, be regarded as a commentary upon his autobiography; and there is no reason for questioning his sincerity	78
As a Breton, he possessed a vivid yet chastened and inexpansive imagination; while to the Gascon blood, which came to him through his mother, he owed " une certaine habileté dans l'art d'amener le cliquetis des mots et des idées," and "le penchant à trancher beaucoup de difficultés par un sourire"	80
Everything in his early years seemed to indicate for him a modest ecclesiastical career in Brittany	81
And during his time at the Little Seminary of St. Nicholas du Chardonnet, no question as to his vocation to the priesthood occurred to him	83
But in the course of his four years at the Grand Seminary of St. Sulpice, the physical sciences — especially general natural history and physiology — greatly attracted him, and his studies in this department shook his confidence in metaphysics	84
Later on in his career at the Grand Seminary, he devoted himself specially to Theology and Biblical Exegesis, and gradually became convinced of the impossibility of demonstrating that the Christian religion is, more specially than any other, divine and revealed; further, it appeared to him certain, that, in the field of reality accessible to our observation, no supernatural event, no miracle has ever occurred	87
Again, historical facts seemed to him absolutely irreconcilable with the theory that the doctrines of Christianity, as they were defined at Trent, or even at Nicæa, were what the Apostles originally taught	87

xx   *SUMMARY.*

                                                              PAGE
While his mind was revolving these matters, he betook
   himself to the study, first of Hebrew, and then of
   German, which introduced him to the new exegesis
   distinctive of the nineteenth century; the result
   being that "the traditional thesis" as to the date,
   authorship, and inerrancy of the Hebrew Sacred
   Books—a thesis which he had been taught to consider
   essential to Christianity—soon grew incredible to
   him   89

The conclusion of the whole matter for him was that
   "his direct study of Christianity, undertaken in the
   most serious spirit, did not leave him enough faith
   to be a sincere priest; while, on the other hand, it
   inspired him with too much respect to allow of his
   resigning himself to play an odious comedy with
   beliefs most worthy of respect"   .   .   .   89

He had the courage of his convictions; and on the 6th
   of October, 1845, he quitted Saint-Sulpice, leaving
   behind him the faith which he had once hoped to
   teach   89

M. Renan was what he called himself, "un prêtre
   manqué:" and the work of his life was to engraft
   modern criticism upon his religious temperament.
   The faith of his childhood dwelt with him as a
   sentiment. Its poetry survived, side by side with the
   criticism which had been fatal to it as a creed. His
   utterances differed, according as it was the poet, or the
   critic, that spoke   92

He was, in fact, a poet penetrated by the beauty, dominated
   by the majesty of the religious sentiment. He was
   also a critic whose last word was that the Object of the
   religious sentiment—if Object there be—is beyond

SUMMARY.

our knowledge : that we can affirm nothing of it, not
even its existence 97

But his scepticism was not confined to the domain of religion.
In the province of morality he found the same fundamental doubt. Here, too, his first dogma was the
rejection of all dogmas. "Sa pensée de derrière la
tête, c'est que la vertu, non plus que toute autre chose
ne supporte l'examen; on soulève le voile et, là
comme partout, ou découvre qu'il n'y a rien dessous."
Critical Agnosticism is as fatal to the idea of Duty as
is the most dogmatic Atheism . . . 98

His ethical Agnosticism sprung from his religious Agnosticism. And of his religious Agnosticism he has
himself given us the history. Like so many others
in this age, in unlearning Christianity he unlearned
Theism. He illustrates, in a very striking manner,
Cardinal Newman's dictum that " to deny revelation
is the way to deny natural religion " . . . 105

We have seen that the reasons why he ceased to believe
in Christianity were, mainly, two: his inability to
receive " the traditional thesis" regarding the date,
authorship, and inerrancy of the Sacred Books of
Christianity, and his conviction that miracles never
have happened and never can happen . . 105

With regard to the first of these, it must be frankly
admitted that if Christianity depended upon a pseudo-
scientific view of certain venerable documents, formed
at an unscientific period, and irreconcilable with the
conclusions of true science, Christianity would be
doomed 106

But to suppose Christianity founded upon that collection

of ancient documents called the Bible is historically false. It is certain that no authorized New Testament canon existed until the latter half of the second century. It is equally certain that the mission of the Author of Christianity was not to promote the formation of a volume, which, long centuries after, should become " the religion of Protestants," but to establish a society. The Bible is, in fact, the creation of the Catholic Church, from which other varieties of Christianity have received it. And the Catholic Church, while declaring it in all matters of faith and morals divinely inspired throughout, has never pronounced how far that inspiration extends—has never formally committed herself to " the traditional thesis," which has come down from uncritical ages . . . 107

Next, as to M. Renan's peremptory declaration that "there never has been a supernatural fact," " Quod gratis asseritur, gratis negatur," would, in good logic, be a sufficient reply. It is a question of evidence . 110

M. Renan, in terms, acknowledged this, and professed to repudiate the *a priori* argument. But, as is clear from many passages in his writings, he was, consciously or unconsciously, under its influence. It was a first principle with him that a supernatural fact — a miracle—is impossible, because it would be abnormal: an infraction of the order of the universe: a violation of law 110

But everything depends upon what is meant by "norm," "order of the universe," "law." The invincible prejudice against the miraculous, now so common, is, in truth, an expression of that abounding materialism which denies the spiritual principle in man and in

SUMMARY. xxiii

PAGE

nature, and which, identifying law with physical necessity, issues in physical fatalism . . . 111

Again, " What are miracles for us, that is, what are they for the practical use of our understanding, but events in the world with the laws of whose working we are, and must always remain, utterly unacquainted?" . 111

That such events have occurred, and do occur, seems absolutely certain; and when intelligent men are found dogmatically asserting that they do not occur, we can only suppose that these dogmatists have not looked into the evidence, or that they are under the influence of a first principle which disqualifies them for weighing it 112

M. Renan constantly speaks of the miraculous as "irrational" and "absurd." But "irrational" means contrary to reason; "absurd" means contradictory, impossible. Do we assert that which is contrary to reason, or contradictory, or impossible, when we say that there are events with the laws of whose working we are, and ever must remain, unacquainted? . 115

The criticism whereon M. Renan founded the Agnosticism of which we have taken him as a typical exponent, is inadequate to support the vast edifice of doubt which he reared upon it 115

CHAPTER IV.

SCIENTIFIC AGNOSTICISM.

The Scientific Agnosticism, which is the subject of this chapter, will be best viewed as exhibited by Mr. Herbert Spencer, who is generally recognized as its most complete and methodical expositor . . 117

xxiv   *SUMMARY.*

                                                                    PAGE

Mr. Spencer bestows upon his speculations the name of
"The Synthetic Philosophy;" and philosophy he
defines as "completely unified knowledge;" his
Scientific Agnosticism proposes to give a solution of
The Great Enigma: to explain the source of life, the
meaning of life, the end of life, and the conduct of
life 120

The foundation of Mr. Spencer's philosophy is the distinction between the Unknowable and the Knowable.
The sentiment of a First Cause, infinite and absolute,
he considers the eternal and secure basis of all
religion. This Deity, whom, hidden more or less
under anthropomorphic disguises, the votaries of all
creeds ignorantly worship, declares he unto them as
"The Unknowable" 121

Next, turning to the physical sciences, he regards all
forces as manifestations of the dynamic energy everywhere diffused, which co-ordinates the whole range
of phenomena, past, present, and future: an energy
the essence of which escapes us. Thus the last
word of physical science, as of religion, is that "the
Power which the Universe manifests to us is inscrutable:" and in "the ultimate truth" of The Unknowable he finds "the basis of their reconciliation" 122

We can know, he holds, in the strict sense of knowing,
only the phenomenal manifestations of The Unknowable, and these we can know only as purely relative
and subjective realities. "Even the highest achievements of science are resolvable into mental relations
of co-existence and sequence, so co-ordinated as
exactly to tally with certain relations of co-existence
and sequence that occur externally" . . . 123

SUMMARY.

These manifestations, "called by some 'impressions' and 'ideas,'" Mr. Spencer prefers to distinguish as "vivid" and "faint;" manifestations that occur under the conditions of sensuous perception being "faint," and such as occur under the conditions known as those of reflection, or memory, or imagination, or ideation being "vivid" . . . 123

"This profoundest of distinctions between the manifestations of The Unknowable," he continues, "we recognize by grouping them into *self* and *non-self*. These faint manifestations, forming a continuous whole, differing from the others in the quantity, quality, cohesion, and condition of existence of its parts, we call the *ego*: and these vivid manifestations indissolubly bound together in relatively immense masses, and having independent conditions of existence, we call the *non-ego*; or rather, and more truly, each order of manifestations carries with it the irresistible implication of some power that manifests itself; and by the words *ego* and *non-ego* respectively, we mean the power that manifests itself in the faint forms, and the power that manifests itself in the vivid forms" 123

"The totality of my consciousness," he further writes, "is divisible into a faint aggregate which I call my mind; a special part of the vivid aggregate cohering with this in various ways, which I call my body; and the rest of the vivid aggregate which has no such connection with the faint aggregate. This special part of the vivid aggregate, which I call my body, proves to be a part through which the rest of the vivid aggregate works changes in the faint, and through which the faint works certain changes in the vivid." And, "the root-conception of existence, beyond consciousness, becomes that of resistance, *plus* some force which the resistance measures" . 124

Mr. Spencer's philosophy, in fact, requires as "a primordial proposition," as "a datum," the acceptance of these two separate aggregates, as constituting the world of consciousness, and the world beyond consciousness, and the ascription of both to the action of one single cause, which he terms, The Unknowable. Thus is "the unification of science complete," and "philosophy reaches its goal" . . . 124

Mr. Spencer's theory may be shortly and accurately described as an attempt to find the solution of the problem of the universe in a sole law: the persistence of force under multiform transformations. Physical forces, vital forces, mental forces, social forces, are all only different manifestations of the selfsame force. Cosmology, Biology, Psychology, Sociology, Ethics— all are to be explained by the persistence, under various modifications, of that manifestation of The Unknowable. The Spencerian philosophy is, in fact, a vast system of speculative physics . . . 125

There are three fundamental doctrines upon which it rests: his doctrine of Causation, of the Relativity of Knowledge, and of The Unknowable. Each will be examined in detail 129

First, then, as to Causation. The unity of natural forces is by no means established, and the correlation of mental and physical forces is a mere nude hypothesis. No equivalence can be shown between neurosis and psychosis; nor can life and energy be brought under Mr. Spencer's doctrine of the Per-

SUMMARY. xxvii

sistence of Force, which, as taught by him, is an amalgam of physical dogmatism and metaphysical error 129

Mr. Spencer's doctrine of the Relativity of Knowledge is, in substance, this: "That what we are conscious of as properties of matter, even down to its weight and resistance, are but subjective affections produced by objective agencies that are unknown and unknowable." But perception is a much more delicate matter than Mr. Spencer imagines. Passive sensation does not constitute knowledge in the true sense. The instrument of knowledge is thought. There is a perception of sense: there is an analytical interpretation, an intellectual appropriation of that perception. The idea which the intellect obtains concerning its various objects is not wholly relative. Mr. Spencer ignores the fact that the relations of things are rational; that is, that they possess an element of objectivity. He does not recognize the category of Being 138

Next as to The Unknowable, Mr. Spencer teaches that "though the Absolute cannot in any manner or degree be known, in the strict sense of knowing, yet we find that its positive existence is a necessary datum of consciousness: that, so long as consciousness continues, we cannot for an instant rid ourselves of this datum: and that thus the belief which this datum constitutes, has a higher warrant than any other whatever." But the very nature of intelligence forbids such a conception of the Absolute as this. All knowledge, according to Mr. Spencer, is relative. It is rigidly restricted to phenomena. If this is so, if our knowledge is limited to conditioned experience,

xxviii   *SUMMARY.*

                                                                                                                PAGE

we cannot possibly know, in any sense of knowing, the unconditioned. All consciousness, according to Mr. Spencer, is constituted under forms and limits: it belongs to the phenomenal order. That is for him the one mode of consciousness. If you abolish the limits, you abolish the consciousness . . 145

The truth is, that as Mr. Spencer's erroneous theory of relativity has led him to label the Supreme Object of knowledge Unknowable, so a true theory of relativity would have saved him from the antinomies in which he is hopelessly involved with regard to this matter. The more the manifold relations of things are examined, the more clearly are they seen to be rational: they testify of Objective Reason. Mr. Spencer's Scientific Agnosticism is an outrage upon reason. He puts aside the self-affirmations of the intellect—those *a priori* or necessary truths which are laws of thought because they are absolute uniformities, intuitively known as self-evident—and these are the primary sources of all knowledge; they are "what God eternally thinks." In them, and not in any collocation and displacement of molecules, is the ultimate basis of metaphysics . . 152

But Mr. Spencer's Scientific Agnosticism is not merely speculative. He preaches new morals as well as a new faith. He considers that since "moral injunctions are losing the authority given by their supposed sacred origin, the secularization of morals, the establishment of rules of right conduct on a scientific basis, is a pressing need," lest "by the disappearance of the code of supernatural ethics" a moral "vacuum" should ensue 157

SUMMARY. xxix

PAGE

Mr. Spencer, however, greatly errs—as has been pointed out in Chapter I.—in supposing transcendental moralists to regard divine commands as the only possible guides in morals. The old *data* of ethics which have guided the civilized world for so many generations are not "supernatural," though they are supersensuous 159

This, by the way. We proceed to examine that "fitter regulative system of conduct" which Mr. Spencer invites mankind to accept 161

There are, in truth, only two great schools in ethics. There is the school which seeks to ascertain morality from the spiritual nature of man by methods purely rational. There is the school which denies the transcendental ground of man's being, and which seeks to derive morality from his animal nature, by methods merely physical. There is the school which finds the real aboriginal principle of morals in pleasure or agreeable feeling. There is the school which finds it in intuitions of equity, held to be primordial and independent elements of our nature . . . 161

There can be no question to which of these schools Mr. Spencer belongs. His philosophy, viewed as a whole, is, as we have seen, an attempt to construct a complete scheme of the universe by means of the persistence, under various transformations, of that manifestation of the Unknowable which he calls Force; to unify knowledge of phenomena, the only knowledge held by him to be possible, and to trace everywhere the one cosmical *processus*. "Moral phenomena" he considers as phenomena of evolution; and he expressly tells us that "a redistribution of matter and motion constitutes evolution." He attempts

xxx SUMMARY.

PAGE

to construct a science of morals out of physical elements by means of his one formula . . 162

Such is Mr. Spencer's method in moral philosophy. We proceed to consider his application of it, and to see how he manufactures morality from prior conditions that were unmoral 167

He tells us "Ethics has for its subject-matter that form which universal conduct assumes, during the last stage of its evolution." By "conduct" he means "acts adjusted to ends, or else the adjustment of acts to ends." And "always acts are called good or bad, as they are well or ill adjusted to ends." Conduct which subserves "the welfare of self, of offspring, and of fellow-citizens" "is regarded as relatively good:" but "evolution becomes the highest possible when the conduct simultaneously achieves the greatest totality of life in self, in offspring, and in fellow-men:" the reason being that in Mr. Spencer's philosophy life is regarded as the highest good . 167

Moral good, then, according to Mr. Spencer, does not differ *essentially* from physical good. The goodness of a hunter and the goodness of a hero, the goodness of a sausage and the goodness of a saint, are for Mr. Spencer, *in kind*, identical. And the test of goodness is always the same: not the character of the agent, not the quality of his intention, but the pleasurable tendency of his acts. Virtue possesses for Mr. Spencer no primordial and independent character. It is whatever, as a means, promotes, on the whole, the supreme end—pleasure 169

This is Mr. Spencer's treatment of the fundamental question wherewith ethics is concerned: the nature of moral good: the difference between right and wrong. Further, he believes "that the experiences of utility organized and consolidated through all past generations of the human race, have been producing corresponding nervous modifications, which, by continued transmission and accumulation, have become in us certain faculties of moral intuition—certain emotions responding to right and wrong conduct, which have no apparent basis in the individual experiences of utility." "The moral motive," he lays down, "is constituted by representations of consequences which the acts naturally produce." "These are the restraints properly distinguished as moral." And "since with the restraints thus generated is always joined the thought of external coercion, there arises the notion of obligation;" a notion which he afterwards interprets as equivalent to the indispensableness of any means towards a given end,—the means being that which we are obliged to employ, if we would secure the end 170

He further pronounces it "evident" that when the human machine is perfected by evolution, "that element in the moral consciousness which is expressed by the word obligation will disappear," and "the moral sentiments will guide men just as spontaneously as do now the sensations" 174

Upon these fundamental positions of the "fitter regulative system" proposed to us by Scientific Agnosticism in the place of the rule of right and wrong hitherto received, it may be observed—

First, that there is an absolute contradiction between Mr. Spencer's hedonistic morality and his great law of evolution 175

xxxii   *SUMMARY.*

                                                                                            PAGE

Secondly, that Mr. Spencer's teaching depends, essentially, upon quite arbitrary assumptions 178

Thirdly, that Mr. Spencer's moral philosophy is hopelessly vitiated by his misapprehension of the subject wherewith such philosophy is concerned—moral goodness . 182

Fourthly, that it is no less fatal to the concept of moral obligation than it is to the concept of moral goodness 190

The "fitter regulative system" which Scientific Agnosticism proposes to substitute for the old data of ethics is a mere abortion of moral philosophy; just as its doctrine of The Unknowable is a mere abortion of natural theology 196

Mr. Spencer's portentous generalities, with their integrations and disintegrations, leave the mystery of "the immeasurable world" precisely where they found it. The key to the problem of existence is not sensation, but personality. And it is to be sought, not in the charnel-house of Physics, but in the spiritual temple of Reason 199

CHAPTER V.

RATIONAL THEISM.

The next step in the present inquiry is, whether Theism is, in fact, so hopelessly discredited as is frequently and confidently alleged 200

The antitheistic current of contemporary thought is a

sort of intellectual epidemic. The vast majority of those who are infected by it could give no coherent account of their scepticism 200

It is, no doubt, largely due to the stupendous advance of the experimental sciences. And this is natural enough. For those sciences dwell in the sphere of physical uniformity. They are nothing but a knowledge of the relative; and exclusive devotion to them tends to shut out the idea of a First Cause . . 201

Existence presents two problems—the how and the why. To explain the how of things, we must discover those uniformities of sequence or co-ordination which we call their laws. That is the province of physics. And with all beyond that, physical science, as such, is not concerned 202

But contemporary masters of physical science often display a desire, and more than a desire, to bring everything within its boundaries; to restrict our ideas to generalizations of phenomena; to erect experimental observation into the sole criterion of certitude . . 204

No doubt there is a true, a close analogy, between physical and intellectual laws, both being manifestations of the same Reason. But it is most necessary to resist the application—misapplication—of the physiological method to the mental and moral order: the claim that purely intellectual questions shall be determined by the laws of matter . . . 205

In this chapter the special character of the antitheistic current of thought, in these days, will be specially kept in view. The reader will be asked to consider first what are the reasons specially urged why we

xxxiv SUMMARY.

PAGE

should abandon Theism; and next, what Reason, freely exercised according to the methods now specially prized, and without any reference to systems of religion professing to be revealed, makes evident, unless we stultify its teaching, concerning the existence and character of the Supreme Reality . 206

We are told that if men will go on believing in God, it is "in spite of science and the laws of consciousness." We will proceed to see what reasons in support of the antitheistic argument "science and the laws of consciousness" supply 208

The antitheistic argument from physical science specially relied on, in the present day, is the argument from the apparent failure and waste in the phenomenal world. We are told, "The early glimpses of the marvels of Nature afforded by modern science undoubtedly were favourable to natural theology in the first instance. Knowledge revealed so many wonders which had not been suspected by ignorance, that a general increase of reverence and awe for the Creator was the natural though not very logical consequence. But a deeper philosophy, or rather biology, has disturbed the satisfaction with which 'the wisest and most exquisite ends' were once regarded. It is now known that for one case of successful adaptation of means to ends in the animal world, there are hundreds of failures. If organs which serve an obvious end justify the assumption of an intelligent designer, what are we to say of organs which serve no ends at all, but are quite useless or meaningless?" . . 208

In answer to this it may be said—
First, that though we may not be able to argue, solely from the phenomena of the physical world, to an absolutely

wise and all-powerful First Cause, yet the progress of
physical science has not disproved, and does not tend
to disprove, thought, order, purpose . . . 211

Secondly, that, in strictness, there is no such thing as
failure known to us, because there may be always
ends which are hidden from our eyes. We can affirm
order, because that is a thing positive. But to affirm
disorder, absolute and final, is like attempting to
prove a negative 211

Thirdly, that theories borrowed from the economical
schools of the day are not the proper measure of
finality in the universe: nor can the standard supplied by Utilitarianism be accepted as the rule of all
things in heaven and earth 212

Fourthly, that the doctrine of organic evolution does not
in the least conduct us to the necessity of modern
phenomenists as the true explanation of the universe.
Necessity is a question-begging word. If blind
necessity is meant, such necessity assuredly could
not produce the diversity, the succession, the return
of phenomena. But if necessity is not blind it is
merely another name for law; and law implies an
abiding and unchanging self, a spiritual principle . 212

Fifthly, that the question of a First Cause is one with
which the physicist, as such, is not concerned. His
domain is the sphere of sense perception . . 213

Next, the antitheistic argument from the laws of consciousness amounts to this: that the antithesis of subject
and object, never to be transcended while consciousness lasts, renders impossible all knowledge of the
Ultimate Reality, in which subject and object are
transcended; that we can believe in a Divine con-

	PAGE
sciousness only by refraining from thinking what is meant by consciousness, and that the condition of believing in a Divine will is similar . . .	214
But this argument is vitiated hopelessly and radically— First, by assumptions, of the most arbitrary *a priori* description, concerning the Ultimate Reality, whose existence and attributes reason seeks in some degree to know	217
Secondly, by utter misconception of what is meant by the faculty of abstraction	218
Thirdly, by failure to apprehend the essential nature of intellect	219
We go on to the next point : What grounds for belief in God are afforded by reason freely exercised, according to the methods specially prized in these days? .	220
It must be frankly admitted that the strongest grounds for such belief are inexpressible, because they transcend the logical understanding. But we may claim to have done enough in satisfaction of the debt which we owe to all men, if we show that our faith, so far from being unreasonable, does, in fact, sum up the conclusions to which reason points; that the language in which we clothe it, although infinitely inadequate, is the nearest approximation to the truth possible to us	220

Let us start, then, from the way of thinking just now so much in credit. The popular philosophy of the day is a philosophy of relativity, employing as its most valued instrument comparative analysis. No doubt, to reduce the complex to the simple, the phenomenon to the law, the special law to the general law, is, so far as it goes, an explanation. And if universal being were merely monotonous and inflexible mechanism, such would be the whole explanation. But universal being is not merely that. It is also organic. And the tendency of lower forms to pass into higher, implies something else than mechanism; a system of definite directions is merely a synonym for finality 221

Correlation cannot be essence. It is a logical impossibility for the Relative to exist alone. It presupposes the Absolute. To the Absolute the whole series of relative realities tends. 222

Phenomena, apprehensible by the senses, must have a reason which is not a phenomenon, and which therefore is "beyond the probe of chemic test" . . 223

If it be objected, from Kant, that the principle of causality is purely subjective, and that we must not venture with the speculative reason beyond the limits of sensible experience, the reply is that though the subject imposes its own form on knowledge and makes it subjective, subjectivism does not necessarily follow from this. The phenomena of the external world are not merely abstract signs, like algebraic symbols. They are instinct with life: they obey law: they are disposed in a wonderful order. The life, the law, the order, demand explanation. And for this explanation the principle of causality is necessary. "It is by an *a priori* axiom of the understanding, that we apply the causal relation to the external world" . . . 223

If Kant's teaching be viewed as a whole, it cannot be believed that he held the law of causation to be

xxxviii SUMMARY.

PAGE

wholly subjective. Nor is there any way out of Nihilism for his disciples, save to take the Supreme Principle which is beyond sensible experience, and to build on that 225

What, then, can we know about this Supreme Principle? this Ultimate Reality? As we saw in the last chapter, Mr. Spencer, while pronouncing it Unknowable, predicates of it not only being, but causal energy, eternity, omnipotence; recognizes it as "the basis of intelligence," and holds it to be "manifested" "through phenomena," to our "consciousness." Let us see what these manifestations amount to . . 225

What does the external universe manifest to our consciousness of the Power which, as Mr. Spencer tells us, "persists unchanging under these sensible appearances?" If we look around us and above us, we find everywhere what we term mind and matter. Surely we may say with Fénelon that the Ultimate Reality "is not indeed mind or matter, but is all that is essential in mind and matter" . . . 227

What is essential in mind is reason. And if there is any lesson taught more clearly than another by the recent researches of physicists, it is the intelligibility of the universe. Reason everywhere—such is the lesson which we see writ large in Nature. Its laws are identical with the laws of the human intellect. Reason is the constituent element of reality. And does not this point to the Supreme Cause as Objective Reason? Surely it is an irrational doctrine that the unintelligible is the primary source of the intelligible 228

Reason, then, the essence of mind, is what sensible phenomena disclose to us, ever more clearly. And what is essential in matter? It is given us only as the union of two forces—the force of expansion and the force of attraction. It is the visibility of force . 231

But force is only a resultant; nor, if we go by experience, have we knowledge of any other primary cause of force than volition. This is the only possible name under which we can gather up the mighty forces ever energizing throughout the universe. Matter, therefore, is merely a manifestation of Will . . 231

Reason and Will are inseparably united in the universe as they are in idea. But the union of reason and will it is which constitutes personality . . 232

This is perhaps as far as external nature enables us to go. But the phenomena of the external world are not the only channels through which the Ultimate Existence is manifested to consciousness. We must also take into account the lessons of what the somewhat slipshod language of the day calls "mental phenomena." Mr. Spencer tells us that the Ultimate Existence is "the basis of our intelligence." Let us see what our intelligence tells us concerning its basis 232

What is the primary fact which the intellect reveals to us, as soon as the act of thinking takes place in our own consciousness? Unquestionably it is the distinction of self and non-self. And, as unquestionably, this distinction is *accompanied* by the idea of moral obligation. It is also matter of fact that the source of that obligation has ever been felt to lie in a mysterious and hyper-physical Entity whereon man depends 234

SUMMARY.

This is the common factor of all creeds. They all proclaim, however rude or refined, grotesque or sublime their symbolism, the absolute dominion of the moral law, as a perpetual obligation binding upon all possible intelligent beings, and therefore, as a Transcendental Reality, a manifestation of the Eternal under the condition of time. They point to the Ultimate Reality which is "the basis of our intelligence" as law moral 234

It appears, then, that as external phenomena manifest to our consciousness the Ultimate Reality as Law, which is another name for the union of Reason and Will, wherein consists Personality, so do "mental phenomena" also, adding this further revelation first of all: that the Law is just, the Reason right, the Will ethical, the Person holy 237

But further: the primary fact revealed to us by reason, as soon as the act of thinking takes place in our consciousness, is the distinction of self and non-self. Intellect, then, manifests to me myself. The perception of selfhood is the very fundamental interior fact of which I am conscious. The *Ego*, upon its own self-testimony, is a something which is one, identical, permanent, rational, volitional, and free—not, of course, absolutely, but relatively free—a something which is the principle and cause of our acts. But these facts are manifestations to our "consciousness" of the Ultimate Reality, which is "the basis of our intelligence." And they manifest that Reality as possessing, in some transcendent and incomprehensible way, those qualities which are the self-affirmations of the intellect: Substance, Causality, Being, and all else included in the metaphysical conception of Personality . . 238

SUMMARY.

If it is objected that there is a contradiction in conceiving the Absolute as personal, the answer is that personality does not mean limitation. In the proper sense of the word, Personality—Für-sich-sein—can be predicated only of the Infinite. "Ipse suum esse est." Perfect selfhood means immediate self-existence. The idea of Personality, like all ideas, is realized only in that Self-Existent—the Original of all existence—which transcends those ideas, indeed, but in transcending, includes them . . . 241

We may say, then, that the Ultimate Reality is manifested to our consciousness as the Original of the law physical, which rules in the phenomenal world, and of the law moral written on the fleshly tables of the heart; as the Supreme Good, in whom all ideas are realized; as the First Cause and Final End of the universe, where all is causation and finality; as the Self-Existent, and therefore a Person, or rather *the* Person, from whom all personality is an effluence; as "the basis of our intelligence," of all intelligence. Such are the conclusions which we must accept upon the testimony of intellect. The only alternative is to deny the validity of intellect altogether 242

It may indeed be objected that the conception of God involves us in invincible antinomies. No doubt that is so. We should remember, however, that while in the finite contradictories are in opposition, in the Absolute they find their union . . . 244

It must not for a moment be supposed that our human and relative notions are the measure of the Absolute and Divine. The Infinite and Eternal is not "a magnified, non-natural man;" nor can our speech do more than most dimly adumbrate Him. All our words, essentially phenomenal and relative, are but sensuous symbols of the great Noumenal Fact. But surely there is some mean between knowing all about a thing and knowing nothing about it . . 244

The popular god, in all religions, is a thing of shreds and patches, a vice of gods, and cannot possibly be other. Still, we are too apt to undervalue that exceeding great multitude of people who are simply good and religious-minded, wholly undisturbed by Theistic problems. They are not intellectually considerable. But to them are ofttimes revealed things hidden from the wise and prudent 246

Unquestionably, of all those problems the most terrible is the existence, not of the Absolute, but of the Perfect Being. It is hard to conceive how the Supreme Self, in whose unmoved and immovable calm all ideals are realized, could have become an active cause. It is infinitely harder to conciliate the existence of a Perfect Creator or First Cause with the existence of such a world as this . . . 249

Nor is there any alleviation of the burden and the mystery save in the certitude that justice rules the world, and that we *can* follow the law within. In this certitude the wisest and best of our race have ever found "amid the encircling gloom" "a light unto their feet." That light will be spoken of in the next chapter 253

CHAPTER VI.

THE INNER LIGHT.

Mysticism is the proper complement of the Rational Theism considered in the last chapter; its office to point from the phenomenal to the noumenal, from that which seems to that which is. It is based upon the indubitable fact, that the spirit of man comes in direct contact with the Supreme Object, to which neither the senses nor the logical understanding can attain: whose manifestations carry with them their own proof, and are moral in their nature, are out of time and place, are enlightening, purifying, and are therefore, in a true sense, ascetic . . . 255

In this chapter the four chief systems in which the mystical doctrine has been clothed will first be surveyed; and then the especial significance of the expression which it has found in modern philosophy will be considered 256

The most perfect specimen of Hindu mystic philosophy is the *Katha Upanishad*, in which Yama, answering the questions of Nakiketas concerning "the Self and that which dwells in the Great Hereafter," expounds the doctrine of *Âtman*—infinite, invisible, divine; life of the world and life of our life; of whom many are not able to hear; whom many, even when they hear of Him, do not comprehend; and who is reached, not by the *Veda*, not by understanding, not by much learning, but only through the spiritual insight of him who has ceased from evil, and who is concentrated, and whose mind is quiescent 256

xliv   SUMMARY.

                                                                    PAGE
Greek mysticism is substantially the development of the
    same thought, from its earliest expression by
    Pythagoras to its full development by the Neo-
    Platonists   259

And the root idea of Moslem mysticism is identical with
    the root idea of the Upanishads   .   .   . 262

The fourth great mystical school—the Christian—is clearly
    marked off from these three other schools, which are
    all more or less Pantheistic, by its doctrines of the
    Trinity and creation   265

Still, Christian, like all other mysticism, aims at grasping
    the Ultimate Reality, at direct communion with the
    Highest; and professes to open a way of escape from
    the blinding tyranny of sense, to transcend the veil
    of illusory phenomena, and to set free its votaries
    by an inward vision. Its central doctrine is that
    which is so emphatically enforced by the great non-
    Christian schools of mysticism, that the Being of
    Beings is cognizable only by the purified mind   . 265

At first the Supreme Reality appears to the inner eye as
    darkness, whence Dionysius the Carthusian tells us,
    "Mystica theologia est ardentissima divini caliginis
    intuitio." This apparent darkness is, however, in
    itself light, dazzling and blinding in its splendour,
    and it gradually becomes visible as such, when the
    spiritual vision is purged and strengthened and
    renewed by the stripping off of all love for the
    relative, the dependent, the phenomenal, and by the
    assiduous practice of all moral virtues   .   . 267

To this Purgative way succeeds the Illuminative way,
    and to that the Unitive way, whereby the soul attains
    to that union with its Supreme Object which is called
    "transformation"   268

SUMMARY.

PAGE

The dangers incident to mysticism are obvious: on the one side lie the deep gulfs of madness: on the other, the abysses of sensuality 269

It is, however, a fact, worthy of being deeply pondered, that in the Catholic Church mysticism has been incomparably more healthy, more sober, more beautiful, than anywhere else. Her symbolism, historical, social, visible, has provided for its highest aspirations congruous expression, and restrained them within the bounds that may not be passed in this phenomenal world. While as the type of Christian mysticism, practically exhibited "for human nature's daily food," it is enough to point to *The Imitation of Christ* . 270

Noteworthy, too, is it that when the paramount authority of dogmatic theology has been lost sight of, the speculations of medieval and modern transcendentalists have usually issued in Nihilistic Pessimism . 270

Our present concern is, however, with the normal aspects of mysticism which is a fact of human nature, exhibited at all times in history, and confronting us to-day. We go on to inquire what is the peculiar significance of contemporary mysticism, when viewed in the light—or darkness—of modern philosophical speculation 272

European thought, after a century of not very fruitful wanderings, is going back to Kant. His *Critique of Pure Reason* deals precisely with the question, What are the limits of sane affirmation? Without entering upon an examination of that work, and assuming, for the sake of the present argument, that its theory of cognition is substantially correct, where are we in regard to The Great Enigma of which man ever seeks the solution? the question which Nakiketas put to Yama about the Self and that which dwells in the Great Hereafter? 272

The Critique of Pure Reason is essentially a doctrine of nescience. The human understanding, Kant insists, is shut up within the circle of our sensations. These reveal to it merely phenomena. And beyond phenomena all is a void for it. Noumena may exist, or they may not exist. All that is certain is that no faculty of the human understanding can discover anything about them. The issue clearly is to annihilate dogmatism, affirmative or negative, and to warn us against venturing with the speculative reason beyond the limits of experience . . . 273

The effect of this doctrine upon the ordinary "proofs of the existence of God" is evident. Kant insists that no unity of thought and being is knowable save the unity of experience, and that this is the sole realization, cognizable by the speculative reason, of the ideal to which men have ascribed the name of God . 275

Thus does Kant lead us into what may be called "the dark night of the soul." *The Critique of Pure Reason* presents a striking parallel to the *Via Purgativa* of the mystics. The illusoriness of the phenomenal world, the impotency of the mere understanding to penetrate beyond it to the vision of a Reality transcending sense—these are its main lessons. Kant employs the word noumenal to express a limitary conception. He gives it a negative use. But it is worthy of notice that this is pretty much the sum of the knowledge of God to which, as the mystics of all schools teach, we can attain by means of the phenomenal order.

SUMMARY. xlvii

PAGE

And hence the phrase common to them all: "The Divine Darkness." Is there any way in which this darkness may be made light for the disciple of Kant? 275

The philosopher has answered that question in *The Critique of Practical Reason*, a work which he tells us is the necessary complement of the first: another storey of the same edifice. He knew well that there is far more in the human consciousness than is explicable by "the pure forms of intuition," the concepts of the understanding, the ideas of reason; and that to shut us off from the intelligible world, is to doom us to moral and spiritual death. The opening into this transcendent region he finds in the concept of Duty; a concept marked off from the notions of space, of time, of substance, and the like, by vast differences which prove its objective character. Here is for him the creative principle of morality, of religion. "We recognize," he says, "in our moral being, the presence of a power that is supernatural." It is the Kantian equivalent of the Illuminative Way of theology: and here Kant is at one with the mystics of every age in pointing to the Inner Light guiding from the phenomenal to the noumenal world 277

The intuition of duty is, however, but one of many faculties independent of sense perception which, as a matter of fact, exist in human nature. That power within us which discerns the axioms of eternal righteousness is the very same, in root and substance, which grasps the facts and interprets the laws of a world beyond appearances 280

It remains to consider two objections. The first is that "whether in the Vedas, the Platonists or the Hege-

xlviii　　　　　　　SUMMARY.

PAGE

lians, mysticism is nothing more nor less than ascribing objective existence to the subjective creation of our own faculties, to mere ideas of the intellect" 284

Surely this is a tyrannous *ipse dixit*, if ever utterance deserved to be so called. Why should we believe, upon the authority of those who confessedly do not speak as experts, that the choice specimens of human wisdom and virtue in all ages have been wrong, when they thought themselves in communion with a world transcending sense? It is impossible for one who has held high converse with the sages of the *Upanishads*, with Plotinus, with Jelâl, with St. Teresa, to believe that what those great souls accounted the prime and only Reality was wholly unreal 284

The second objection is based upon the discrepancies and contradictions of mysticism 286

This objection seems to fade away, when it is fairly considered. The primary position of the mystics is that highest truth is not so much intellectually known as spiritually felt: " cognoscendo ignoratur et ignorando cognoscitur." The accounts of the mystics are necessarily discrepant, and the discrepancy is due to the varying symbolisms used by them: symbolisms, for the most part traditional, inherited from the nation or school to which they belong. The Divine Secret cannot be congruously conveyed in the language of sense perception: " transumanar significar *per verba* non si poria." The very incongruity of human words as a vehicle of transcendental truth, accounts sufficiently for defects in its presentation . . 286

No doubt, in the more vulgar manifestations of religion,
that is to say, the religion of the great majority, the
mystical element, which is its life, will assume the
most unlovely forms. But it is still there, potent in
its divine virtue to slake the thirst of human nature
for a great good transcending sense . . . 288

CHAPTER VII.

THE CHRISTIAN SYNTHESIS.

Shall we say, then, that the solution of The Great
Enigma is given by what is called Theism of the
natural order—a Theism at once rational and
mystical? Or is there, among the world's religions,
any to which, without making our reason blind, or
our conscience dumb, we may join ourselves, as
filling up the revelations of the external and internal
universe? 290

It is held by many excellent and distinguished persons
that this last question must receive a negative
answer. They make of religion merely an emotion,
an aspiration, and of religions merely temporary and
fluxional hypotheses which have served to render
the ideal accessible to the multitude. They preach
an abstract, a subjective and unhistorical religiosity,
which makes God into an impersonal force, with no
objective character at all, or, at all events, undis-
tinguishable from human impulses . . . 290

But man never is abstract self-consciousness: he belongs
to the world of time; he is individual, concrete, *hic*

SUMMARY.

PAGE

et nunc. And the religious faith which binds him to a present Deity must have the same character. Faith, if it is to be anything more than a blind instinct, must involve assent to propositions. And that it should likewise involve assent to historical truths, is simply of a piece with the laws by which man lives, and moves, and has his being . . 294

It is precisely because this is the nature of man, and of the religious instinct in man, that we are led to form ecclesiastical associations . . . 294

To speak of Christianity alone, it will be found impossible, in fact, to separate the idea of Christ from the person of Jesus, and to live by the one without believing in the other. It is to the combination of eternal truth with the details of the evangelical history, that we must ascribe the influence of Christianity over the hearts and lives of men . . 295

And it is enough, for our present practical purpose, to confine ourselves to Christianity. Few people, probably, would seriously maintain that any other of the world's creeds can really dispute with it the world's future 296

But what do we mean by Christianity? There are so many kinds of Christians! Perhaps we may say that Christianity is, in its simplest reduction, the doctrine concerning God summed up in the baptismal formula—the most ancient and, in a sense, the most authoritative, of all its formulas—the acceptance of which has, from the first, been required as a condition of admission into the Christian society. And the question to be discussed in this chapter is

SUMMARY.

whether there is anything irrational, and therefore immoral, in accepting The Christian Synthesis as affording the best answer to The Great Enigma . 297

First, then, as to belief in an Almighty Father, of whom, and through whom, and to whom, are all things, it may suffice to refer to what has been said in previous chapters of this volume. If the intellect is valid, the true conclusion can never be Atheism or Agnosticism, but must be Theism of some kind . 298

The conclusions of Reason are certain. But they leave us cold. Objective Reason, Eternal Energy, Supreme Cause, Absolute Being, Perfect Personality—these conceptions, august as they are, by no means suffice for the needs, either of our intellect or of our emotions. We want "a God that can interest us." Our conceptions of Him are, and cannot keep from being, anthropomorphic: that is to say, they are conditioned by the essential limits of our nature. It may, in a sense, be said, that we incarnate God by a necessity of our intellectual and spiritual existence. "Humanity will have a God at once finite and infinite, real and ideal. It loves the ideal, but it will have that ideal personified. It will have a God-man" 299

The claim of Christianity is definitively to satisfy this longing. It presents Christ to the world as "the image of the invisible God," in whom the eternally ideal has become the historically real: the Λόγος Θεῖος, the thought of the Infinite and Eternal, made flesh and dwelling among us: the realization of the Divine will in the moral and religious order: "the desire of all nations" 300

SUMMARY.

                                            PAGE

And this claim is as prevailing now as it was eighteen hundred years ago. In the Divine Founder of Christianity we have an "ideal of humanity valid for all men, at all times, and throughout all worlds" . 304

But external nature and human history are not our only sources of knowledge. One of the primary facts of consciousness is the feeling of ethical obligation. As surely as consciousness reveals to me, in the ordinary exercise of my faculties, myself, and an objective world not myself, so surely does it reveal to me, through that feeling of ethical obligation, a Higher than I, to whom that obligation binds me . . 305

"The moral law first reaches its integral meaning when seen as *impersonated* in a Perfect mind, which communicates it to us, and lends it power over our affections, sufficient to draw us into Divine communion." The direct revelation of the personal God is that which is made to the personality of man. "Spiritus Domini replevit orbem." The article of the Apostles' Creed, "I believe in the Holy Ghost," stands as firmly now as it did eighteen hundred years ago. How can it pass away? We have "the witness in ourselves" 307

It must not be supposed that an endeavour is being made to *prove* the Christian doctrine of the Trinity by appealing to the facts of physical nature, history, and consciousness. It is merely contended, for the purposes of this *argumentum ad hominem*, that there is nothing in those facts inconsistent with the theistic conception of Christianity, but that, on the contrary, they clearly harmonize with it . . 309

SUMMARY. liii

PAGE

It will, however, be said that Christianity, as it comes before us, means a great deal more than this: that it is not merely a religion, but has become a theology: that the difficulty really lies in the vast accretion of dogma, to excise which from Christianity would be to perform a mortal operation upon it . . 309

No doubt that is so. Christianity comes before us "rich with the spoils of time." We may take it or leave it. But if we cannot take it as it is, with its doctrines and its traditions, we had better leave it. It is hard to imagine anything less satisfactory than the results attained by the method called rationalistic, which, in fact, seems extremely irrational . . 310

No intelligent man can candidly deny that we may sometimes find difficulties in reconciling the positions of dogmatic theology with the exigencies of criticism. But those difficulties are such as we may rightly discount when we are unable fully to solve them 310

It must be remembered that, *philosophically* considered, a dogma is the result of several factors. There is the original idea, there is the concrete image, and there is the logical deduction. The facts of the Divine Life, with their redemptive and recreative energy, are not the subject of evolution. The Confessions, in which we sum up our appreciation and interpretation of those facts, are slowly elaborated by the human intellect 311

Doctrine is the vertebration of religion, and is as essential to it as words are to thought. There is something in us which compels us to reduce to system the various aspects of truth. But our synthesis must necessarily be imperfect. "Verba sequuntur non modum essendi qui est in rebus, sed modum essendi secundum quod in nostra cogitatione sunt." To which we must add that human language has an essentially physical, sensual, materialistic character. And our theological theories expressed in words are but imitations of the inimitable. Christian teaching is professedly symbolical. And the symbolized is greater, and deeper, and older than the symbol . 312

In the moral order truth is apprehended not only by the intelligence, but by the whole soul. The credentials of Christianity are sufficient for "men of good will." But they "are not of so imperative a character as to impose themselves on reluctant wills. They are, in fact, moral and not mathematical or experimental" 314

It must be further remembered that " quidquid recipitur secundum modum recipientis recipitur." Christianity is one thing. Popular conceptions of it are another 316

The contention in this chapter is that, while no one pretends that Christianity offers us a complete explanation of the scheme of things, there is no more reason in the nineteenth century than there was in the first, why its message should not be received by cultivated and intelligent men, who feel their need of it, and who will carefully and candidly examine its claims for themselves. We may call Christianity, if we will, "a chapel in the infinite." Still it is a sacred shrine where life and death are transfigured for us, where we may gaze into the eternal realms of Spirit and Deity, where wise and learned, foolish and ignorant, alike, may handle everlasting realities, and realize in their deepest experience, the powers of the world to come . 317

THE GREAT ENIGMA.

CHAPTER I.

THE TWILIGHT OF THE GODS.

JOUBERT, in one of the neatest of his Aphorisms, thus sums up philosophy: "Je, d'où, où, pour, comment, c'est toute la philosophie : l'existence, l'origine, le lieu, la fin et les moyens." In truth this is The Great Enigma with which the generations of mortal men have ever been confronted —What am I? Whence am I? Why am I? What is my final end? What the means to it? There is something in human nature which forces man to ask these questions. Hence he has well been termed "a metaphysical animal." That it is which clearly marks him off from the rest of sentient existence. Schopenhauer has strikingly expressed this truth in words from which I shall borrow, as I cannot hope to better them :—

"With the exception of man, no being wonders at its own existence." "Only to the brute, which is without thought, do the world and life appear as a matter of course. To man, on the contrary, it is a problem whereunto even the coarsest and most narrow-minded becomes vividly alive in some brighter moments. It enters distinctly and permanently into the consciousness of each of us, in proportion as that consciousness is clear and considerate, and has, through culture, acquired food for thought. In those higher minds which are naturally fitted for philosophical investigation, it becomes the 'wise wonder' of which Plato spoke." "For the great majority, who cannot apply themselves to thought, religion very well supplies the place of metaphysics." "If anything in the world is worth wishing for—so well worth wishing for that even the coarse and stupid herd, in their more reflective moments, would prize it beyond gold and silver—it is that a ray of light should fall on the obscurity of our being, and that we should gain some explanation of the riddle of existence." "Temples and churches, pagodas and mosques, in all lands, at all times, bear testimony by their splendour and vastness to this metaphysical need of man." *

It is no doubt true, as Schopenhauer here intimates, that religions are the philosophies of the vulgar. It is also true that philosophy, in that highest sense rightly put upon it by the thinkers of the antique world, includes all wisdom: by wisdom being understood, according to the definition of Cicero in the *De Officiis*, "the knowledge of things divine and human, and of the causes by which they are determined." Causation is the great problem both of philosophy and of religion, but they approach it from different sides. Philosophy endeavours to explain man. Religion pro-

* *Die Welt als Wille und Vorstellung.* Ergänzungen zum ersten Buch. Kap. 17.

poses to reveal God. It is, however, in the Divine, that philosophy seeks the ultimate source and fount of the human. It is to man, "the true Shekinah," as St. Chrysostom writes, made in the Divine image and likeness, that religion turns for an adumbration of the attributes of the First Cause. In both provinces the logical method must be followed; no other will serve in controversy. It is a postulate of Christian apologists, from Justin Martyr down to Cardinal Newman, that between the teachings of religion, rightly understood, and the conclusions of philosophy, properly apprehended, there can be no contradiction. A bold and original French writer has spoken of "les grandes verités qui composent la partie supérieure et vraiment métaphysique du Christianisme." And the world's greatest intellects, from Plato to Hegel, have held, with one consent, that those supreme verities are bound together in links of necessary thought, which are the common ground and the last explanation both of philosophy and religion, and which make a philosophy of religion possible. For there is only one Truth, and there is only one way of discerning what is true. "That intellectual light," writes St. Thomas Aquinas, "that is within us, is nought else than a certain participated likeness of the Uncreated Light, in which are contained the eternal reasons."*

* *Summa*, I. 1æ, q. 84, a. 5.

It is in religions, then, and in the religion which is behind all religions, however puerile or debased their theologies, however sanguinary or obscene their ritual, that mankind, speaking generally, has hitherto sought the solution of The Great Enigma. They have explained the human by the superhuman. They have contained—even the poorest and lowest of them—an ethical element in virtue of which this life was viewed, more or less clearly, as a period of probation. But in Christianity this ethical element assumes a very different character from what it possesses in any other mode of faith. Christianity proclaims that man is made and fashioned by the hands of the Divine Creator; that he is capable of the perfect felicity of the Beatific Vision which is his true end, and that the way to that end is by a right ordering of his will in this state of moral discipline. This is the solution of The Great Enigma taught, in the Catechism, to every Catholic child: "Why did God make you?—To know Him, love Him, and serve Him in this world, and to be happy for ever with Him in the next." Such a view of life and the end of life was assuredly new to the masses of that vast Roman empire who first had the gospel preached to them, however nearly the nobler schools of philosophy may have approached to it. Mr. Lecky is well warranted when he writes, "To amalgamate the two spheres of ethics and worship, . . . to incorporate moral culture with religion, was among the most important achievements of Christianity:" an achievement whose practical issue is, that "doctrines concerning the nature of God, the immortality of the soul, and the duties of man, which the noblest intellects of antiquity could barely grasp, have become the truisms of the village school, the proverbs of the cottage and of the alley."*

We live, however, in an age when religions—Christianity among them—are widely supposed, in Mr. Leslie Stephen's phrase, to have been "found out." From the very first mankind has desired an explanation of them. "Whence the gods severally sprang? whether they had existed from all eternity? what form they bore?" were questions, Herodotus relates, to which he sought answers when he visited Dodona. The priestesses at that hallowed shrine appear to have been able to give him little information beyond the assurance, whatever it may have been worth, that the names of the Hellenic deities came from Egypt. The problems which thus occupied the inquiring mind of the father of history have been discussed, with little definite result, from his day to ours. But at last, we are told by a school of writers whose wide learning and indefatigable industry are beyond

* *History of European Morals*, ch. iv.

dispute, at last the solution has been found. Religions are now studied in the scientific spirit, and the mystery which once enshrouded them is dispelled. They are the accidents of periods: the poems in which man, at sundry times and in divers manners, has enshrined his ideals of the Divine, his aspirations towards the Unseen. Professors of the science of religion confidently undertake to explain these "phenomena," and to deduce the laws regulating their manifestation and development. They inform us that the great Olympic gods, like the *Dii Consentes* whose gilded statues adorned the Forum, were personifications of the powers of Nature, while the domestic deities, the πατρῶοι θεοί, the θεοὶ σύναιμοι of the Greeks, the *Lares* and *Penates* of the Romans, were merely deified ancestors. The innumerable denizens of the Hindu Pantheon are similarly explained. The Allah of Islâm is the Sheikh of the spirits worshipped by the Arabs, but invested with attributes borrowed by Mohammed from the Jews. Thus does the new science deal with the theistic conceptions of one religion after another, nor does it stop short at the Christian Trinity. The Third hypostasis of the Sacred Triad, it will have to be merely the personification of a metaphor. The Second it accounts of as the deification, under Platonic influences, of the Son of Mary. The First is subjected to a long and painful process of criticism which strips off the ecumenical attributes wherewith He had been invested by Jeremiah, the Babylonian Isaiah, and the later prophets, and reveals Him as the national God of a small tribe of Western Semites. Even His name is not left Him. The worshippers who bow " before Jehovah's awful throne " are told that the consecrated appellation is a barbarous forgery composed of the consonants of one word and of the vowels of another. They are bidden to say Yahveh: and Yahveh, they are assured, was originally merely the Sky God, and then the God of the Sky, a primitive conception of a primitive people. "Praise Him in His name Jah," sang the Hebrew bard. But this is pronounced to be a borrowed designation. Jao, or Jah, according to some great authorities, who found themselves upon the cuneiform inscriptions, is, in truth, the fire-god of the Chaldees, adopted at one time by the Israelites and invoked as Hallelu-Jah. Curious starting-point for the Paschal Alleluia, the Hallelujah Chorus, and the Hallelujah Sals and Bills who make day hideous beneath the standard of " General " Booth.

Such is the account of the God of Christianity often presented to us in the name of the science of religion. And then its professors apply themselves to the revered documents which are, in a sense, the credentials of that faith, and invite us to consider candidly what they are really worth. " Ye have Moses and the Prophets," it was said of old. What is left of Moses and the Prophets by the criticism usually called "higher"? The Pentateuch it pronounces to be really the Hexateuch shorn of its tail, the Book of Joshua, an operation performed when the legendary name of Moses was given to the collection, because it would have been too much to expect even Apella the Jew to believe that the law-giver wrote not only the account of his own death and burial, but also the history of his successor's conquests. Does any good easy-going Christian exclaim, "Well, Hexateuch if you will; what does it matter?" Nay, but the Hexateuch itself is exhibited as mainly based upon the fusion of two narratives—which indeed extend beyond it—the Jehovistic and the Elohistic: collections of the primitive cosmogonies brought by the Hebrews with them from Mesopotamia, "the most ancient portion of their traditional baggage," of ethnographic myths, of ritual prescriptions, of moral precepts, of popular ballads celebrating the exploits of national heroes. The fusion is referred to the reign of Hezekiah— B.C. 725–696—a time of great literary activity, which displayed itself chiefly in compilation. The real beginning of the Old Testament, we are told, was a long-perished *Book of Legends of the Israelites*, the choicest treasure of this singular people; the source to which we owe the charming romance of Joseph, the touching history of Ishmael, the incomparable tale of Jacob, "at once so sublime and so gross, so concrete and so ideal," and those many other exquisite and perfect stories, breathing all the freshness of the world's springtime, "which have made the literary fortune of the Bible." I do not discuss these views. I simply expound them. They may, at least, serve to illustrate the remark of a recent writer, "On ne fait pas d'exégèse impunément." Of Moses, then, the "higher" criticism makes a mere mosaic. The Prophets fare as badly at its hands. It sometimes dissolves the most venerated personalities, as when it insists upon two Isaiahs. It radically reforms chronology. It rejects, as spurious, writings bearing the most hallowed names. It finds that the vaticinations most confidently relied upon by Christian apologists had really reference to secular and contemporary affairs, and will no more see in such a text as "Out of Egypt have I called my Son" a reference to the Messiah, than it will see in the verse of Scott, "The sun shines fair on Carlisle walls," a reference to the sage who dwelt in Cheyne Row. Nor does the New Testament come off much better than the Old. Not to speak of revolutionary views as to the date and origin of its several books, the supernatural element is eliminated from it. Miracles are pronounced to be the residuum of religions, although it is admitted that at the epoch when Christianity arose they passed for the indispensable mark of the Divine, and for the sign of the prophetic calling. The old hypothesis of fraud is now little employed for their explanation. But it is declared that the apostles and evangelists lived in a state of poetic ignorance, at least as complete as that of St. Clare and the Three Companions, and so found it quite natural that their Master should have interviews with the imaginary personages Moses and Elias, should command the elements and raise the dead. The divine radiance dies away from the Crucified, to whom the hearts of eighteen centuries have gone out with adoring love. "All very well," says the vivisecting surgeon in Lord Tennyson's most pathetic poem—"All very well, but the good Lord Jesus has had His day."

After this manner does modern criticism explain the Christian Deity and His religion. And, as if that were not enough, the stupendous conquests achieved by physical science in this new age have introduced us to quite other conceptions, both of man and of his place in the universe, than those more or less closely interwoven with the old theological dogmas. Cosmogony, geology, palæontology, and physiology have simply revolutionized our thoughts about the world in which we live. As we all know, it is a favourite doctrine with many physicists of authority that "in fluid heat this earth began," and that after its detachment from the solar nebula, an unimaginable period of time passed away—three or four hundred millions of years they tell us—before it condensed into globular form, cooled, solidified, and became habitable. Then, as the new Book of Genesis teaches, for ten or twelve millions of years it was the seat of primitive organisms, of inferior species, algæ and the lower invertebrata. Another ten millions of years are calculated to have elapsed from the appearance of animal life, and of the higher vegetable forms, to the advent of man. It was some thousand centuries ago, as would appear, since this most highly specialized of mammals found himself upon the earth. And what a picture rises before us of those strange and monstrous forms of sentient existence, which were the predecessors and the necessary precursors of humanity! The trumpet of science has sounded through their sepulchres in all lands, and they have risen at its compelling summons, to give account of themselves to Man. From their graves beneath the rivers, or under the mountains, or deep down in the recesses of mines, they have come together, bone to his bone. And the naturalist prophesies, and lo! the sinews and the flesh come upon them, and the skin covers them above, and they stand in our galleries and museums an exceeding great army. Those huge dinosauri, those grotesque pterodactyls, those formidable megalosauri—the originals of the griffins, the vampires, the dragons of fable—were once the lords of the earth; and they are our ancestors: the far-off fathers of the savants who have raised them up from their long sleep. Certain it is, science declares to us, as she surveys the past, that from the simplest forms of animate existence, from plants leafless, flowerless, fruitless, from animals headless, sexless, motionless, the ascent of life runs unbroken, through innumerable minutest gradations, on manifold lines, until it reaches its utmost differentiation, its completest personality, in man. As certain is it, she prophesies, as she sets her face towards the future, that man as he now exists, is not the supreme product of evolution, the ultimate result of the law of progress: that the inexhaustible fecundity of the Mighty Mother has in store nobler types: that it was no idle fancy, but a true forecast, which inspired the vision of the crowning race, no longer half-akin to brute:—

> "Of those, that eye to eye shall look
> On knowledge: under whose command
> Is Earth and Earth's: and in their hand
> Is Nature, like an open book."

This is the answer which the revelation of science makes to the question, What is man? And yet, not the whole answer. She bids us lift our eyes to the heavens, and read what is written there regarding the human race and the globe it doth inhabit. Of those celestial bodies which gravitate, in majestic harmony, through infinite space, some are suns first bursting into flame, others are suns well-nigh burnt out. Here are worlds which are the cradles of life. There are worlds which are its tombs; vast nameless sepulchres, black and frozen, minatory of the end to which our terrestrial home is surely hastening. This earth is but a diminutive islet in the boundless celestial archipelago, which has its centre everywhere and its circumference nowhere: one of the least considerable planets of our vast solar system, which again is a mere speck in the illimitable ocean of space. Who can believe that all the boundless universe, except this infinitesimal constituent of it upon which we live, is merely monotonous mechanism? that the millions of world-systems, lit by suns before whose splendour ours pales its ineffectual fires, are unpeopled solitudes, desert and sterile from everlasting to everlasting? Reason revolts at such a conclusion. It demands a reasonable purpose in the universe. We argue, and justly, concerning other world-systems from the analogy of our own. It has been said, and perhaps not too strongly, that the existence of ultra-terrestrial life is the capital synthesis and the definite conclusion of all astronomy. "The wave of life which is now passing over our earth is but a ripple on the sea of life within the solar system; and that sea of life is but as a wavelet on the great ocean of life that is co-extensive with the universe." Not eternal death, but life eternal, wraps us round.

And what can we conceive concerning the denizens of those other worlds? Even upon the earth the reign of man is but a short episode in its history. The races now peopling this globe are quite different from those found in it under other conditions. Certain it is that in the infinite diversities of environment in other worlds, organisms quite unlike our own must be evolved. Nor, from our inchoate civilization, the product of a few thousands of years, can we even conjecture of the progress achieved in longer periods, by beings endowed with faculties, unlike and, no doubt, often transcending ours. All this, we are told, is incontestable by the wise. And we are asked, How can we reconcile it with that theory of final causes, which accounts of this inconsiderable speck in the infinite universe as the end of the wondrous All? How do the old religions of mankind, with their infantine cosmogonies, their mythical anthropologies—mere dreams which have visited the cradles of races—look in the light now shed from those "innumerable, pitiless, passionless eyes" in the heavens, which "burn and brand his nothingness into man"? Professor Huxley has not a doubt about the answer. "Astronomy," he assures us, "more than any other science, has rendered it impossible for men to accept the beliefs of their forefathers." What is man, do we demand? Why, man, they tell us, the whole race as the individual, is but an ephemeral atom in the universe, where all is movement, all is transformation. Yes, *all*. The physical formation of the earth, as of the infinite series of worlds, the conditions of life, the organisms which environment insensibly, but completely, modifies, habits, language, laws, all are in perpetual metamorphosis: and so are religions too. Are the generations of men like the generations of leaves? Even so are the generations of gods. Even so. And M. Renan takes up his parable and declares that this is well. "All here below is symbol and dream. Gods pass away like men; and it would be ill for us if they were eternal. The faith which we have once had should never be a chain. We have paid our debt to it when we have reverently wrapped it round in the shroud of purple where the dead gods sleep."

I do not think that any one who carefully follows the course of European thought from the days of Kant and Goethe (I might say from the days of Galileo and Spinoza) can doubt that it has conducted multitudes to the conclusions which I have depicted in rough, but, as I trust, clear outline. I am not, at present, inquiring how far they are warranted. I am merely pointing to the undeniable fact that they are very widely diffused. They are, so to speak, in the air. People can no more escape from them than from cholera or influenza: nay, less; for thought is the most contagious thing in the world. They darken the dim minds, and thwart the dull lives of millions who could give no coherent account of them. Current literature everywhere exhibits evidence of their activity. Nor is the general doubt merely about this or that dogma. Unquestionable is it, that as the old creeds have lost their hold upon men's minds, the Theistic conception which they, more or less worthily enshrined, has become faint. The public mind is confused with the speculations upon this high theme which so many learned men, and so many men who are not learned, place before us. God, one writer avers, did not create man, it is man who creates Him; He does not think, but is thought; He is the category of the ideal, the symbol of the truth which we conceive, the beauty which we imagine, the good which we long for. Another, while bidding us purge our minds of the phantom of personality, the ghost of individuality, makes of man "a wandering sorrow in a world of dreams," and of God one of those dreams projected upon nothingness. There are those who bid us be of good comfort, because, although God does not yet exist, He will exist some day; He is being made or is making Himself, they assure us; is, if I may so speak, on the road. The author of *Natural Religion* invites us to think of God as the "unity which all things comprise, in virtue of the universal presence of the same laws;" a difficult thing to do, as it seems to me: I wonder whether he has ever himself succeeded in doing it. Then there is the ultra-Hegelian school, which will have it that God is personal only in man, and that man is personal only in God; a dark saying which I do not pretend to understand. The practical issue is that, for vast multitudes,—

"He is now but a cloud and a smoke, who once was a pillar of fire;
The guess of a worm in the dark, and the shadow of its desire."

When Pierre Leroux offered his article "Dieu" to the *Revue des Deux Mondes*, it was returned with the observation, "La question de Dieu manque d'actualité." The voice of the *Zeitgeist* spoke by the mouth of Buloz.

But it is not only in the domain of religion that the general mind is "clouded with a doubt." Victor Hugo truly tells us, " Tout aujourd'hui, dans les idées comme dans les choses, est à l'état de crépuscule. Un point d'interrogation se dresse à la fin de tout."* The scepticism of the age extends to all first principles, and is nowhere more signally manifested than in the sphere of ethics. "Bound to believe and to do" was the conviction which dominated former generations. The obligation to right action is as much called in question as the obligation to a right creed. Nor is this to be wondered at. Christianity has hitherto claimed to instruct the nations both in faith and morals. And it is natural that the darkness which has overshadowed its theology should fall also upon its ethics. Professor Seeley has

* Preface to *Les Chants de Crépuscule*.

recorded his opinion that "never was the English mind so confused, so wanting in fixed moral principles, as at present."* Doubt concerning Deity has generated doubt concerning duty.

From one point of view, indeed, it is extremely illogical that the decay of religious belief should affect ethical convictions, for the spheres of theology and of moral philosophy are, in themselves, distinct. It may, perhaps, be well here to enlarge a little upon this truth, which appears not to be apprehended by various influential writers who certainly ought not to be ignorant of it. Thus, Mr. Herbert Spencer seems to suppose that transcendental moralists inculcate " a code of theological ethics," and think " Divine commands the only possible guides."† More crudely still, but in the same spirit, Mr. Leslie Stephen describes that school as affirming that morality is " the product of a particular creed : " that it is " caused by belief in Christianity : " that " it dropped from the clouds eighteen hundred years ago."‡ This representation of the view held by transcendental

---

* See his very interesting paper on " Ethics and Religion " in the *Fortnightly Review*, of April, 1871, p. 505.

† *Data of Ethics*, pref., p. iv. Elsewhere in this volume he writes, " Religious creeds, established and dissenting, all embody the belief that right and wrong are right and wrong simply in virtue of Divine enactment," that " moral truths have no other origin than the will of God."

‡ See his article, " Belief and Conduct," *Nineteenth Century*, September, 1888.

moralists is so utterly incorrect that one can hardly understand how an intelligent person can in good faith have made it. In its really philosophical aspect, our morality appeals to metaphysical, not to theological principles. The ethical precepts of Christianity are independent of its mysteries. As a matter of fact, they have been largely derived from non-Christian sources. Jesus Christ left no code of ethics.* He left the record of a life of lives, where the moral ideal is realized: a supreme example, an all-sufficient pattern. He preached perfection and exhibited Himself as the embodiment of it. But it is impossible to formulate from the Gospels, even if we add to them the Epistles, the elements of a scientific morality. I shall not be supposed to undervalue the direct contributions made to morals by the New Testament. I think it is the fashion, at the present day, largely to undervalue them. But the great work of Christianity for ethics was to fecundate it by the supreme ideal of self-sacrifice presented by Him, who " pleased not Himself," and to elevate it by the exhibition of man's true end and supreme good,

---

* So Suarez: "Christus non tradidit Præcepta moralia Positiva, sed Naturalia illa magis explicavit."—*De Legibus*, lib. 2, c. 15, n. 9. And in his tenth book (c. 2, n. 20) he quotes the dictum of Aquinas: "Legem novam esse contentam præceptis moralibus Naturalis Legis, et articulis Fidei et Sacramentis Gratiæ." The "Lex Naturalis" is a permanent revelation of the Reason, indicating "quid sit per se malum vel bonum homini."

the enjoyment by the soul, purified through the truth, of the Absolute Truth in the Beatific Vision. And when, in the expanding Christian society, the need arose for a scientific synthesis, recourse was had to the great philosophers of Greece: to Aristotle and Plato: to the Stoics and the Epicureans. It is to the inexhaustible fount of wisdom opened by Hellenic thought, that we owe the clearness, the precision, the wealth of psychological analysis which characterize the ethical teaching of the great medieval schoolmen and of their modern continuators. For them, the moral law depends, not upon the command of a supreme legislator, but upon "those dictates of natural reason" which, in the words of Suarez, "are intrinsically necessary and independent of all volition, even of the Divine."* Upon these dictates do we ground morality. From the very nature of man do we ascertain it. The moral eye of the sage ($\phi\rho\acute{o}\nu\iota\mu os$), as Aristotle teaches, is an original source of knowledge, through its inward intuitions. Ethical science proceeds from those intuitions as directed upon the manifestations of the moral nature. We start from the facts of personality, will, consciousness. And we work up to principles. The moral law, as we conceive of it, is a transcendental, universal order, good in itself, as being supremely reasonable; the rule of

* *De Legibus*, c. 6, n. 1. I need hardly observe that this is also the teaching of Plato.

what *should be*, as distinct from what *is*. To that rule our own individual reason gives testimony: for the moral order of the macrocosm is mirrored in the microcosm. This is what St. Paul calls our "consent unto the law that it is good," our "delight in it, after the inward man." We have the witness in ourselves to that *should be*. Necessity is laid upon us. The Categorical Imperative "Thou oughtest" means "As a rational agent thou must." The goodness of man consists in his voluntary submission to that Imperative: in his allowing the higher law by which he feels himself involuntarily conditioned, to prevail over "the law in his members." The true end of man is moral perfection, not pleasure. And it is in bringing the animal nature into obedience to the rational, the particular will into subjection to the universal, that he advances towards that end. The moral quality, subjectively considered — of course the act has also, or rather primarily, a moral quality—resides, not in the result achieved, nor in the end pursued by him, but in the motive which prompts him: in the inner spring of action, in volition. The only real and absolute good for man is a good will: that is a will determined by the moral law. The desire to do right, as right, is morality. No act is really ethical which is not motived by Duty, by obedience to the moral law. And that law, as Kant admirably teaches, is not a higher self, but an independent reality, which evokes the higher self within us. Human conscience is the entering into the individual of the objective law of right, the authority of which is intrinsic and unconditioned: which is its own evidence, its own justification; and which would subsist to all eternity, as it has subsisted from all eternity, though Christianity, and all other religions, were swept into oblivion. I do not deny, but strenuously maintain, that the ideas of God and Immortality are the crown of the moral law. True is it, that this law, written on the fleshly tables of our heart—"the law of virtue which we are born under"—links us with the whole moral order of the universe, and with the Infinite and Eternal, its final end and ours, in whose Divine Reason, as Plato teaches, it is contained. But it is also true that this law is in itself independent of religion: that if we prescind from, if we make abstraction of the formal idea of God,—

> "Duty exists: immutably survive
> For our support, the measures and the forms,
> Which an abstract intelligence supplies."

The very knowledge which we have, by our natural reason, of justice and injustice suffices to give rise to a strict ethical obligation. "N'y eût-il même point de Dieu saint et bon, n'y eût-il que le grand être universel, loi de tout idéal, sans hypostase ni réalité, le Devoir serait encore le mot de l'énigme et l'étoile polaire de l'humanité en marche."

Such is the moral law, as we account for it. And, being such, it assuredly merits the homage which Kant has paid it, in a magnificent passage where that most sober of philosophers seems, as it were, caught up into the realms of Spirit and Deity, and labouring to express in human speech those "unspeakable words which it is not lawful for men to utter" that fell upon his trembling ear. "Two things fill the mind with ever new and increasing wonder and reverence, the more frequently and the more closely reflection occupies itself with them, the starry heaven above me, and the moral law within me. Neither may I search after and merely guess concerning them, as though veiled in obscurities, or in the transcendental, beyond my range of vision. I see them before me, and connect them immediately with the consciousness of my own existence. The first originates from the position which I occupy in the outer world of the senses, and augments into immeasurable greatness the connection (*Verknüpfung*), wherein I stand, with worlds on worlds and systems on systems, in the illimitable ages of their periodical movements, their beginning, and their duration. The second originates from my invisible self, my Personality; and places me in a world which has the true unendingness, but is apprehensible only by the understanding, and with which I recognize myself to be connected, not . . . only accidentally and through the position which I chance to occupy in the world of sense, but universally and necessarily."* Duty, then, for the sake of duty, is the true principle. But it is a principle "too bright and good for human nature's daily food." For those who, by defect of will and nature, cannot rise to the height of this great argument, there is need of retributive happiness and suffering, of "deos aliquos et subterranea regna"† to keep them in the right way. That a rule is conformable with reason is not sufficient to insure obedience to it. Nor can we, indeed, think of the absolute and unconditioned authority of the moral law as proceeding from an abstraction. It implies a Person, the object of love, veneration, and fear; it witnesses to One with whom we have to do, holy, just, retributive; and—such is our nature—it is precisely because it bears this witness that it rules our will. "Religion, subjectively considered," is defined by Kant as "the recognition of all our duties as Divine commands." Assuredly

* *Kritik der praktischen Vernunft*, Beschluss.

† To obviate any misconception of my meaning, let me here cite a few words from Dr. Martineau, with which I substantially agree. "If there were no *award* of retributory happiness and suffering, the moral law would be curtailed of its adequate supports: not, however, because right and wrong are revealed, or even in themselves distinguished, only by their consequences, and by the erasure of these would be equalized, but because with our reflective knowledge of the better and the worse are connected secret auguries of joy and sorrow, the failure and falsehood of which would throw discredit on the whole announcement of the inner oracle."—*Types of Ethical Theory*, vol. ii. p. 105.

it is this, whatever else it may be. And here is the effective sanction of the moral law, by which it is made an operative and living reality in the lives of men. As the same philosopher writes, "Without a God and without a world, not now visible to us, but hoped for, the glorious ideas of morality are indeed objects of approbation and of admiration, but cannot be the springs of purpose and practice." * Hence the ideas of moral good and evil, and of rewards and punishments beyond the grave, the presentiment of which forms part and parcel of human nature, properly find place in dogmatic religious teaching, nay, constitute one of its principal spheres. Christianity is, and cannot keep from being, a vast system of moral discipline. For a thousand years it has taught the foremost nations of the world what "to believe and to do." And, assuredly, its rules of action must share in the discredit cast upon its articles of faith. It is impossible practically to view any ethical problem apart from The Great Enigma of the meaning and end of life which fundamentally underlies all morality.

Now, in this book I propose, in the first place, to assume, for the purpose of my argument, that the solution of that Enigma offered by Theistic belief,

* *Kritik der reinen Vernunft.* Methodenlehre, 2 Haupst., 2 Abschn.

and especially by Christianity, is discredited, and to consider, both in their theoretical and practical aspects, the other solutions offered us instead. I shall then ask my readers to weigh with me the question whether Theism in general, and the Christian religion in particular, are, in Heine's phrase, so utterly "played out" as is very generally contended. Such is the scope of the present book. And here let me observe that I am writing it for the benefit, not of those who are already of my opinion, but of those who are not. I cannot conceal from myself that there is a great and growing multitude of cultivated and virtuous men and women, earnestly desirous to follow truth, who, in the increased capacities for doubting which this new age confers, are unable—honestly unable—to use the old religious symbols. Yet they feel acutely "that unless above himself he can erect himself, how poor a thing is man!" They suffer from what George Sand called "the remorse of religion and the recklessness of thinking." It is of no avail to say to them, with a vigorous disputant of the present day, "A man who cannot occupy his mind with love, friendship, science, literature, art, politics, trade, and a thousand other matters, must be a poor kind of creature." This truculent dictum—happily an extra-judicial utterance of the learned judge who delivered himself of it—does not in the least touch them. They feel that it is as though a deaf man should revile the portentous folly of all who are moved with concord of sweet sounds: as though a blind man should proscribe the pictorial art as idle daubing. They feel that the exact contrary is true; that a man who can wholly occupy his mind with such things—even though he put money in his purse thereby—must be "a poor kind of creature;" because precisely in proportion to our elevation in the scale of being is our inability to appease with finite husks the infinite hunger that is in us. To such I especially address myself in what I am about to write. I shall endeavour to put myself in their place, to see with their eyes, to feel with their sentiments. I say to them, Setting aside altogether the stock arguments—if I may so speak—usually relied upon by Christian apologists, prescinding from the "evidences" commonly adduced in favour of what is called "revealed" religion—arguments and evidences which you *ex hypothesi* find insufficient—let us see, first, what is the real value of the answers to The Great Enigma of human life offered us in the place of such religion, and, next, whether its essential verities do not rest upon a basis of adamant, against which the dynamite of modern physicists, historians, and critics is powerless.

There are really, as it seems to me, in good

logic, only two answers besides Theism to this great problem of man's existence—Atheism and Agnosticism: terms which, before I go further, I ought to define. Atheism has been employed in many different senses. Thus St. Paul speaks of the Polytheistic Greeks as Atheists in the world (ἄθεοι ἐν τῷ κόσμῳ), and the Eastern Fathers after him do the like. Clement of Alexandria, for example, describes the Bacchic orgies as "the mysteries of Atheists." On the other hand, the primitive Christians were reproached with Atheism, as Socrates had been reproached before them, and some of the early apologists apply themselves to a refutation of that charge.* The sense in which the word is used has gradually been narrowed; and should, as I think, be still further restricted. Theologians classify Atheists as practical and theoretical, systematic and non-systematic, direct and indirect. Littré defines an Atheist as "one who does not believe in God." But there are many who, like Faust, are unable, for one reason or another, to say, "I believe in God," and who strongly object to inclusion in the same category

* Athenagoras is one of these. He writes (Legatio 10): "I have sufficiently demonstrated that they are not Atheists who believe in One who is unbegotten, eternal, unseen, impassible, incomprehensible, and uncontained; comprehended by mind and reason only, invested with ineffable light and beauty and spirit and power; by whom the universe is brought into being and set in order and held firm, through the agency of His own Logos."—Quoted by Hatch, *Hibbert Lectures*, p. 253.

with those who in terms deny Him. Doubt, suspension of judgment, ignorance, they maintain, represent a very different attitude of mind from negation. And it appears to me that they are well warranted in their contention. I think they are most correctly described by the name of "Agnostic," invented by Professor Huxley for their benefit; and I shall so describe them. The term "Atheist," I shall restrict to the dogmatic denier of God. Of Agnosticism, again, there will be found to be two varieties, which, for very practical reasons, ought to be distinguished: the merely critical and negative, and the scientific or affirmative. There are those who maintain that we cannot know whether or no a Divine Noumenon exists. And there are those who assert His existence, but deny that He can be known.

I shall return to this distinction hereafter. My present point is that to Atheism or Agnosticism all antitheistic theories may be reduced. This is clearly true of Pantheism, which is really such.* I add the qualifying words, because what is often called Pantheism is merely the presentation—the one-sided presentation, it may be—of the great Theistic verity, too often ignored, upon

* Mr. Downes, in his interesting article in the *Encyclopædia Britannica*, defines Pantheism as "that speculative system which, by absolutely identifying the subject and the object of thought, reduces all existence, mental and material, to phenomenal modifications of one eternal self-existent Substance, which is called by the name of God."

which Plato insisted when he taught the men of Athens "all things are full of divinity, full of soul;" which St. Paul recalled to them when he declared on Areopagus, "In Him we live and move and have our being." Pantheism, that is really such, in all the manifold forms which it assumes—for it is a very Proteus—will be found rather a term than a terminus of human thought, its ultimate resolution being the cancellation of the Theistic idea. Such, I maintain, is the logical value of the doctrine which sees in the universe only the self-evolution of the Infinite, and in man only that point in such self-evolution at which the Infinite attains self-consciousness. To deify the totality of things is to annihilate Deity, for it empties the Divine Noumenon of the elements of personality and morality; while it is no answer at all to The Great Enigma wherewith we are concerned: "to call the world God," Schopenhauer has well observed, "is not to explain it; it remains a riddle under the one name as under the other."*

* The following terse and cogent remarks, from the *Bampton Lectures* (1866) of my lamented friend Dr. Liddon, may fitly find place here: "In conceiving of God, the choice before a Pantheist lies between alternatives from which no genius has as yet devised a real escape. God, the Pantheist must assert, is literally everything; God is the whole material and spiritual universe; He is humanity in all its manifestations; He is by inclusion every moral and immoral agent; and every form and exaggeration of moral evil, no less than every variety of moral excellence and beauty, is part of the all-pervading, all-compre-

The principal other antitheistic theories before the world are Materialism, Positivism, Secularism, and Pessimism. Concerning these it will be sufficient here to remark that Materialism,* like Pantheism, is a name covering a vast variety of opinions, all of which will be found to issue in the denial of Deity in the universe, or in the denial that anything transcending the senses can be apprehended by man. Positivism, whether in its more materialistic form, originally taught by Comte, or as modified in an idealistic sense by later exponents, should, I suppose, since it repudiates absolute Atheism in terms, be held to be a variety of Agnosticism. The same, it would seem, must, in

hending movement of His universal life. If this revolting blasphemy be declined, then the God of Pantheism must be the barest abstraction of abstract being; He must, as with the Alexandrian thinkers, be so exaggerated an abstraction as to transcend existence itself; He must be conceived of as utterly unreal, lifeless, non-existent; while the only real beings are those finite and determinate forms of existence whereof 'nature' is composed. This dilemma haunts all the historical transformations of Pantheism, in Europe as in the East, to-day as two thousand years ago. Pantheism must either assert that its God is the one only existing being whose existence absorbs and is identified with the universe and humanity; or else it must admit that He is the rarest and most unreal of conceivable abstractions; in plain terms, that He is no being at all" (p. 393).

* In its proper sense Materialism means absolute Atheism; for it is the doctrine that in matter is the foundation and explanation of the universe, and that life is merely a form of mechanical and chemical force. It denies the existence of God and of the soul.

fairness, be said of Secularism,* although Mr. Bradlaugh laboured abundantly to show that its principles are essentially atheistic. Finally, Pessimism, in what are called the "reasoned" forms of its contemporary presentation, is irreconcilable with any form of the Theistic idea. It denies "all that is called God or that is worshipped," and exhibits as the answer to The Great Enigma a blind irrational entity, denominated by Schopenhauer, Will; and by Hartmann, The Unconscious. I am very far indeed from saying that this judgment holds good of all Pessimism. On the contrary, Buddhism, which certainly exhibits a pessimistic view of the world, recognized the innumerable divinities of the Hindoo Pantheon. That is clear from its canonical books. Equally clear is it that the Buddhist missionaries adopted, or, at the least, respected the gods honoured in the countries which they evangelized. It is perfectly true that Buddhism does not possess the conception of the supreme creative Deity of Monotheism. But its

* "The *Secularist* is an exponent of that philosophy of life termed Secularism, which deprecates the old policy of sacrificing the certain welfare of humanity on earth to the merely possible and altogether unknown requirements of a life beyond the grave; which concentrates human attention on the life which now is instead of upon a dubious life to come; which declares science to be the only available Providence of man, which repudiates groundless faith and accepts the sole guide of reason; and makes conduciveness to human welfare the criterion of right and wrong."—Prospectus of *The Secularist*, quoted in Mr. Gladstone's *Gleanings*, vol. iii. p. 129.

very foundation is belief in a supersensuous Power ruling absolutely over gods and men and all sentient existence; and that Power a perfectly just and holy Law. And this is the source of its sublime morality. Christianity, again, has almost as much in common with Buddhist pessimism as with Buddhist ethics. It is essentially a doctrine of renunciation based upon the verity succinctly formulated by the apostle—"Mundus totus in maligno positus est;" "The whole world lieth in wickedness:" a verity true not of an age but for all time. It is a doctrine of abstinence, not only from all things which it brands as positively sinful, but from pleasant things in themselves licit. It is a doctrine which exhibits as the way to perfection the denial of man's strongest instincts, through voluntary poverty, voluntary chastity, voluntary obedience.* "The world, which St. John exhorts his disciples not to love, because the love of it is incompatible with the love of the Father, which he describes as lying in the wicked one, which

* St. Thomas Aquinas writes: "The perfection of man consists in a total adhesion to God. . . . The religious life is instituted principally for the gaining of perfection by means of certain exercises whereby the obstacles to perfect charity are removed. . . . [It is] an exercise and training by which men arrive at the perfection of charity. For this it is necessary totally to withdraw the affection from worldly things." And he goes on to point out that the instruments of such withdrawal are poverty, chastity, and obedience solemnly vowed. "By these three vows the religious state is suitably set up in its integrity."—*Summa*, 2. 2æ. q. 186, a. 1-7.

over and over again in the New Testament the disciples of Christ are bidden to forsake and overcome, and which—such is the vitality of phrases—stands, even in our own day, for the complete antithesis of the Church, is the present visible frame of things, doomed, as those early preachers believed, soon to pass away with the lust thereof: the flesh, in which St. Paul declared no good thing to dwell, which it was his daily endeavour to keep under and to bring into subjection, is the whole of man's lower or animal nature. Whatever is doubtful, this is clear."* The smug optimism, which is now frequently paraded as Christianity, exhibits what Dean Church has well called " a strange blindness to the real sternness, nay, the austerity, of the New Testament." †

So much may suffice to indicate generally—which is enough for our present purpose—my reasons for holding that the various antitheistic theories current at the present day are reducible to Atheism or Agnosticism. I now go on to consider the former of these answers to The Great Enigma.

* I am quoting from my *Chapters in European History*, vol. i. p. 85.

† *The Oxford Movement*, p. 19.

CHAPTER II.

ATHEISM.

I HAVE defined Atheism as the dogmatic denial of God. But, before I go on to discuss it, I ought to indicate what I understand by God. When I use that great name, I mean by it, with Kant, "a Supreme Being, the First Cause or Creator of all things, by free and understanding action;" and with Dr. Martineau, "a Divine Mind and Will, ruling the Universe, and holding Moral relations with mankind." By an Atheist I understand one who denies this highest generalization of Monotheism. Theistic belief has, of course, a history. The concept of Deity has been slowly evolved. Among our own Aryan ancestors it " was at first a generic conception. It applied not to one power, but to many. Even when the human mind tried to combine the idea of supremacy, and therefore of oneness, with that of Deity, this was done, at first, by predicating supremacy of single *devas* or gods only, each supreme in his own domain. After this stage, in which we find a number of single gods, neither co-ordinate nor subordinate, there follows the next, in which all the single gods were combined into a kind of organic whole, one god being supreme, the others subject to him, but to him only, and standing among themselves on a certain level of equality. After these two stages . . . follows in the end that of real Monotheism, a belief in one God, as excluding the very possibility of other gods."* For our present purpose we may put aside the tribes of men who are still in the stage of Henotheism or Polytheism. We are not concerned with them. And it is not worth while to fight as one that beateth the air. The Atheists with whom we are brought into contact are not the gainsayers of the gods many and lords many worshipped by those dwelling on the lower levels of religious thought. They are the dogmatic deniers of a Supreme Agent, above and behind but distinct from nature, who makes all things to be, and " with whom we have to do."

It may indeed be objected that such dogmatic denial is not worth answering. No doubt, in one sense, this is so. The Theistic idea is a living

* F. Max Müller, *Anthropological Religion*, p. 75. Professor Max Müller truly adds, " These stages in the development of the idea of the Godhead are not merely theoretical postulates. They are historical realities, which we may watch in many religions, if only we are enabled to follow their history in literary documents."

form of thought, not in the least affected by verbal negations. These merely touch the word. The concept remains inviolate—

> "For it is, as the air, invulnerable:
> And our vain blows malicious mockery."

Hence the Hebrew poet appears to be perfectly well warranted when he charges with folly the man who says in his heart there is no God. "Dixit insipiens in corde suo, non est Deus." The absolute and dogmatic Atheist usually founds himself upon the argument that there can be no God, because He is not found as a finite force in the universe, and cannot be weighed or measured; because He is not apprehensible by the senses, and cannot be seen, heard, touched, smelt, or tasted. What is one to say to a disputant who relies upon this absurdest of absurdities? It is surely enough to send him to school to Voltaire for half an hour. Let him read, mark, learn, and inwardly digest the article "Dieu" in the *Dictionnaire Philosophique*, and unless he is impervious to common sense, he will hardly dissent from that sage's conclusion: "A demonstrative proof of the non-existence of God assuredly no one has ever found nor will find." But indeed the rage of these fetid blasphemers—chiefly represented by the medico-atheistic school now so powerful in France—is in itself suspicious. "Does any one take God *au sérieux?*" one of them asked me not long ago. And I ventured to reply,

"At least, you and your friends would seem to do so: else you would not hate Him so bitterly." Surely this intellectual and moral *canaille* merits no serious consideration from any thinker. To glance at it and pass by would be enough, save from one very practical consideration. We live in an age when "the masses" (as the phrase is), who have hitherto been nothing in the public order, have become everything, or are fast becoming everything. Political power has everywhere passed, or is passing, into the hands of those who are "as incapable of thinking as they are of flying." And among the masses the propagandists of Atheism are, everywhere, most active and most successful. Their methods differ in different countries, but in all worketh one and the selfsame spirit. In Germany it has assumed the form of that crassest, coarsest and most consistent Materialism which Heine declares, in his *Confessions*, scared him back into Deism; and it is closely allied with a political party which aims at the entire overthrow of the public order, and the reconstruction of society upon a basis of Socialism. "These troops of destruction, these sappers whose axe threatens the whole social edifice, are immeasurably superior to the Chartists of England and the levellers and revolutionists in other lands, by reason of the terrible thoroughness (*Konsequenz*) of their doctrine; and in the madness which impels them there is, as Polonius would say, method.

Their more or less secret leaders . . . are, without doubt, the most capable heads and the most energetic characters of Germany." * These words of Heine are as true now as when they were written, nearly four decades ago.

In England the Atheistic propaganda chiefly takes the form of an attack upon the Sacred Books of Christianity. The doctrine of the plenary inspiration of those venerable documents is the very corner stone upon which the popular religion of Great Britain rests. Dr. Bain, if my memory is not at fault, somewhere tells us of a worthy man, "a citizen of Edinburgh," who was a firm believer in Christianity, until he acquired a smattering of geology, when, being unable to reconcile the assertions in the first chapter of Genesis with the facts of that science, he applied to the whole Bible the rule "falsus in uno, falsus in omnibus," abandoned his belief in God, and became a zealous Atheist. It is an instance of what is commonly happening in this country, and "the open Bible theory"—as the phrase is—must be held largely responsible for it. I am far indeed from questioning the value of the religious and moral and intellectual culture resulting from the familiar acquaintance with the sacred volume possessed by all classes in this land. But there is another side to the matter. To place the Bible, without note or comment, in the hands of all able to read it, assuring them of its

* Heinrich Heine's *Sammtliche Werke*, vol. xiv. p. 275.

complete verbal inspiration and absolute inerrancy, of its all sufficiency as a revelation of the Divine Will, so perfectly intelligible, that "a wayfaring man, though a fool," shall not err in interpreting it, is assuredly, in this age of ours, to play into the hands of the propagandists of Atheism. And of this they are quite well aware, for wellnigh all their publications—a considerable number of which lie before me, as I write—are directed to show the scientific and historical untrustworthiness of the sacred volume, and so to discredit the Deity, whose very voice it is alleged to be. The note and comment which Exeter Hall withholds, the apostles of what calls itself Free Thought supply; the result being a wide diffusion of bitter and blasphemous Atheism, the fierce unintelligent denial of those who conceive themselves deceived by a false theophany, and who hasten to burn what they have adored. "The common people," writes Mr. John Morley, with a significant touch of Voltairian scorn for the *ignobile vulgus*, "are wont to crave a revelation, or else they find Atheism a rather better synthesis than any other. They either cling to the miraculously transmitted message, with its hopes of recompense, and its daily communication of the Divine voice in prayer or sacrament, or else they make a world which moves through space as a black monstrous ship with no steersman." *

* *Voltaire*, by John Morley, p. 278.

It is, however, to France that we should turn for the completest view of the Atheistic propaganda. And what Atheism is in France, it is in the Latin races generally. I do not know where a better revelation is given of it than in certain catechisms which have been prepared as instruments for the atheizing of that country. If we would learn how the various forms of Christianity are apprehended and assimilated by the popular mind, there is no safer way than by consulting the hornbooks and manuals in which the dogmas of that faith are reduced to their essential elements, and expressed in the simplest statements. Thus, should a Protestant desire to know what Catholic teaching practically is, he will naturally consult Catholic catechisms—the most authoritative of which is, of course, that set forth by the desire of the Council of Trent. So the Shorter Catechism, prepared by the Assembly of Divines at Westminster, provides the best summary of the dogmas held by Presbyterianism and its kindred sects; while, if we would discover the secret of the wholesome influence exercised by Anglicanism upon the general mind of this country for generations, we shall find it in those pages of the Book of Common Prayer which put before us "a catechism, that is to say, an instruction, to be learnt by every person before he be brought to be confirmed by the Bishop:" a beautiful document, in which primary verities of Christian faith and morals are impressed upon the tender mind, in language at once simple and stately as that of the English Bible. And let no one suppose that the age of Catechisms is past. The Apostles of Atheism in France know better. They have discerned, rightly, that the catechetical form is unique in its adaptation to the wants of the masses; and they have displayed much practical wisdom in availing themselves of it. Three works lie before me, which have of late years been given by them to the world, in order to the rearing of the youth of their country in the tenets which they desire to substitute for the old doctrines of religion and morality. The smallest of these works—I will take them in order of size—is a duodecimo of eight pages, entitled, *Le Petit Catéchisme du Libre-Penseur*. It is authorized, I observe, "pour le colportage"—a fact worth noting—and has been very widely disseminated since it was published about ten years ago. The *Catéchisme Populaire Républicain*—a somewhat larger treatise—was given to the world some thirty years since, and has had a large sale (the edition before me is the thirtieth), although it is now, perhaps, a little out of date: events have moved fast during the last three decades. But both these compilations are as the Catholic *Penny Catechism* is to the *Catechism of the Council of Trent*, in respect of M. Edgar Monteil's *Catéchisme du Libre-Penseur*—a work which its author describes as "destiné à porter au milieu des masses la vérité sur des matières que la crédulité humaine maintient fort enracinées, à pénétrer dans les couches de la société moderne exploitées par la superstition." The studies of which his Catechism is a *résumé*, would have filled folios, he tells us. It would have cost him less pains, he asseverates, to have presented in ten volumes what he has here compressed into three hundred pages: three hundred pages, so to speak, of the essence of Atheism. But his object was to be a connecting link (*trait d'union*) between *savants* and the populace; to put before the world a "condensed book, within the grasp of the ignorant, intelligible to everybody." It will be seen that M. Monteil has well grasped the right conception of what a Catechism ought to be. It is clear, too, that in executing his arduous labour he was cheered and sustained by the true spirit of faith. "Quant à nous," he writes, "notre récompense se trouvera en nous-mêmes si par la publication de ce catéchisme nous pouvons inciter les auteurs à renouveler par des livres conformés aux idées modernes, les livres qui corrompent l'homme dès l'enfance, et si par-dessus tout, nous avons contribué, encore plus que par nos œuvres antérieures, à extirper l'erreur et à faire triompher la vertu." Such were the beautiful aspirations with which M. Monteil betook himself to the composition of his Catechism. Regarding the probabilities of its achieving the success which he desiderates in extirpating error and promoting the triumph of virtue, my readers shall presently judge for themselves. Meanwhile, let me observe that the author already has his reward, to some extent, not only in the wide circulation of his work among an appreciative public, but in the plaudits of his fellow Atheists. Among other testimonies of great weight is that of the *République Française*, which solemnly blesses it, and pronounces it to be the best and most meritorious composition of its kind extant. And now, having thus surveyed the work from the outside, let us look a little at its contents, and learn from it what French Atheism is, illustrating M. Monteil's teaching, where necessary, from the smaller compilations of which mention has been made.

One indubitable merit of M. Monteil's book is its admirable arrangement. He begins at the beginning and does not leave off until he has conducted us to the logical conclusion. As he well observes in his preface, "Il fallait être systématique, absolu, pour que ce livre fut à son adresse." "Systématique" and "absolu" he accordingly is. His work is divided into three sections. The first treats of God; the second of Religion; the last of Morals. And in following this order M. Monteil has evidently had in mind the maxim, "Fas est et ab hoste doceri." The religion which he seeks to replace rests upon the idea of God. Thus, the Church Catechism leads the child from his own name and the manner of its imposition to the conception of a Divine paternity; and thence to the duties—religious and ethical—which flow from his relationship to the ineffable Being whom he has learnt to call "Our Father." M. Monteil must, then, I think, be credited with much astuteness in beginning with the primary tenet of all Theism, and so going to the root of the matter. Here are the four questions and answers wherewith he initiates his work. I reproduce his typography:—

" *Q.* What is *God?*

" *A.* God is an *expression.*

" *Q.* What is the exact value of this expression?

" *A.* The exact value of the word NATURE.

" *Q.* What is Nature?

" *A.* The totality of all we know to exist in the infinite Universe.

" *Q.* What other definition can you give of Nature?

" *A.* It is the material world, and ALL *is matter*" (p. 14).

The *Petit-Catéchisme* gives to its teaching upon this high theme a political turn so deliciously grotesque that I must here quote it, although at the sacrifice of laying aside M. Monteil's work for a moment. "Do you believe in a Supreme Being?" that manual inquires of the neophyte. And the reply which it puts into his mouth is as follows:—"I only believe what my reason permits me to believe, and my reason refuses to admit the principle of the 'Government of Nature' by any being whatsoever. I am persuaded that Nature always has been, is, and always will be, republican, and consequently fitted to govern herself" * (p. 19).

Verily, to speak in the gorgeous language of Oriental metaphor, which alone is adequate here, this author has strung a pearl of the first water upon the chaplet of Atheism.

But to return to our *Catéchisme du Libre-Penseur*. "The learned, then, have not found out God?" it goes on to ask. The answer is, "No, they are all agreed in denying His existence;" a somewhat sweeping proposition, it must be confessed, but M. Monteil's experience as a journalist in the *République Française* and other newspaper organs of Atheism has doubtless taught him the value of a slashing style. Nor, indeed, is there wanting high authority by which he might

---

* Compare the *Catéchisme Populaire Républicain*:—"Ceux qui prétendent que Dieu a créé l'homme afin d'être connu, aimé et servi par lui n'exigent pas autre chose de l'homme que de renoncer à sa raison, à son intelligence, à sa liberté morale, de se nier soi-même et de s'anéantir en face d'une puissance absolue dont il ne lui est accordé de comprendre ni la nature ni la justice" (p. 19).

vindicate his contempt for exact accuracy. Thus he might appeal to the doctrine of the Patriarch of Ferney, so faithfully carried out by that great man upon many occasions:—" Mentez, mes amis. Il faut mentir comme un diable, non pas timidement, non pour un temps, mais hardiment et toujours. Le mensonge n'est un vice que quand il fait du mal." Any stick Voltaire considered was good enough to beat *l'Infâme;* and doubtless M. Monteil thinks so too; "the disciple is not above his master." The *Catéchisme du Libre-Penseur*, however, goes on to anticipate and dispose of the familiar argument, old as the days of the Hebrew Psalmist, and, probably, as the infancy of the human race : " Cœli enarrant ; " the testimony of " the spacious firmament " and " shining heavens " to " their great Original," who, " in the beginning created the heavens and the earth."

" *Q.* If there is no God, who then created the heaven and the earth?

" *A.* Neither the heaven, nor infinity, nor the earth has been created.

" *Q.* Who created man and woman?

" *A.* Neither man nor woman has been created.

" *Q.* There is no First Cause, then?

" *A.* No; for all that we cannot prove scientifically has no existence, and may be denied until proof of the contrary " (*et se nie jusqu'à preuve du contraire*, p. 16).

This last sentence leads us to fear that, in the

vast range of M. Monteil's studies, logic must have been overlooked. On the next page he proceeds to another objection which, as he sagaciously discerns, will present itself to the inquiring minds that he desires to form.

"*Q.* How is it, then, that there are gods?

"*A.* Because man has invented them" (p. 18).

And so the *Petit Catéchisme:* " God is a spectre invented by priests to frighten timid minds (*les faibles d'esprit*) in order that these latter may cast themselves into their arms and endure more easily their domination."

The *Catéchisme du Libre-Penseur* goes on to press the argument from the presence of evil in this imperfect world. It concludes from this that "the divine individuality is a lie," that "we ought not to believe in the existence of the individual named God that most religions have presented to us" (p. 24). "Such a God has no existence, and it is not to an independent and creative Will that we can attribute this universal harmony" (p. 26), M. Monteil insists. It will be remembered, however, that at the opening of the *Catéchisme du Libre-Penseur* the exact value of the expression God was stated to be the exact value of the word Nature; and now after thus accomplishing the purely iconoclastic part of his work, M. Monteil takes up this theme. It is significant that while teaching the crassest Atheism, he nowhere expressly avows it. He prefers to mask it under the name of Pantheism. That, he tells us, is the true faith. And, by way of definition of Pantheism, he gives us the following question and answer:—

"*Q.* What do you mean in the present day by Pantheism?

"*A.* There is an all (*un tout*)—the all of forces, the all of beings, the all of forms—which is God. He gives not, he receives not, he constitutes not, he is constituted (*il ne constitue pas, il est constitué*). He is neither a force nor a form; by himself he is nothing at all (*par lui même il n'est que néant*). He is no more one thing than another, but the whole (*l'ensemble*) of the objects and the worlds in infinity" (p. 32).

Obviously this new deity, in vindication of whom M. Monteil approvingly cites Holbach and La Mettrie, is (to quote one of Lord Beaconsfield's happy phrases) merely "Atheism in domino." But let us follow our author as, with his usual prevision, he proceeds to anticipate and answer the gainsayer:—

"*Q.* Is Pantheism consistent with our scientific knowledge?

"*A.* Yes.

"*Q.* And yet it is not admitted by our two principal philosophic sects—that of the Positivists and that of the Materialists?

"*A.* True; but this is by reason of sectarian exclusiveness (*par l'exclusivisme de secte*).

"*Q.* Explain yourself."

M. Monteil then proceeds to explain himself at some length, the upshot being that in what he is pleased to call Pantheism is to be found the reconciliation of these two sects of "modern thought." Here are the two questions and answers in which he disposes of this subject:—

"*Q.* How does the Pantheist reconcile the Positivist and Materialist?

"*A.* By arguing to them thus: 'Your supreme law is science?'* 'Yes.' 'Do you either find or place science outside Nature?' 'No.' 'It is then in Nature?' 'Yes.' 'It is, therefore, incorporate with Nature?' (*Elle fait en conséquence corps avec la nature?*) 'Yes.' 'It proves to you the existence of natural things?' 'Yes.' 'Do you know of anything that is, or can be outside Nature?' 'No.' 'Then, if that is so, everything may be summed up in the term *Nature*, and you are at one with the Pantheists.'

"*Q.* Can they, then, admit that Nature is God?

"*A.* Doubtless, for it is then no more than a matter of expression. It is enough that they should be so obliging as to use the term *God* as well as *Nature*, admitting the two terms to be absolutely synonymous" (p. 35).

Atheistic Pantheism, or Pantheistic Atheism,

---

* It is hardly necessary to remark that by "science" M. Monteil means physics. Neither he nor his Positivist and Materialistic friends recognize any sciences except the physical.

with a tendency to a generous minimism which shall embrace Positivism, is, according to M. Monteil, the true solution of The Great Enigma. And now, having thus emancipated the neophyte from the old superstition about God, and reduced Him to something which is not either a force or a form, and which, taken by Himself, is nothing, the *Catéchisme du Libre-Penseur* proceeds to deal with that part of man hitherto popularly supposed to be immortal. It is related of Tom Moore, the poet, that upon one occasion, when plied with Atheistic discourse by Sir Charles Morgan, he remonstrated, "Pray, my dear Morgan, consider my immortal soul." To whom the irascible surgeon: "Damn your immortal soul, sir; listen to my arguments." The adjuration was more vigorous than timely, and failed to reassure the trembling bard. M. Monteil is more considerate. His scholars may listen to his arguments without any terror, and may take his word for it that the soul is even a more absolute nonentity than the Pantheistic deity to whom we have been introduced. In the following trenchant manner does he dispose of this subject:—

"*Q.* What is the soul?

"*A.* Nothing.

"*Q.* It is not a thing then, existent in Nature?

"*A.* No.

"*Q.* What is the distinction between soul and body?

"*A.* The distinction between soul and body is a simple analytical process (*un simple procédé analytique*).

"*Q.* What is generally understood by the word *soul?*

"*A.* Thought independent of matter is what is generally understood by it.

"*Q.* Can such independence exist?

"*A.* No: since everything belongs to the material order.

"*Q.* The soul, then, does not return to God who is all?

"*A.* No: For God is formed of that which exists, and the soul does not exist" (p. 36).

Such is the simple syllogism wherewith M. Monteil reassures us upon this grave matter. The *Petit Catéchisme*, providing, so to speak, "milk for babes," expresses itself even more bluntly, as follows:—

"*Q.* What is man?

"*A.* Man is one of the most favoured products of the earth; but Nature makes no more account of him than of the smallest insect. In consequence of his material conformation, he possesses a stronger dose of intelligence (*une plus forte dose d'intelligence*) than any other animal. But it is no less a fact that he exists by virtue of the same principle as the most vulgar companion of St. Anthony."

The world has travelled far since the question,

What is man? was asked by the royal poet of the Hebrews. "Quid est homo, quod memor es ejus? aut filius hominis, quod visitas eum?"— man, made a little lower than the angels, and crowned with glory and worship. How are the mighty fallen! A few words of these sages of Atheism, and, as by a touch of Circe's wand, the glory and worship die away, and we are reduced to our proper rank among the swine. It was a right apprehension of "the spirit of the years to come," a true prescience of the impending needs of the world, which led Mr. Carlyle to embody, in the *Latter-Day Pamphlets*, his invaluable "Pig Propositions."

So, then, according to the Atheistic gospel, there is no soul in man; and, if no soul in him, then no future life for him. But M. Monteil, with his usual care to be thorough, is explicit upon this latter point:—

"*Q.* The materiality of the soul, then, involving its negation, there is no future life?

"*A.* No: as the soul no longer constitutes for us an independent and imperishable individuality, there is no future life" (p. 38).

M. Monteil here favours us with an elaborate note to prove that the immediate consequence of belief in a future life is suicide. It is true that the facts do not bear him out, such belief having been pretty general in the world for a good many ages, and not having resulted in universal *felo de se.* But so much the worse for the facts, which, it must be allowed, have a most coarse, inconsiderate way of deranging the neatest Atheistic arguments. It is not M. Monteil's fault if people were too stupid to follow out their own principles. He returns, however, to his point:—

"*Q.* There is, then, no future life?

"*A.* No: there is no future life; unless, indeed, it be that we continue to live on by our works. What we leave behind us of our labour, what we bequeath of our thought, what we sow of our body, what is incarnate in our children, after having been incarnate in us—that is the only future life" (p. 40).

M. Monteil's practical conclusion is: "We must apply to the real world, to the earth, which we see, and which we enjoy, the belief in eternity which in Theism is applied to a fiction" (p. 55).

Pass we now to Part II. of the *Catéchisme du Libre-Penseur*, in which M. Monteil devotes some hundred and fifty pages to the subject of religion. He divides this portion of his volume into three sections. In the first he deals with the theology of the Christian Church; in the second, with its moral philosophy; in the third he is at the pains to summarize in a sort of discourse or homily the opinions exposed in the two preceding sections. It might at first seem, to shallow judgments, as though this part of his work were superfluous: since, if there be no undying soul in man, and no God to whom we shall give account for the deeds done in the body, it is but lost labour to attack Christian theology, which is the science of God, or Christian morals, which take account of His existence and His attributes. But, as I have said, one great characteristic of M. Monteil's work is its thoroughness; and in a note (p. 69) he tells us, "The object of this part of the Catechism is to establish the historic truth about the Christian religion, and to show that a system at once philosophic, and moral, and rational may be substituted for it." According to M. Monteil, then, Christianity, like other religions, has proceeded (*découlé*) from the foolish Theistic hypothesis. It is a purely human work. It has brought into the world no new truth. Considered as a fiction, it is but a pantheistic theory. Considered as a social religion, its results have been disastrous indeed, for it has retarded civilization by fifteen hundred years; meanwhile conducting men to the brutality, to the prostrate degradation of the most revolting immorality. Nor let any one say, our teacher protests, that this is the work of its ministers; that it is a good religion in itself, but that it has been spoilt by priestcraft. No; M. Monteil is indeed anti-clerical to the very marrow of his bones, as becomes the friend and brother in journalism of the late MM. Paul Bert and Gambetta. But he allows that the priests—so much the worse for them—are "dans la logique de la religion." "It is the religion itself," he urges; "it is the Old, it is the New Testament, as well as the Popes and Councils, that have accomplished the fine work" above mentioned. "It is the religion itself which is baneful, deadly; in Jehovah as in Jesus, in the Pentateuch as in the Gospels."*

* It may be well to subjoin the text of the passages I am quoting:—"La Terre avait peuplé le Ciel, elle se dit que c'était le Ciel qui l'avait peuplée. De l'hypothèse déiste ont découlé les religions, et le christianisme n'a été, comme les autres inventions, qu'œuvre humaine ; seulement il n'a apporté dans le monde, en religion comme en morale, aucune vérité nouvelle. Considéré comme une fiction, le christianisme n'est qu'une théorie panthéistique ; considère à la lettre c'est un monothéisme devenu un polythéisme anthropomorphiste. . . . Si l'on considère le christianisme comme religion sociale, on doit admettre que ses résultats ont été désastreux, qu'ils ont reculé la civilisation de près de quinze siècles. . . . En effet, ce n'est pas le clergé uniquement qu'il faut accuser de conduire l'homme à une bestialité, à un anéantissement de la plus révoltante immoralité, c'est la religion elle-même, c'est l'Ancien, c'est le Nouveau-Testament, ce sont les pères de l'Église tout autant que les Papes et les Conciles qui ont accompli cette belle œuvre. Ne tenons donc jamais ce langage ; la religion est une bonne chose en elle-même, ce sont les prêtres qui la gâtent. Non, les prêtres sont dans la logique de la religion. Tout ce qu'on peut exiger des prêtres, c'est un compte sévère de leurs plus minces actions. . . . Mais on ne saurait empêcher leur action dissolvante et pernicieuse sur les consciences, c'est-à-dire véritablement anéantir les prêtres, qu'en les frap-

Such is the succinct view of Christianity put before the neophyte of Atheism by his father in the faith. Let us glance at the pages in which it is worked out in detail. Those which deal with the Founder of Christianity I prefer, indeed, to pass over. But I must note the apology with which we are presented for the persecution of His primitive followers. These martyrs and confessors, M. Monteil would have us know, " professed sentiments of revolt against classes of society other than their own, and practised a communism which was the very negation of the domestic hearth, so honoured at Rome ; " " their common meals or *agapes* soon degenerated into shameful concubinage ; " they " turned everything into ridicule, broke the laws, and despised all that attaches one to life ; " thereby justly incurring both the imputation of "odium humani generis," fastened upon them by the philanthropic pagans of the decadent empire, and the severities which followed. And such conduct, M. Monteil points out, was quite congruous with the " exitiabilis superstitio " as which he paints their religion.

pant dans leur sacerdoce même, c'est-à-dire en frappant la religion, car c'est la religion qui est nuisible, funeste, dans Jehowah comme dans Jésus, dans le Pentateuque comme dans les Evangiles. Il faut prendre le mal dans sa racine et couper la racine. Le clergé forme les branches et les feuilles chargées de répandre le poison contenu dans le tronc, que le tronc s'abatte donc, et les branches et les feuilles se dessècheront. Toute tentative de conciliation est désormais impossible " (pp. 198–203).

The following cullings from his Catechism may serve to indicate the outlines of his picture:—

"*Q.* Is the Christian religion the source of all morals?

"*A.* No; for it does not contain a single trait of morality which is peculiar to it, and which is not derived from the religions or the philosophies which preceded or accompanied it.

"*Q.* Is not, then, that which is peculiar to the Christian religion moral?

"*A.* For the most part, no.

"*Q.* Does the Church regard men as of an elevated nature or a high morality?

"*A.* No. From Genesis onward the Lord proclaims: 'The spirit of man and all the thoughts of his heart are inclined to evil from his youth upward.' *

"*Q.* How does the Church regard woman?

"*A.* The Church hates, execrates, abominates woman" (p. 155).

"*Q.* What is this first result of this hatred of woman?

"*A.* The first result of this abasement of woman is to favour concubinage.

"*Q.* Does not the Church prohibit concubinage?

"*A.* No.

"*Q.* Does the Church admit marriage?

---

* M. Monteil is by way of quoting the Vulgate, Gen. viii. 21: "Sensus enim et cogitatio humani cordis in malum prona sunt ab adolescentia sua."

"*A.* She admits it, but she detests it" (p. 158).

"*Q.* Has not the Church blessed incestuous marriages?

"*A.* Yes; the Church has gone so far as to bless marriages between brothers and sisters.

"*Q.* Does the Christian religion inspire a child with respect and love for his parents?

"*A.* No. The ancient Law said, 'Honour thy father and mother so as to live long upon earth.'* But since the coming of Christ, one must no more live long (*il ne faut plus vivre longuement*). The anticipation of death is a happiness, and the titles of father, mother, brother, sister, given by Nature, count for little. Jesus said, 'Call no one on earth your father, for you have only one Father who is in Heaven.' † St. Paul says, 'Obey your parents, but only according to the law of the Lord.'

"*Q.* The Church, debasing man and woman and detesting marriage, is evidently contrary to the spirit of the family (*l'esprit de famille*)?

"*A.* Yes: and this is how the Son of God has come to consolidate the family, and to bring peace into the world, 'Think ye that I have come to bring peace upon earth? No, I tell you, but divisions. . . . The father shall be divided against the son, and the son against the father; the mother against the daughter, and the daughter

---

* "Ut sis longævus super terram."—*Vulgate.*

† "Vous n'avez qu'un père qui est dans le ciel:" Unus est enim Pater vester, qui in cœlis est.

against the mother; the mother-in-law against her daughter-in-law, and the daughter-in-law against her mother-in-law. The brother shall deliver his brother to death, and the children shall rise up against their fathers, and cause them to be put to death.'

" Q. Has the Church established equality among men and destroyed slavery?

" A. No. Those are two profound errors. The Church has never established equality among men, either in this world or the other, and nothing is more false than to attribute to Christianity the abolition of slavery. . . . 'Christ,' says J. J. Rousseau, 'preaches nothing but servitude and dependence. His spirit (*esprit*) is too favourable to tyranny that it should not always profit thereby. True Christians are made to be slaves' (p. 165).

" Q. Does the Church honour labour?

" A. No.

" Q. Does the Church allow of property?

" A. No; the Church does not allow of property.

" Q. Why?

" A. Because Christianity is eminently communistic.

" Q. On what words do you found this assertion?

" A. Christ knows of nothing but misery and bareness. Many times did he repeat that the rich should not enter into the kingdom of heaven. He says, 'Whosoever does not renounce all that he possesses cannot be my disciple. Sell all that you have.' There is no greater negation of property than Christianity. The first disciples of Jesus bring to the feet of the apostles all that they possess. . . . There are sects of Christians who, founding themselves on certain verses of the Gospels, have carried—nay, still carry—communism so far as to apply it to women. Common possession (*la communauté*) administered by the priest is the only true way of living Christianly. Every Christian who is a proprietor is no Christian at all; and 'a camel should sooner pass through the eye of a needle than a rich man should enter into the kingdom of heaven'" (p. 168).

It must be owned that M. Monteil has here displayed the wisdom of the serpent. The peasant proprietors of France, among whom his Catechism has been largely circulated, however little they may make of much of it, can hardly fail to be touched closely by this part, or to turn the eye of distrust upon M. le Curé, as the minister of a religion which proscribes equality, and is incompatible with property. And, like a skilful general, the preacher of Atheism follows up his advantage. "All kinds of violence," he asseverates, "hatred, vengeance, murder, incest, joined to avarice (that characteristic vice of the clergy) are the special endowments of the clerical body" (p. 174). "Pleasures, fortune, rule—such are their morality." His practical conclusion is that the world must break off for good and all from the Christian faith

(p. 203). "Let us abandon," he pleads; "let us abandon religion completely, and take refuge in PHILOSOPHY—the product of all reason, and the source of all morality" (p. 207).

And now let us glance at the philosophy of Atheism: the source of all its morality. "Philosophy," M. Monteil postulates, "must not be separated from human nature." Few will refuse to go this mile with him. But he would have them go twain; and his next, to feebler spirits, will appear a long mile. "Don't let us believe," he urges, "that people can't be wise unless they are ascetic or live without passions. No: the passions of man are his surest and most faithful guide." And of these passions, M. Monteil regards what he calls love (meaning thereby the sexual instinct*) as the chief, and, as of right, predominant. Upon this theme he rises to lyric enthusiasm. "C'est par l'amour qu'il peut sentir, comprendre: c'est par l'amour qu'il étend son individu à l'humanité toute entière." In the passions, then, as the budding Atheist learns, he will find the source of true philosophy: "they open to the reason all the gates of morality, of science,

* "L'amour est une inclination réciproque de l'homme et de la femme, dont tous les sens physiques réunis forment l'attache la plus puissante," &c. (p. 219).

of beauty, and of love"* Thus does *la libre pensée* justify its name and prove itself a true emancipating agency. The old repressive morality, acknowledged throughout Europe for so long, rested on conscience as "the Voice of God in the nature and heart of man;" the Divine Law, identical with the Supreme Being Himself, implanted in the intelligence of all His rational creatures, against which it is never lawful to go, since, as the Fourth Lateran Council says, "Quidquid fit contra conscientiam, ædificat ad gehennam.'" M. Monteil makes as short work of conscience† as he does of gehenna. In its place, as the rule of life, Atheism enthrones concupiscence.‡ The criterion of right and wrong is

* "Ne séparons point la philosophie de la nature humaine, et n'allons pas croire qu'on ne peut être sage qui si l'on est ascète et si l'on vit sans passions, dans l'inertie. Les passions de l'homme lui sont le guide le plus sûr et le plus fidèle, c'est par elles qu'il apprend à se servir de toutes les richesses de son cœur et à répandre les lumières de sa raison. C'est par l'amour qu'il peut sentir, comprendre, c'est sur l'amour qu'il doit méditer, c'est par l'amour qu'il étend son individu à l'humanité toute entière. Que la raison tempère la violence de la nature, rien de mieux, si la nature est violente, mais que les passions ouvrent à la raison toutes les portes de la morale, de la science, de la beauté et de l'amour" (p. 208, note).

† I am aware that he uses the word once or twice; but he uses it in an entirely different sense from the theological, as will be seen hereafter.

‡ I use the word in its proper theological sense: "Sciendum est concupiscentiam esse commotionem quamdam ac vim animi, qua impulsi homines quas non habent res jucundas appetunt." —*Cat. Concil. Triden.*, pars. iii. c. x.

thus succinctly laid down for the catechumen: "All that man desires and seeks out of self-love (*par amour de lui-même*) is good; and evil all that is contrary to his nature" (p. 238). Good, in fact, is what we like; evil what we dislike. In the following three questions and answers this matter is very clearly put:—

"*Q.* What is good?

"*A.* Good is the development of the faculties of man in conformity with his nature. 'Good,' says Jean Reynaud, 'is the sole principle of which our nature does not weary, and, sooner or later, evil, with the consequences of various kinds which it engenders, fatigues or repels Nature.'

"*Q.* How do we discover the principles of good?

"*A.* In the study of Nature.

"*Q.* What is the good given to man?

"*A.* Laromiguière tells us: 'Pleasures of the senses, pleasures of the intellect (*de l'esprit*), pleasures of the heart—these, if we knew how to use them, are the good things scattered in profusion across the path of life'" (p. 241).

Such is the glorious liberty of Atheists. In them a great work is wrought, exactly the contrary of that spoken of by St. Paul. Being made "liberi justitiæ," free from the bugbear called righteousness, and the rule of the imaginary "individual named God," they have their fruit unto gratification of the passions, and the end—why, that is in itself the end.

"O pleasure, you're indeed a pleasant thing,
 Although one must be damned for you, no doubt,"

sighed Lord Byron, haunted by dim reminiscences of "creeds that refuse and restrain." But only let Atheism have its perfect work, and the instinct of retributive justice, however "deep-seated in our mystic frame," shall be eradicated, and the bold human appetite shall be freed from its last restraints. Does any colder and more cautious spirit shrink from the probable consequences to society of this consummation? Let him be of good cheer: let him know that human nature is essentially good (p. 215), that man, unspoilt by religion, is just, loving, and lovable, whatever the phenomena of life may seem to teach to the contrary. Let him leave the beggarly elements of concrete fact, and betake himself to "the high *priori* road;" let him enter into his chamber and be still, and then, shutting out the world and opening his Rousseau, reassure himself, if not by the example, at all events by the rhetoric of that evangelist, from whom M. Monteil cites an appropriate text (p. 216).

Man, then, according to the Atheistic philosophy, is naturally good: the passions are the true guides of human life: their gratification is the true end of human life: and other life there is none. This being so, morality, duty, and law are very simple matters, and are soon disposed of. Morality—with which, as M. Monteil tells us, conscience is one (*la morale et la conscience ne font qu'un*, p. 242)—is "the sentiment that prescribes to us prudent conduct" (*une sage conduite*),* and is "determined by the reason" (p. 242), which, apparently, is nothing but phosphorus.† "Duty consists in rendering us devoted (*devoués*) to our affections, and to the laws to which we have consented, and rebellious against oppression" (p. 244). "The law is a natural verity, which people formulate, and to which they consent to conform their conduct" (p. 245). It is "based on right;" and the principal rights of man are those proclaimed in the "Declaration" of "the immortal French Revolution, to which the inhabitants of the whole world (previously slaves) owe it that they are citizens" (p. 246).

This is the New Gospel which the poor have preached to them: an Atheistic Materialism which is practically the negation of all ethics. I say "practically," for I do not deny that a dogmatic Atheist might insist upon the supreme authority of the moral law, the essential difference between right and wrong. But, as a matter of fact, in the

* Compare the sixth of the "Pig Propositions:" "The pig knows the weather; he ought to look out what kind of weather it will be."

† "La raison, a dit je ne sais plus quel physiologiste, c'est du phosphore," p. 212, note.

vast majority of instances, dogmatic Atheists lose this transcendental idea, with all other transcendental ideas. Their Atheism means a crude disbelief in all that lies out of the senses' grasp: it means the most crass and vulgar animalism. The overwhelming majority of men are not, and cannot be, philosophers. For them, in the Theistic concept, is the source of all justice, the type of all virtue, the sanction of all ethics. Mazzini did but point to an indubitable fact when he wrote—" The idea of an intelligent First Cause once destroyed, the existence of a moral law supreme over all men, and constituting an obligation, a duty imposed upon all men, is destroyed with it." That idea alone supplies an effectual *frenum cupiditatum*. Deprived of it, men, in general, find no sufficient motive for thwarting their inclinations, opposing their desires, subduing their passions. And, indeed, here is one of the greatest recommendations urged in favour of Atheism by those who preach it *ad populum*. Formerly, its propagandists endeavoured to veil the demoralizing results of their dogma. In our day these results are boldly proclaimed as an evidence of its superiority over a Theism which reasons of righteousness, temperance, and judgment to come. This is a sign of the times well worthy of being pondered. Certain it is, that in proportion as Atheistic doctrines spread in any land, there is an absence of repugnance to, and remorse for vice. How widely these doctrines have been disseminated of late years, in well-nigh every country, is notorious. To use the elementary schools as a means for inculcating them, has been the cherished object of the antichristian sectaries who have so largely obtained political power throughout Europe. Well-nigh half a century ago M. Gustave Flourens wrote—"Our enemy is God. Hatred of God is the beginning of wisdom. If men would make progress, it must be on the basis of Atheism." A great deal of such "progress" has been achieved by the malignant irreligion which dominates the ministry, the parliaments, the municipal institutions in France, in Italy, and in the Latin races generally. It has laboured abundantly, and with only too much success, to atheize the countries in which it has obtained the upper hand: to banish the idea of God from public and private life; and it has rightly discerned that the most effective means of compassing that end is to shape in its own image and likeness popular education. It is training the coming generation to believe that the answer to The Great Enigma is not moral, but material: to put aside faith in the Divine as a senseless and servile superstition; to find the rule of right and wrong in self-interest; to see in ethics but a regulation of police; to acquiesce in physical fatality; and to practise a brutal egoism. Such are the human animals, with the wild beast unchained in them, which Atheism is rearing as the sovereigns of the democratic future.

And this in the name of liberty! As though liberty were possible without religion respected, duty revered, charity practised: in a word, without virtue, and the self-sacrifice which virtue involves, recognized as the necessary bonds of the social organism. As though brute force, and the slavery which brute force implies, were not the only regimen possible for the *bête humaine*, deprived of "the mighty hopes that make us men." "La France en mourra, peut-être, mais ce sera une expérience curieuse pour l'humanité," observed M. Renan, as he meditated upon these things. The prognostication of that sage cannot be far wrong, whatever we may think of his attitude of scientific dilettantism towards the future of his country.*

* Fortunately, M. Renan's philosophic calm on this important subject is not universal among his more intelligent countrymen. A French correspondent sends me, with other weighty evidence to the contrary, the following resolution recently passed by the Conseil d'Arrondissement de Nantes:—

"Le conseil, considérant que l'expérience prouve de plus en plus l'insuffisance de l'enseignement de la morale dans les écoles primaires, s'il ne prend comme base essentielle les devoirs envers Dieu et l'obéissance due à sa loi; considérant que cette insuffisance ressort clairement des rapports et des documents officiels par lesquels l'Administration elle-même a voulu se renseigner; considérant, en outre, que le compte rendu général de la justice criminelle démontre une progression lamentable dans les crimes et délits commis par les enfants et les jeunes gens, dont près de 29,000 ont été traduits devant les tribunaux pendant la seule année 1887 (la dernière dont les résultats aient été publiés);

"Considérant que les suicides d'enfants et d'adolescents, naguère encore presque inconnus parmi nous, se sont multipliés à tel point depuis plusieurs années, qu'ils ont atteint le chiffre effrayant de 443 pour la même année 1887 ; considérant qu'on est d'autant plus fondé à voir une étroite corrélation entre cette douloureuse statistique et le développement du nouveau système d'éducation primaire, que l'instruction morale donnée à l'enfant reste évidemment dépourvue de toute autorité et de toute sanction, si elle ne s'appuie tout d'abord sur les grands principes de l'ordre religieux, notamment : la connaissance de Dieu comme règle de toute justice et comme souverain maître des hommes, la pleine obéissance due à sa loi, la nécessité d'une vie future où chaque créature entre dans la destinée définitive qu'elle s'est elle-même préparée ici-bas par ses œuvres ;

"Considérant qu'une pareille situation révèle un péril social et national de la plus haute gravité, qu'il est urgent de conjurer ;

"Considérant que le conseil est fondé d'une façon plus spéciale à donner son avis sur les questions intéressant particulièrement l'arrondissement de Nantes,

"Emet le vœu que, dans les écoles primaires de l'arrondissement, la morale ne reste pas séparée de la religion ; que l'enseignement des devoirs envers Dieu y soit pris comme base fondamentale et nécessaire de tous les devoirs qui incombent à l'homme, et qu'à cet effet les lois sur l'instruction publique reçoivent toutes les modifications nécessaires."

CHAPTER III.

CRITICAL AGNOSTICISM.

THE name of M. Renan, with which I ended the last chapter, might, not improperly, stand at the head of this. He is the very type of the variety of Agnosticism which I propose now to discuss. For, as I have already said, I distinguish between two types of the Agnostic doctrine: the merely sceptical or critical, which is content with professing nescience of God, and the positive or scientific, which erects a system of belief upon the foundation of that nescience. The former of these varieties—it might not improperly be called, even at the cost of a pleonasm, Negative Agnosticism— and its answer to The Great Enigma, I shall consider in the present chapter. I do not think a better view of it can be obtained than that which is exhibited by M. Renan's career and writings. Joubert observes that "the authors who have most influence are merely those who express perfectly what other men are thinking; who reveal in people's minds ideas or sentiments which were tending to the birth." These words admirably indicate the chief cause of M. Renan's immense popularity. His spiritual history is the spiritual history of millions writ large. He used his incomparable literary skill to interpret the mind of his generation to itself. Hence it is that he is a prophet so abundantly honoured in his own country, and wherever the language and literature of his country are known. His sound has gone out into all lands. It would be difficult to mention any writer whose influence in the civilized world is just now more diffused and more penetrating and more effective.

For nearly thirty years that influence has been at work. It dates from the publication of his *Vie de Jésus*, which may be said to have taken the world by storm. The effect produced by that work on the public mind may be judged of from the fact that, in France alone, fifteen hundred books or pamphlets about it were published within twelve months from its appearance; most of them, I need hardly add, attacking it with extreme severity. But whether men applauded or anathematized the *Vie de Jésus*, none could deny the high gifts of which it made full proof. It may, or it may not have been, what is called "an epoch-making book." It certainly made the literary fortune of its author. Not even the most superficial of "general readers" could be insensible to its delightful phrases, so finely chiselled, to its flowing and harmonious periods—recalling the cadences of music—to the artistic perfection of its word-painting, to the exquisite grace of its delicate dilettantism, to the seductive sweetness of its sceptical piety. Savants might gibe at it as mere literary perfumery, fit only to titillate the nostrils of the multitude. But they have had to reckon with it. Not even the most orthodox of subsequent commentators on the evangelical history have written as they would have written before it was published; while those of doubtful orthodoxy, or of no orthodoxy at all, have found in it a rich mine of ideas, a full fountain of inspiration. But although the most popular of M. Renan's works—some three hundred thousand copies of it have been sold in France alone—I feel sure that its author would not have deemed it the best, and that no competent critic would so deem it. The *Essay on Averroes*, the *General History of the Semitic Languages*, the *Studies in Religious History*, the work on the *Book of Job*, the *Ethical Essays*—all published before the *Vie de Jésus*—are of more account than it from the point of view of scholarship, and certainly are not inferior to it in literary workmanship. The same may be said of the remaining volumes of the *Sources of Christianity*, of the *Philosophical Dialogues*, of the very striking dissertations entitled *Contemporary Questions*, of the *History of the People of Israel*.

The mere mention of these works—and they are by no means a complete list—is enough to indicate another of the causes of M. Renan's influence. One of the most opulent natures that have adorned modern literature, he takes captive his readers by the breadth of his erudition and the abundance of his ideas, no less than by the magic of his style. A philologist—he was that first and foremost—an historian, a theologian, a philosopher, a publicist, he appealed to thoughtful men of every variety of intellectual character. And he seldom appealed in vain. It is hard for even the most inveterate prejudice to refuse to hear the voice of the charmer; the more especially as to his *illecebræ suaviloquentiæ*—to use St. Augustine's phrase—is joined the fascination of subtle and stimulating paradox. Mordant irony lurking beneath the most ingenuous candour, voluptuous sensism extracted from the purest idealism, universal pyrrhonism expressed in the language of religion—such is the piquant ragout which M. Renan served up, in the lordly dish of his superb French, to the jaded palate of the nineteenth century. It is not difficult to understand how the century has relished it. But it is very difficult to bring so unique an artist within the ordinary formulas of criticism; or adequately to form a general estimate of his multiform achievements. M. Sainte-Beuve felt the difficulty. "Pour parler convenablement de M. Renan," he writes, "si complexe et si fuyant quand on le presse et quand on veut l'embrasser tout entier, ce serait moins un article de critique qu'il conviendrait de faire sur lui qu'un petit dialogue à la manière de Platon." Similarly, M. Renan himself judged that, in the present state of the human intellect, the dialogue alone was suitable for the exposition of his philosophic ideas. "Truths of this order," he writes, in the Preface to *Le Prêtre de Némi*, "should be neither denied nor affirmed directly. They are not the subject of demonstration. All we can do is to present them in different aspects and to exhibit their strength or their weakness, their necessity, their equivalence." Unquestionably this form of composition suited M. Renan admirably, and he used it with supreme skill to exhibit himself according to his own humorous description, as "a tissue of contradictions, one half of him engaged in demolishing the other half, like the fabulous beast of Ctesias, who ate his paws without knowing it." "The clear perception of a truth," he tells us, "does not in the least hinder one from discerning the opposing truth, the next minute, with just the same clearness." The contradictions with which his writings are replete, are no accident. They were a habit; nay, more, they were a law of his nature. Indeed, he found in them an evidence of veracity: "Malheur à qui ne se contredit pas une fois par jour." No doubt all this may be, to some extent, conceded. Certain it is that the mere juxtaposition of divergent elements of thought often gives us more help towards grasping the verity underlying them, than that which would be afforded by a premature and arbitrary synthesis. But the dialogue has peculiar dangers and temptations of its own for a mobile and subtle intellect. Even Plato himself did not altogether escape them. They are dangers and temptations to which a Frenchman is especially exposed. For, as Amiel says, truly enough, " the Frenchman's centre of gravity is always outside himself; he is always thinking of others; always playing to the gallery." M. Renan throughout his brilliant volume of *Dialogues Philosophiques* reminds me of one of Moore's nymphs—

> " Lesbia has a wit refined ;
> But when its points are gleaming round us,
> Who can tell if they're designed
> To dazzle merely, or to wound us ? "

There was a marvellous coquetry in his intellect; at one moment dallying with materialism, at the next fondly embracing the ideal; now, passionate in professions of mysticism; then, cold and disdainful in negation or indifference. Yes; the dialogue was admirably suited to M. Renan's genius. And no doubt it would serve excellently well for an entertaining and instructive exhibition of him as an artist. But for the sober estimate of him as a teacher, which I am about to essay, the beaten track of criticism, in spite of the difficulties pointed out by M. Sainte-Beuve, is the more excellent way. It leads more surely than the dialogue to definite conclusions.

In order to appreciate M. Renan's influence as a teacher, it will be well to inquire first into the intellectual constituents of his character. And here we shall derive signal help from his intensely interesting volume, *Souvenirs d'Enfance et de Jeunesse*,—a work, which, as he tells us, he wrote "in order to transmit to others the theory of the universe which he carries in himself;" which we may indeed take as presenting his answer to The Great Enigma. The book is full of charms of every kind; admirable bits of description, as the pictures of old Brittany; masterpieces of rhetoric, as the famous prayer on the Acropolis; finished pages of irony, as the account of M. de Talleyrand's conversion. But, to my mind, its greatest charm lies in its veracity. In this species of composition it is very difficult to avoid the artistic insincerity of which, perhaps, the most conspicuous example is afforded by Rousseau's *Confessions*. Throughout M. Renan's *Souvenirs*, there breathes that antique candour which so mightily fascinates us in a very different book—Cardinal Newman's *Apologia*. I may remark, in passing, upon the curious and instructive parallel which these two works offer, both of them of the highest value as documents for the spiritual history of the nineteenth century. I may observe, too, that all the other writings of both masters may, in a true sense, be regarded as commentaries upon, or explanations of, their autobiographies. There is not a page of Cardinal Newman which is not a real revelation of its author. The same may be said of the works of M. Renan, who, very early in life, felt, that "to write without expressing something of one's own personal thought was the vainest exercise of the intellect." Of course M. Renan did not mean us to suppose that everything in his *Souvenirs* is to be taken absolutely. Like the author of *The Pilgrim's Progress*, and the Hebrew prophet whose example Bunyan imitated, he used similitudes. "All that I have written is true," he testifies, "but not of that kind of truth which is required for a *Biographie Universelle*. Many things have been introduced to provoke a smile (*afin qu'on sourie*); and, if only custom would have allowed, I should have written here and there, in the margin, 'cum grano salis.'" Nay, as he tells us elsewhere, he indulges sometimes in "little literary evasions (*petits fauxfuyants littéraires*) required by the view of a higher truth, or by the exigencies of a well-balanced phrase." If, after these admonitions, the reader chooses to misapprehend the candid author, why he must thank his own dulness for his mistakes. We may, on the whole, fully credit M. Renan when he claims for himself, "Dans mes écrits j'ai été d'une sincérité absolue." Indeed, it is this very sincerity which is his greatest offence in the eyes of some of his critics. He is "the candid friend," in whom the Anti-Jacobin poet discerned the worst of foes.

And now, in considering M. Renan a little more closely, it will be well, according to the fashion of the day, to begin with heredity, the force of which, indeed, in the determination of moral and mental qualities, no candid investigator can deny. M. Renan was a Breton. And in him, as in Chateaubriand and Lamennais before him, the qualities of his race were strongly marked. Physically, he resembled hundreds of good curés who may be seen in Lower Brittany. A friend of my own, indeed, some years ago, was greatly astonished at finding, as he thought, in one of the parish churches there, the author of the *Vie de Jésus* clad in strange ecclesiastical costume, and devoutly sustaining some humble part in the offices of religion. He rubbed his eyes, and after a few minutes discerned his error. It was an obese and orthodox beadle whom he had mistaken for the Administrator of the College of France. The characteristics of the Breton were as clearly imprinted upon M. Renan's intellectual constitution as upon his physical form. One of the chief of them is a vivid yet chastened and inexpansive imagination, the heritage of the people dwelling in that land of mysterious ocean, and melancholy plains, and grey skies, and desolate rocks, which M. Renan himself so admirably described in his *Poésie des Races Celtiques:* "Quelque chose de voilé, de sobre, d'exquis, à égale distance de la rhétorique trop familière aux races latines, et de la naïveté refléchie de l'Allemand." But M. Renan had also Gascon blood in him through his mother, whom he describes as lively, candid, and inquisitive (*curieuse*). To her he owed, as he tells us, "une certaine habileté dans l'art d'amener le cliquetis des mots et des idées," and "le penchant gascon à trancher beaucoup de difficultés par un sourire," "but for which," he piously adds, "my salvation would have been better assured." In this complexity of origin he found the source, to a great extent at all events, of his apparent contradictions. "I am double," he writes; "sometimes one part of me laughs while the other weeps. That is the explanation of my gaiety. As there are two men in me, there is always one who has reason to be satisfied."

Ernest Renan was born in 1823, in Tréguier, a small town which had grown up under the shadow of a vast monastery founded in the last year of the fifth century, by St. Tudwal. The monastery has disappeared, but the cathedral remains, "chef d'œuvre de légèreté, fol essai pour réaliser en granit un idéal impossible." This architectural paradox, he tells us, was his first master. Under its vaulted roof he passed long hours, breathing the monastic atmosphere in this highly unmonastic age. The town and its neighbourhood presented the same ideal and religious character. It was a great school of faith and reverence, in which his childhood was passed. His father, the master of a small coasting boat, was drowned when Ernest was three years old. And this misfortune, doubtless, served to enhance the piety of the devout household. The boy grew up with the fixed determination to be a priest. Good and devout, he accepted the faith of his fathers, as "the absolute expression of truth," "the supernatural summary of what man ought to know." His state of mind at twelve, nay at fifteen, was precisely " celui de tant de bons esprits du xviie siècle, mettant la religion hors de doute." His intellectual superiority over his comrades was marked from the first. Criticism and philosophical sagacity, of course, did not enter into the instruction of those excellent priests who were his first masters, he tells us. "But they taught me," he adds, "what was worth infinitely more: love of truth, respect for reason, the seriousness of life." Everything in his early years seemed to indicate for him a modest ecclesiastical existence in Brittany. "I should have made a very good priest," he continues; "indulgent, paternal, charitable, blameless in my life and conversation. My career would have been on this wise. At twenty-two I should have been Professor in the College at Tréguier. At fifty, Canon, and probably Vicar-General at St. Brieuc: very conscientious, much respected, a good and safe director. No very enthusiastic admirer of the new dogmas, I should have dared to say, like many worthy ecclesiastics after the Vatican Council, 'Posui custodiam ori meo.' My antipathy for the Jesuits would merely have led me not to speak of them. A substratum of modified Gallicanism would, however, have lain concealed under a profound knowledge of canon law." Such was the prospect before M. Renan, when, at the age of fifteen, a slight incident completely changed his future.

That incident was that his success at the College at Tréguier, where he had carried off all the prizes of his class, attracted the notice of the Abbé Dupanloup. This eminent ecclesiastic—subsequently famous as Bishop of Orleans—had been appointed, by the Archbishop of Paris, Superior of the Little Seminary of St. Nicholas du Chardonnet, and was anxious to fill his house with promising recruits. He offered Ernest Renan a place there, and the offer was accepted. At first, the change did not suit the young Breton. He fell ill. It was the Abbé Dupanloup's care of him, he thinks, which saved his life. He gradually became accustomed to the routine of seminary existence. M. Dupanloup he found "un éveilleur incomparable," absolutely unrivalled in the power of drawing out what was best in each of the young students. The education of St. Nicholas was literary to an extent very unusual in Catholic seminaries. M. Renan tells us that he had come to Paris "morally formed, but as ignorant as he well could be." He now learned "that something existed besides antiquity and the Church; that there were contemporary French authors worthy of some attention." Despite its claim to be an asylum "far from the madding crowd's ignoble strife," the atmosphere of the century circulated pretty freely in St. Nicholas. It was M. Dupanloup's wise design to form priests who should be not merely theologians with Moses on the mount, but "learned in all the wisdom of the Egyptians" among whom their work was to lie. To St. Nicholas du Chardonnet, M. Renan owed his initiation into modern literature. But if "the superficial humanism" which he acquired there destroyed the first *naïveté* of his faith—as he thought it did—it by no means planted in his mind anything that could properly be called doubt. When, at the end of his first year in the college, "a full *bourse*" was awarded him, and he was told that it was given with no restriction as to his future career, he replied calmly, "I shall be a priest." And during the whole of his course there, no question as to his vocation to the ecclesiastical state occurred to him.

When his three years at the Little Seminary were completed, M. Renan quitted it for the

Grand Seminary of Saint Sulpice, where four years more of training awaited him. The first two of these were spent at the "succursale" of Issy, and were devoted to philosophy. The philosophy taught was scholasticism in Latin; "not the barbarous and infantine scholasticism of the thirteenth century, but what may, perhaps, be called the Cartesian Scholasticism, which was generally adopted for ecclesiastical instruction in the eighteenth century, and stereotyped, so to speak, in the three volumes known as *La Philosophie de Lyon*. "I owe," M. Renan testified, " the clearness of my intellect, and in particular a certain skill in division—an art of the first importance, for it is one of the conditions of the art of writing—to the scholastic exercises, and above all to geometry, which is the application par excellence of the scholastic method." Here M. Renan obtained some acquaintance with the philosophical writings of Cousin, and of Jouffroy, and heard rumours of German thought. But the authors he read habitually were Pascal, Malebranche, Euler, Locke, Leibnitz, Descartes, Reid, Dugald Stewart. The physical sciences—especially general natural history and physiology—greatly attracted him, and his studies in this department shook his confidence in metaphysics. "J'aperçus l'insuffisance de ce qu'on appelle le spiritualisme: les preuves Cartésiennes de l'existence d'une âme distincte du corps me parurent toujours très faibles: dès lors j'étais idéaliste et non spiritualiste, dans le sens qu'on donne au mot. Un éternel *fieri*, un métamorphose sans fin me semblait la loi du monde. La nature m'apparaissait comme un ensemble où la création particulière n'a point de place, et où, par conséquent, tout se transforme." Do we ask how it was that these conceptions did not banish from M. Renan's intellect scholasticism and Christianity, with which they are clearly at variance? He replies: "Parce que j'étais jeune, inconséquent, et que la critique me manquait."

But others, or at least one other, already saw in M. Renan, what his youth, his want of logic and of criticism, prevented him from seeing in himself. His professor of philosophy, M. Gottofrey, observed him narrowly; and, with the instinct of piety, divined the true state of his mind. At last, upon a certain occasion, M. Renan was engaged in a public disputation, on some philosophical matter; when the vigour of his objections to the orthodox position, his manifest dissatisfaction with the arguments traditionally accredited and received, provoked a smile from some of the listeners, and M. Gottofrey, who was presiding, stopped the argument. In the course of the evening, the professor sent for the too candid disputant, and, with the eloquence of deep conviction, warned him that overweening confidence in reason was contrary to the spirit of Christianity—that rationalism was incompatible with faith. Growing strangely animated, M. Gottofrey went on to reproach the young man with his too exclusive devotion to study. "Research? What is the good of it? All that is essential has been already found. It is not by science that souls are saved." And then, gradually becoming more excited, he said, in passionate accents, "You are no Christian."

"I have never in my life," M. Renan tells us, "felt more fright than that which I experienced on hearing those words uttered in a ringing voice. I tottered, as I left the room. And all night long 'You are no Christian' resounded in my ears like a great peal of thunder." The next day he poured his trouble into the ear of his confessor, an excellent man, who saw nothing, and wished to see nothing; who soothed him with words, and bade him dismiss the matter from his mind. "He did not in the least understand the character of my mind, nor divine its future logical evolution. M. Gottofrey did. He saw clearly enough. He was right; fully right. I now recognize it completely. Writing thirty-five years afterwards, I discern the deep penetration of which he made proof. He alone was clear-sighted, for he was quite a saint. It needed his transcendent illumination of martyr and ascetic to discover what completely escaped those who directed my conscience with so much sincerity, so much goodness, in other matters."

Yielding, then, to the counsels of his confessor,

M. Renan put aside, for the time, the revelation of himself made to him by M. Gottofrey; and when his two years at Issy were accomplished, proceeded for his theological studies to Saint Sulpice. There, his conduct was irreproachable, as it had been throughout the whole of his previous career, and in due time he received the tonsure and was admitted into minor orders. Theology and Biblical exegesis were now his chief subjects of study, with results which all the world knows. I am concerned, for my present purpose, to indicate how those results were reached. At the basis of dogmatic theology lies the thesis *De Vera Religione*, the object of which is to prove the supernatural character of the Christian religion —that is, of the canonical scriptures and the Church. The next step is to prove the dogmas of the Church by Scripture, the Councils, the Fathers, and the theologians. M. Renan gradually became convinced of the impossibility of demonstrating that the Christian religion is, more specially than any other, divine and revealed; nay, further, it appeared to him certain, that in the field of reality accessible to our observation, no supernatural event, no miracle has ever occurred. He was led to the conclusion of M. Littré, that "investigate as you will, you will never find that a miracle has been wrought under conditions where it could be observed and verified." Again, historical facts seemed to him absolutely irreconcilable with the theory that the doctrines of Christianity, as they were defined at Trent, or even at Nicæa, were what the Apostles originally taught. While his mind was revolving these weighty matters, he betook himself to the study, first of Hebrew, and then of German, which introduced him to the new exegesis distinctive of the nineteenth century, and led him to apply to the Semitic documents of Christianity the grammatical and historical interpretations which are applied to the other books of antiquity. The result was that "the traditional thesis" as to the date, authorship, and inerrancy of the Hebrew Sacred Books —a thesis which he had been taught to consider essential to Christianity—soon grew incredible to him. But let me, in this connexion, quote his own words:—

"Dans un livre divin, en effet, tout est vrai, et, deux contradictoires ne pouvant être vraies à la fois, il ne doit s'y trouver aucune contradiction. Or l'étude attentive que je faisais de la Bible, en me révélant des trésors historiques et esthétiques, me prouvait aussi que ce livre n'était pas plus exempt qu'aucun autre livre de contradictions, d'inadvertences, d'erreurs. Il s'y trouve des fables, des légendes, des traces de composition tout humaine. Il n'est plus possible de soutenir que la seconde partie d'Isaïe soit d'Isaïe. Le livre de Daniel que toute orthodoxie rapporte au temps de la Captivité, est un apocryphe composé en 169 ou 170 avant Jésus-Christ. Le livre de Judith est une impossibilité historique. [L'attribution du Pentateuque à Moïse est insoutenable, et nier que plusieurs parties de la Genèse aient le caractère mythique, c'est s'obliger à expliquer comme réels des récits tels que celui du paradis terrestre, du fruit défendu, de l'arche de Noé. Or on n'est pas catholique si l'on s'écarte sur un seul de ces points de la thèse traditionnelle. Que devient ce miracle, si fort admiré de Bossuet : 'Cyrus nommé deux cents ans avant sa naissance' ? Que deviennent les soixante-dix semaines, bases des calculs de *l'Histoire universelle*, si la partie du livre d'Isaïe où Cyrus est nommé a été justement composée du temps de ce conquérant, et si pseudo-Daniel est contemporain d'Antiochus Épiphane ? L'orthodoxie oblige de croire que les livres bibliques sont les livres de ceux à qui les titres les attribuent. Les doctrines catholiques les plus mitigées sur l'inspiration ne permettent d'admettre dans le texte sacré aucune erreur caractérisée, aucune contradiction, même en des choses qui ne concernent ni la foi, ni les mœurs. . . . Cette théorie d'inspiration, impliquant un fait surnaturel, devient impossible à maintenir en présence des idées arrêtées du bon sens moderne." *

The conclusion of the whole matter for M. Renan was that " his direct study of Christianity, undertaken in the most serious spirit, did not leave him enough faith to be a sincere priest; while, on the other hand, it inspired him with too much respect to allow of his resigning himself to playing an odious comedy with beliefs most worthy of respect." He had the courage of his convictions. On the 6th of October, 1845, he quitted Saint-Sulpice, leaving behind him the faith which he had once hoped to teach. It was with him as with the Patriarch of old, "when with his staff he passed over that Jordan. He parted with all that his heart loved, and turned his face towards a strange land. He went with the doubt whether he should have bread to eat or raiment to put on." " Ceux qui me connaissent," he wrote to his

* *Souvenirs d'Enfance et de Jeunesse*, p. 229.

confessor, "avoueront, j'espère, que ce n'est pas l'intérêt qui m'a éloigné du Christianisme. Tous mes intérêts les plus chers ne devaient-ils pas m'engager à le trouver vrai? Les considérations temporelles contre lesquelles j'ai à lutter eussent suffi pour en persuader bien d'autres; mon cœur a besoin du Christianisme; l'Evangile sera toujours ma morale, l'Église a fait mon éducation, je l'aime. Ah! que ne puis-je continuer à me dire son fils! Je la quitte malgré moi. . . . Le Christianisme suffit à toutes mes facultés, excepté une seule, la plus exigeante de toutes, parce qu'elle est de droit juge de toutes les autres."

Religious unbelief, contemptible when it is—as we considered it in the last chapter—the outcome of animal passions, rebelling against "creeds that refuse and restrain," is, at all events, respectable if it is the result of conscientious inquiry. There is a true sense in the oft-quoted lines of Lord Tennyson concerning the faith that lives in honest doubt. It is not surprising to learn that M. Renan met with nothing but kindness from the worthy ecclesiastics with whom his youth had been passed. M. Dupanloup, in particular, was goodness itself to the ex-seminarist, as might have been expected from so noble and generous a nature. "Are you in need of money?" he wrote. "It may well be that you are. My poor purse is at your service. Would that it were in my power to offer you goods more precious." M. Renan expressed warm thanks for this proposal, as indeed he well might; but he did not avail himself of it. His deeply-cherished sister, Henriette, placed at his disposal twelve hundred francs, which she had saved; and this sum, relieving him from immediate anxiety as to the morrow, was, he tells us, the foundation of the independence and dignity of his life.

It would be beside my present purpose to follow, in detail, M. Renan's subsequent career. At first he felt himself an utter alien—*dépaysé*—in this work-a-day world, where his lot was now cast. It was to him as a cold and arid desert, peopled by pigmies. And his distress was heightened by his mother's unhappiness; her letters rent his heart. She passed her days in singing the old religious verses known as *Les Cantiques de Marseilles*, her favourite among them being *The Song of Joseph*:—

> "O Joseph, ô mon aimable
> Fils affable!
> Les bêtes t'ont dévoré;
> Je perds avec toi l'envie
> D'être en vie;
> Le Seigneur soit adoré!"

"I exerted all my ingenuity," M. Renan says, "in inventing ways of proving to her that I was still the same 'fils affable' as in the past. Little by little the wound healed. When she saw me still good and kind to her, as I always had been, she owned that there were several ways of being a priest, and that nothing was altered in me but my dress, which was indeed the truth."

Yes, that was indeed the truth. "Cucullus non facit monachum." Secular costume does not make the layman. The external change which had passed over M. Renan made no change in his way of thought. "The studies which I had so long pursued at the seminary," he tells us, "had taken such hold upon me that my only thought was to go on with them. The sole occupation which seemed to me worth living for, was to continue my critical researches upon Christianity by the more abundant methods which lay science offered." M. Renan was what he called himself, "un prêtre manqué." "I was born a priest *a priori*," he elsewhere says, and the work of his life was to engraft modern criticism upon his religious temperament. It is a saying of Jouffroy, "Man believes by instinct and doubts by reason." The faith of his childhood dwelt with M. Renan as a sentiment. Its poetry survived, side by side with the criticism which has been fatal to it as a creed. Here is an explanation of the two voices which are constantly heard throughout his writings. His utterances differ, according as it is the poet, or the critic, that speaks. It would be easy to accumulate from his volumes passages breathing the purest spirit of piety; that abnegation, that elevation, that idealism which are the essence of all religion. Indeed, as every one knows, he himself, for some years, cherished the project of extracting from his works a number of edifying extracts which might serve as a book of devotion for fair readers while assisting at Mass. The height of his ambition, he asserted, would be attained if he might thus make his entry into the Church, "sous la forme d'un petit volume in-18, relié en maroquin noir, tenu entre les longs doigts effilés d'une main gantée." Unquestionably, the effect upon these charming devotees might be salutary if the compilation were made with sufficient care.

> "Das ist alles recht schön und gut.
> Ungefähr sagt das der Pfarrer auch,
> Nur mit ein bischen andern Worten,"

says poor Gretchen, after listening to Faust's eloquent exposition of his somewhat nebulous creed. The fashionable lady might say the same of a volume of *Lectures Pieuses* selected from M. Renan's writings. Nay, it may even be conceded that he was not without warrant when he reproached some of the manuals of *la petite dévotion*, which he desired to supersede, as replete "des faiblesses, des erreurs, des choses qui entretiennent la femme dans la fâcheuse habitude de trop pratiquer avec l'absurde." More guarded must be our attitude towards his claim that he alone, in his time, really understood the Divine Founder of Christianity, and the Umbrian Saint, in whom the image of the Crucified seems most perfectly reproduced ("J'ai pu seul en mon siècle comprendre Jésus et François d'Assise"). Still, unquestionably, whatever grave objections may be made, and ought to be made, from the point of view both of critical science and of religious reverence, to the *Vie de Jésus,* there is some warrant for the contention that it presents a *living* embodiment of the purest idealism, where the popular theology had been too apt to offer a dead abstraction. M. Scherer claims for its author: "C'est M. Renan qui, le premier, a fait rentrer Jésus dans le droit commun de l'histoire, et par conséquent dans la réalité. Il a rendu ainsi au Christianisme, au Christianisme durable, au Christianisme spirituel un service."* No doubt this is too strongly put. But there is enough truth in the view which M. Scherer thus expresses to render his words worth citing. And assuredly there are in the *Vie de Jésus,* as throughout M. Renan's writings, many passages which the most orthodox of his critics might be well pleased to have written. How true and how admirably expressed is the following :—

"Ce vrai royaume de Dieu, ce royaume de l'esprit, qui fait chacun roi et prêtre ; ce royaume qui, comme ce grain de sénevé, est devenu un arbre qui ombrage le monde, et sous les rameaux duquel les oiseaux ont leur nid, Jésus l'a compris, l'a voulu, l'a

---

* *Mélanges d'Histoire Religieuse,* p. 132.

fondé. . . . Il a conçu la réelle cité de Dieu, la 'palingénésie' véritable, le [Sermon sur la montagne, l'apothéose du faible, l'amour du peuple, la réhabilitation de tout qui est humble, vrai et naïf. Cette réhabilitation, il l'a rendue en artiste incomparable par des traits que dureront éternellement. Chacun de nous lui doit ce qu'il y a de meilleur en lui. . . . De nos jours mêmes, jours troublés où Jésus n'a pas de plus authentiques continuateurs que ceux qui semblent le répudier, les rêves d'organisation idéale de la société, qui ont tant d'analogie avec les aspirations des sectes chrétiennes primitives, ne sont, en un sens que l'épanouissement de la même idée, une des branches de cet arbre immense où germe toute pensée de l'avenir, et dont 'le royaume de Dieu' sera éternellement la tige et la racine. Toutes les révolutions sociales de l'humanité seront entées sur ce mot-là. Mais entachées d'un grossier matérialisme, aspirant à l'impossible, c'est à dire de fonder l'universelle bonheur sur les mesures politiques et économiques, les tentatives 'socialistes' de notre temps resteront infécondes jusqu'à ce qu'elles prennent pour règle le véritable esprit de Jésus, je veux dire l'idéalisme absolu, ce principe que pour posséder la terre il faut y renoncer." *

How profound again the dictum—which recalls one of Spinoza's weightiest sayings—"La plus haute conscience de Dieu qui ait existé au sein de l'humanité a été celle de Jésus." And once more, how penetrating the appeal in the *Études d'Histoire Religieuse*: "Si vos facultés vibrant simultanément n'ont jamais rendu ce grand son unique que nous appellons Dieu je n'ai plus rien à dire ; vous manquez de l'élément essentiel de notre nature."

True indeed. "Das ist alles recht schön und gut." But now, if we turn from the poet to the

* *Vie de Jésus*, pp. 282–288, 7ème ed.

critic, we learn that it is impossible to say whether this Deity, concerning whom, and whose kingdom, these very excellent things were spoken, really exists. We read in the *Souvenirs* that the clear scientific view of a universe where no volition higher than man's acts in an appreciable manner, was to M. Renan, since the first months of 1846, an anchor of the soul, sure and steadfast. And again, in another page of the same book, we are told, "It is by chemistry at the one end, and by astronomy at the other, it is above all by general physiology, that we truly grasp the secret of existence, of the world, of what people call God." And if we turn to one of M. Renan's most recently published volumes,* as likely to contain the ultimate light which he was able to radiate upon the high theme, we read as follows:—"The word God is in possession of the respect of humanity; it has in its favour a long tradition; it has been employed in the finest poetry. To suppress it, would be to puzzle, to bewilder mankind (*dérouter l'humanité*). Although it is what the scholastics call 'univocal,' it corresponds to a sufficiently precise idea—the *summum* and the *ultimum*: the line at which humanity stops in the ladder (*échelle*) of the infinite . . . God, Providence, Soul, are so many good old words, a little heavy, but expressive and respectable.

* *L'Avenir de la Science: Pensées de* 1848, p. 475. This volume was published in the year 1890.

Science will explain them. It will not, with advantage, find substitutes for them. What is God for humanity but the transcendental summary of its supra-sensible wants, *the category of the ideal*—that is to say, the form under which we conceive the ideal, just as space and time are the categories under which we conceive bodies?" Do we say, Well and good; but are we to understand that this "category of the ideal" exists? "Ce Dieu est-il ou n'est-il pas?" M. Renan replies, "Questions of being are beyond us." (Les questions de l'être nous dépassent). And so elsewhere he writes, "Le problème de la cause suprême nous déborde et nous échappe : il se résout en poëmes (ces poëmes sont les religions) non en lois : ou, s'il faut parler ici de lois, ce sont celles de la physique, de l'astronomie, de l'histoire, qui seules sont les lois de l'être et ont une pleine réalité." *

M. Renan was, in fact, a poet penetrated by the

---

* I quote from the "Table Analytique," and give M. Renan's words as I find them. But when he writes "univocal" I suspect he meant "analogical," which is the proper school term. In his *Philosophic Fragments*, M. Renan tells us, "Toute proposition appliquée à Dieu est impertinente, une seule exceptée: 'Il est.'" But in another place, in the same volume, we read "L'absolu de la justice et de la raison ne se manifeste que dans l'humanité : envisagé hors de l'humanité cet absolu *n'est qu'une abstraction.* . . . *L'infini n'existe* que quand il revêt une forme finie" (p. 326). The italics are my own.

beauty, dominated by the majesty of the religious sentiment. He was also a critic whose last word is that the Object of the religious sentiment—if Object there be—is beyond our knowledge: that we can affirm nothing of it, not even its existence. But his scepticism, wherein, he tells us, he found the happiness of his life, was not confined to the domain of religion. In the province of morality he discovered the same fundamental doubt. Here, too, his first dogma was the rejection of all dogmas. His critical method was fatal to that eternal distinction between Right and Wrong—not made but apprehended by the practical reason—which is the only true foundation of ethics: to the supreme claim of the moral law as a Divine order ruling throughout the universe in voluntary allegiance to which human virtue consists. True, indeed, it is that passages may be found in his writings wherein these august verities are proclaimed. Thus, in his preface to his translation of the *Book of Job*, we read, " Duty with its incalculable philosophical consequences, in imposing itself upon all, resolves all doubts, reconciles all oppositions, and serves as a foundation to rebuild what reason destroys, or allows to crumble away. Thanks to this revelation, free from ambiguity or obscurity, we affirm that he who has chosen the right is the truly wise man." And so in the preface to his *Essais de Morale et de Critique:* " Morality is the one thing eminently serious and true, and, by itself, it suffices to give meaning and direction to life. Impenetrable veils hide from us the secret of this world, whose reality is at once irresistible and oppressive. Philosophy and science will for ever pursue without ever attaining the formula of this Proteus, unlimited by reason, inexpressible in language. But there is one foundation which no doubt can shake, and in which man will ever find a firm ground amidst his uncertainties; good is good and evil is evil. No system is necessary to enable us to hate the one and love the other; and it is in this sense that faith and love, possessing no seeming connection with the intellect, are the true base of moral certainty, and the only means possessed by man of understanding, in some slight measure, the problem of his origin and destiny."

Yes: "le bien, c'est le bien; et le mal, c'est le mal." Most true, indeed; but here, and in other like utterances, which might be cited, especially from M. Renan's earlier works, we must take him to be speaking as a poet. If we turn to the critic, we find that this lofty teaching crumbles away at the annihilating touch of Agnosticism. "The morality of the critical school," he tells us, in his *Philosophical Fragments*, rests, not upon the Categorical Imperative, but upon "a sentiment of the nobility of man." It seems a frail foundation whereon to rear the moral order. Elsewhere he asserts, "le bien et le mal se transforment l'un dans l'autre." In a famous passage of one of his most famous *Philosophical Dialogues,* the ripe sage Prospero, in whose words we may hear the voice of the Master himself, rebukes with mild irony the simple Gotescale who aspires to moralize mankind, and seeks to regenerate the masses by the aid of Temperance Societies. "Priver les simples gens de la seule joie qu'ils ont, en leur promettant un paradis qu'ils n'auront pas!" And he goes on to teach his astonished disciple that if it is well ever to take the more virtuous course, that does not mean that virtue has any reality. "Elle est une gageure, une satisfaction personelle, qu'on peut embrasser comme un généreux parti : mais la conseiller à autrui, qui l'oserait ?" The same thought finds succinct expression in his well-known phrase about "l'énorme duperie qu'implique la bonté." In his Discourse upon the occasion of the reception of M. Cherbuliez into the French Academy, he acquainted the world that his hesitation regarding the question, "Où est le bien ?" arose from "the divine parable of the Prodigal Son." "Le plus bel enseignement du Christianisme," he declares, "est que la vertu consiste moins dans les œuvres que dans les sentiments du cœur, si bien que l'Éternel a des tendresses pour la faute qui vient d'une ardeur généreuse ou d'un égarement d'amour." Remarking, in passing, upon M. Renan's ingenuity in extracting from the parable of the Prodigal Son the doctrine that the Eternal is indulgent towards, not the faulty, but their faults, not the sinner, but his sins, I go on to note, that he was by no means sure how far old-world moralists are well founded in accounting moral perfection our true end. He tells us in his *Souvenirs* of his inability to rid himself of the idea that perhaps, after all, the libertine is right, and practises the true philosophy of life. It filled him with melancholy, as indeed it well might, when he reflected that it took him ten years of profound meditation, and unremitting intellectual toil, to reach a conclusion which the *gamin* of Paris attains at one bound.* M. Scherer, a warm admirer of M. Renan, seems to me to have correctly summed up his friend's real view of ethics. "Sa pensée de derrière la tête, c'est que la vertu, non plus que toute autre chose ne supporte l'examen; on soulève le voile et, là comme partout, ou découvre qu'il n'y a rien dessous."† But whatever may be the real truth about virtue, M. Renan held that beauty is just as good, nay, better. "La beauté vaut la vertu," he declares in his *Marc-Aurèle*.‡ And in his *Souvenirs* he

* "Je n'arrivai pas au point d'émancipation que le gamin de Paris atteint sans aucun effort de réflexion, qu'après avoir traversé Gesenius et toute l'exégèse allemande. Il me fallait dix années de méditation et de travail forcené, pour voir que mes maîtres n'étaient pas infaillibles."—*Souvenirs*, p. 15.

† *Études sur la Littérature*, vol. viii. p. 127.

‡ So also in his *Fragments Philosophiques*:—"Un beau sentiment vaut une belle pensée; une belle pensée vaut une belle action : une vie de science vaut une vie de vertu."—P. 309.

goes further: "La beauté est un don tellement supérieur que le talent, la génie, la vertu même ne sont rien auprès d'elle, en sorte que la femme vraiment belle a le droit de tout dédaigner." M. Renan's practical conclusion is expressed in his declaration to the students at the Grand-Véfour, "The old French gaiety is perhaps the profoundest of philosophies." It is the philosophy practised by himself in the refined and cultivated form of a dilettante epicureanism to which, indeed, he found himself inclined by nature: "le fond de mon caractère est la gaieté et l'acceptation résignée du sort." Of the two men who are in him, the Gascon—*l'homme qui rit*—dominated his life after he left Saint Sulpice; and he indulged to the full his "penchant de trancher beaucoup de difficultés par un sourire." Life, for M. Renan, was a comedy, and he thought himself fortunate in being provided with a comfortable seat in the stalls from which to witness it: "placé au point de vue d'une bienveillante ironie universelle." Assuredly it is M. Renan himself who speaks to us by the mouth of Ganeo, in the *Prêtre de Némi*: "Jouissons, mon pauvre ami, du monde tel qu'il s'est fait. Ce n'est pas une œuvre sérieuse : c'est une farce, l'œuvre d'un demiurge jovial. La gaieté est la seule théologie de cette grande farce." The French clergy may possibly be, as M. Renan alleged, "respectablement bornés" in their view of the universe. But, assuredly, they can hardly be considered wrong in reckoning him among those "inimicos crucis Christi, quorum finis interitus, quorum deus venter est, et gloria in confusione ipsorum: qui terrena sapiunt."

Such is the Agnostic teaching with which M. Renan interested, amused, fascinated the more cultivated minds of his generation, minds which turned in loathing from the coarse egoism, the crass materialism of modern life; which felt a craving for nobler nourishment than that purveyed by Atheistic animalism to the vulgar. To these M. Renan offered his dilettantism, which, at all events, recognizes man's need of a transcendental ideal, even if it does not supply one. And his dilettantism is precisely of the kind to find favour with his more refined countrymen. He has been well described as "the most accomplished of *jouisseurs:*" contributing his part to the great human comedy by playing, not like the more vulgar sophists with words, but with the most sacred ideas and verities. He interested, amused, fascinated his generation, much as Voltaire interested, amused, fascinated the generation which preceded the French Revolution. We may say that in him his admiring countrymen had another and a better Voltaire; a Voltaire with far less *esprit* indeed, but with far wider culture, and with far less sectarian animosity, preaching the same word of wisdom—the dictum of the elder sage, " La vie est un enfant qu'il faut bercer jusqu'à ce qu'il s'endort," sums up the life philosophy of both—and exhibiting to the end the same inexhaustible gaiety—

> " Toujours un pied dans le cercueil,
> De l'autre faisant des gambades."

The very vagueness and indefiniteness of his writings, nay the contradictions in them, have, in no small degree, contributed to his popularity. He was all things to all men. There was in him, he tells us, in an amusing passage of his *Souvenirs*, an irresistible impulse to give to every one that asked of him, just the answer which he knew would be agreeable.* " Vous avez raison," was his habitual response in conversation. The truth is that his moral philosophy is a thing of shreds and patches,† starting from no principles and leading to no conclusions. It makes of ethics merely the fashion of apprehending life : a matter of taste, of sentiment, of artistic sensibility, of æsthetic perception. M. Renan's Critical Agnosticism is practically as fatal to Duty, as is the most dogmatic Atheism. " It is certain," he tells us, in a significant passage of his *Feuilles Détachées*, " that moral values are losing ground." " The day," he

* Page 152.

† He expressly tells us " Saisir la physiognomie des choses, voilà toute la philosophie " (*Fragmens Philosophiques*, p. 299).

thought, "is fast approaching when organized egotism will be installed in the place of charity and devotedness." And he knew, no one better, that his Agnostic doctrine is powerless to supply a remedy. "La vertu," he writes, "n'a pas besoin de la justice des hommes : mais elle ne peut pas se passer d'un témoin céleste qui lui dise, Courage, courage!"*

M. Renan's ethical Agnosticism sprung from his religious Agnosticism. And of his religious Agnosticism he has himself given us the history. Like so many others in this age, in unlearning Christianity he has unlearned Theism. He illustrates, in a very striking manner, Cardinal Newman's dictum that "to deny revelation is the way to deny natural religion."† The same habit of mind, the same mode of arguing, the same *organon investigandi* which led him to throw off the faith of his fathers, led him, further, to regard the existence of God as "an unverifiable hypothesis." We have seen, in a previous page, that the reasons why he ceased to believe in Christianity were, mainly, two: his inability to receive "the traditional thesis" regarding the date, authorship, and inerrancy of the Sacred Books—Biblia Sacra—

---

* *Le Prêtre de Némi*, Act iii. sc. 3.
† *Grammar of Assent*, p. 499 (fifth edition).

of Christianity which we call the Bible;* and his conviction that miracles never have happened and never can happen. Let us examine each of these reasons† briefly. A brief examination will, I think, suffice.

Now, with regard to the first of these, I frankly admit that if Christianity depended upon a pseudo-scientific view of certain venerable documents, formed at an unscientific period, and irreconcilable with the conclusions of true science, Christianity would be doomed. Nor am I in the least disposed to shut my eyes to the real significance of what is called "the higher criticism;" although I may be permitted to observe that much which passes current under that name appears to me not high criticism, in any sense, but low; in no way divine; not in the least an attempt to assign the final cause of the Old or New Testament, or to gauge the depth of significance which there is for mankind in the Person of Christ. I suppose that the most complete and logical statement of "the traditional thesis" is that set forth in the famous Swiss Declaration of 1675, which declares the

* The word "biblia" is properly plural. In the middle ages it was transmuted into a singular noun.

† As to that apprehension of the grand evolution of dogma which M. Renan thinks incompatible with a sincere profession of the Catholic religion, I may here remark that it is, in substance, the foundation of Cardinal Newman's *Essay on the Development of Religious Doctrine*, the orthodoxy of which is unquestionable. I shall have occasion to consider this subject further in chap. vii. of the present work. See pp. 314–316.

Hebrew Scriptures to be "inspired, in their consonants, in their vowels, and in their points, or, at least, in the substance of their points;" and thus to constitute, together with the New Testament, for which, of course, an equally far-reaching claim is made, "the single and uncorrupted rule of faith and life." And such, I imagine, is, or at all events was until lately, the orthodox Protestant view. It is an astounding thesis. And I candidly confess that the disingenuousness—I had almost said the indifference to veracity—displayed by some thick and thin defenders of the old Biblical exegesis fills me with dismay. It suggests to me Bacon's pregnant question, " Will ye offer unto the Author of Truth the unclean sacrifice of a lie?" It appears beyond doubt that modern research has shown us much which is at variance with "the traditional thesis" as to the date, authorship, and relative value of the Christian Sacred Books, just as it has familiarized us with conceptions of the physical universe utterly alien to the minds of their writers. And I can imagine nothing more fatal to the real significance of the venerable text than the Procrustean torture to which apologists of a certain school ruthlessly subject it, in order to make it fit with facts recently ascertained by natural, historical, and critical science. Surely this is a case in which, if in any, the dictum applies "Litera occidit, spiritus autem vivificat." I add that to suppose Christianity based upon the collection of ancient documents called the Bible is historically false. It is certain that no authorized New Testament canon existed until the latter half of the second century. It is equally certain that the mission of the Author of Christianity was not to promote the formation of a volume, which, long centuries after, should become "the religion of Protestants," but to establish a society. "I should not receive the sacred Scriptures," St. Augustine declared, "unless the authority of the Catholic Church moved me to do so." The Bible is, in fact, the creation of the Catholic Church, from which other varieties of Christianity have received it. And the Catholic Church, while declaring it in all matters of faith and morals divinely inspired throughout, has never pronounced how far that inspiration extends—has never formally committed herself to "the traditional thesis," which has come down from uncritical ages. Cardinal Newman, in his most weighty Tractate *On the Inspiration of Scripture*,* lays it down—"The titles of the Canonical books, and their ascription to definite authors, either do not come under their inspiration or need not be accepted literally:" "nor does it matter whether one or two Isaiahs wrote the book which bears that prophet's name; the Church, without settling this point, pronounces it inspired in respect of faith and morals, both Isaiahs being inspired: and if this be assured to us, *all other*

* Published in the *Nineteenth Century* of February, 1884.

questions are irrelevant and unnecessary." * " Numquid eget Deus mendacio nostro ? " There is nothing to prevent a sincere Catholic from going to any length with modern criticism, *which the evidence really warrants*, in dealing with the letter of our Sacred Books. The divine element in those books no criticism can touch. The details over which it has power are as the small dust in the balance in comparison of the idea, over which it is powerless. There is a perspective to be observed in religion as in painting, otherwise we shall get a Chinese world, where things great and small are equally important. Surely Mr. Carlyle is right when he says: "The Bible has, in all changes of theory about it, this, as its highest distinction, that it is

* The italics are mine. As a suggestion of mine was the immediate occasion of Cardinal Newman's writing on this subject (see his letter to me in the *Fortnightly Review* of September, 1890, p. 436), I may be allowed here to state—what is within my personal knowledge—that nothing which ever proceeded from the pen of my venerated friend was more carefully considered, or was given to the world with a deeper sense of responsibility. Every word was scrupulously weighed, and the whole was submitted to the judgment of most competent theological experts before publication. The Cardinal felt fully the gravity of the question, which had much engaged his thoughts for many years, and was most anxious to indicate, before he was called hence, what appeared to him the true mode of dealing with it. At the same time, his usual consideration for weak brethren led him to employ language of extreme caution, and to desire that his friends when discussing, whether in speech or writing, what he had advanced, should imitate his example in this respect. This will abundantly appear from his letters of the year 1884, if his correspondence is given to the world.

the truest of books: a book springing, every word of it, from the intensest convictions, from the very heart's core, of those who wrote it." What a distinction! entitling the Bible of Christianity—at the very least—to a unique place among the world's Sacred Books: justifying us in saying of it, what the Hebrew poet said of a small and comparatively unimportant portion: "Thy word is tried to the uttermost: the righteousness of thy testimonies is everlasting."

So much may suffice concerning "the traditional thesis," which, unfortunately, was such a stone of stumbling to M. Renan. As to his peremptory declaration that "there never has been a supernatural fact," it would, in good logic be a sufficient reply, "Quod gratis asseritur, gratis negatur." It is a question of evidence. M. Renan, in terms, acknowledged this, and professed to repudiate the *a priori* argument.* But, as is clear from many passages in his writings, he was, consciously or unconsciously, under its influence. It was a first principle with him that a supernatural fact—a miracle—is impossible, because it would be abnormal: an infraction of the order of the universe: a violation of law. But everything depends upon

* "Ce n'est point par un raisonnement *a priori* que nous repoussons le miracle: c'est par un raisonnement critique ou historique. Plus on s'éloigne, plus la preuve de un fait surnaturel devient difficile. Pour bien comprendre cela, il faut avoir l'habitude de la critique de textes et de la méthode historique."—*Souvenirs*, p. 238.

what is meant by "norm," "order of the universe," "law." I say, deliberately, that the invincible prejudice against the miraculous, now so common, is merely an expression of that abounding materialism which denies the spiritual principle in man and in nature, and which, identifying law with physical necessity, issues in physical fatalism. Again, what is meant by a miracle? "Le miracle est l'inexpliqué," M. Renan replies, which is not a bad definition, so far as it goes, but it is too brief. Coleridge writes—

"An effect presented to the senses, without any adequate antecedent, *ejusdem generis*, is a miracle, in the philosophical sense. Thus the corporeal ponderable hand and arm, raised with no other known causative antecedent but a thought, a pure act of an immaterial, essentially invisible, imponderable will, is a miracle for a reflecting mind. Add the words *præter experientiam*, and we have a miracle in the popular, practical, and appropriated sense." *

No doubt this is in some respects extremely felicitous; but it is not sufficiently precise. A far more satisfactory account is given by Kant.

"Should it be asked, what is to be understood by the word miracle, then, since all we are concerned to know is what miracles are for us, that is, what they are for the practical use of our understanding, we might define them as events in the world with the laws of whose working we are, and must always remain utterly unacquainted." †

---

* *Literary Remains*, vol. iv. p. 276.

† *Religion innerhalb der Grenzen der blossen Vernunft.* Book II. Apot. 2.

That such events have occurred, and do occur, seems to me absolutely certain. And when I find an intelligent man dogmatically asserting that they do not occur, I can only suppose that he has not looked into the evidence, or that his intellect is under the influence of a first principle which disenables him for weighing it. In this country, especially, the general mind has been much darkened concerning the supernatural by the attitude of popular Protestantism towards it. Relegate miracles to the dim antiquity of two thousand years ago, and Protestantism will perhaps tolerate them, under conditions. Instance them as matters of modern, of contemporary history, and Protestantism will explain them away, referring them to imposture, or at the best to hallucination. The Catholic position in this matter is clearly the more consistent. Indeed, Protestants involve themselves in a manifest contradiction when they admit the miraculous stories in the Old and New Testaments, and reject the precisely similar legends to be found on every page of ecclesiastical history. The Biblical miracles and the ecclesiastical miracles hang together, so to speak; and, as a matter of fact, the prodigies related in the *Acta Sanctorum* are, from the point of view of historical criticism, much better established than the like occurrences in the Bible. With Catholics it is of faith that miracles have never ceased. They appertain to the gift of sanctity, which is a "note" of the Church. The truth of particular miracles is a question of evidence. And I feel bound to say that in some cases which I have carefully investigated, the evidence seems to me overwhelming. But it may be urged that if such events do occur, they are not the product of any one religious system. For example, not to go further afield, evidence, apparently conclusive, is alleged for spiritualistic miracles, in our own day; for, say, the levitation of a Mrs. Guppy; the curing of diseases by the application of a handkerchief from the body of a Mr. Ashman. The answer is that phenomena, apparently miraculous, most certainly are not the monopoly of any particular religious system. "Talia faciunt magi, qualia nonnunquam sancti faciunt," writes St. Augustine in his book *De Diversis Quæstionibus*.* He adds, "Talia quidem visibiliter esse apparent, sed et diverso fine et diverso jure fiunt." But if this be so, it is objected, what becomes of the value of miracles as "credentials" of Christianity? Well, no doubt it is difficult for the modern mind so to regard them. Possibly this may be largely due to forgetfulness of the fact that they must not be taken apart from the doctrine in support of which they are appealed to. Thaumaturgy, in itself, possesses no moral value. It does not speak to the conscience. It does not touch the heart. No reasonable man would receive Mrs.

* *Quæstio*, 79.

Guppy as an ambassadress from the Infinite and Eternal, merely because she was levitated, even if the testimony to that event should be overwhelming. Nor does the fact, if fact it be, that handkerchiefs from the body of Mr. Ashman cured diseases, invest with authority any utterances which that gentleman may make concerning divine things. It is, of course, unquestionable that the sphere of the miraculous, as vulgarly conceived, is contracting every day, through our ever-extending apprehension of the principle of continuity in the phenomenal universe. But why should that blot out for us the vision of the Divine Noumenon, Maker, Guardian, Worker, Perfecter of all things?

"'God is law,' say the wise. O soul! and let us rejoice;
For if He thunder by law, the thunder is still His voice."

"Dieu n'agit que par des volontés générales," says Malebranche. But why may not a general providence be also a particular providence—that is, a miracle? His all-seeing eye discerns the end from the beginning, or rather, all to Him is an eternal Now. There is a striking passage in Amiel, well worthy of being pondered in this connection.

"Le miracle est une perception de l'âme, la vision du divin derrière la nature, une crise psychique analogue à celle d'Enée lors du dernier jour d'Ilion qui fait voir les puissances célestes donnant l'impulsion aux actions humaines. Il n'y a point de miracle pour les indifférents : il n'y a que des âmes religieuses capables de reconnaître le doigt de Dieu dans certains faits." *

---

* *Journal Intime*, vol. i. p. 75.

M. Renan constantly speaks of the miraculous as "irrational" and "absurd." But "irrational" means contrary to reason; "absurd" means contradictory, impossible. Do we assert that which is contrary to reason, or contradictory, or impossible, when we say that there are events with the laws of whose working we are, and ever must remain, unacquainted? Kant well says: "Sensible people willingly admit in theory that miracles are possible; but in the business of life they count upon none." *

It appears to me, then, that the criticism whereon M. Renan founded the Agnosticism of which I take him as a typical exponent, is inadequate to support the vast edifice of doubt which he reared upon it. I may be permitted to add that in treating of questions which involve the spiritual life and death of nations, his *badinage*, however charming in itself, is as little in place as was the

---

* *Religion innerhalb der Grenzen der blossen Vernunft.* Book II. Apot 2. Mr. Mill writes: "There are few things of which we have more frequent experience than of physical facts, which our knowledge does not enable us to account for, because they depend on "laws" which observation, aided by science, has not yet brought to light; and it is always possible that the wonderworker may have acquired (consciously or unconsciously) the power of calling them into action. . . . We cannot, therefore, conclude absolutely that the miraculous theory ought to be at once rejected. . . . Once admit a God, and the production of an effect by his direct volition must be reckoned with as a serious possibility."—*Essays on Religion*, p. 230.

inimitable *persiflage* of Voltaire. There is profound truth in Goethe's dictum, that the mere Understanding finds matter for laughter in everything, the Reason in hardly anything. "Der Verständige findet fast alles lächerlich, der Vernünftige fast Nichts." Reason—"Vernunft"—is an endowment in which M. Renan, like Voltaire before him, was terribly deficient. And it is precisely the quality essential for a just view of those supreme problems with which he has so much occupied himself. Hence it is that he has, practically, left them just where he found them. His Critical Agnosticism, in effect, adds nothing to the doctrine which Voltaire's "esprit infini" taught a century ago. And, to quote certain words of his own, written in another connection, we may say, "Voltaire suffit:" one Voltaire is enough.

CHAPTER IV.

SCIENTIFIC AGNOSTICISM.

LET us now go on to consider that other variety of Agnosticism of which I have spoken, the Scientific, or Affirmative. And it will be well to view this doctrine also, as exhibited by its most effective and accredited advocate. Such, I suppose, Mr. Herbert Spencer unquestionably is. Professor Huxley has recognized in him the most complete and methodical " expositor of the tendencies of scientific thought." And Mr. Darwin has pronounced him " our great philosopher." I must, indeed, be permitted to say that, while fully recognizing the high place held by Mr. Darwin as a diligent, accurate, and candid investigator of a certain class of physical phenomena, I cannot attach much importance to his judgment about philosophy and philosophers. "Cuique in arte sua est credendum:" and philosophy was not Mr. Darwin's art. In mental science he appears to have been absolutely unversed. I question whether he ever so much as looked into a metaphysical treatise. His dialectical powers were extremely feeble. But it is unquestionable that the view expressed by him concerning Mr. Herbert Spencer is widely prevalent. And no doubt the reason is, in great part, this: that Mr. Spencer's theory of man and the universe is recommended as "scientific:" as a brand-new theory formed in independence of the great intellectual traditions of the human race. Few serious students of philosophy, probably, will reckon Mr. Spencer among the prophets. But such students are rare in England. To the vast majority of those who are commonly called "educated men" the very alphabet of metaphysics is unknown. Of the experimental sciences they more commonly possess some tincture. And the fact that Mr. Spencer's method is essentially physical, is *primâ facie* a recommendation to them of his system. Professor Max Müller has well remarked: " It is short and easy . . . to be a philosopher, not by studying Plato and Aristotle, Berkeley and Kant, but by ignoring if not by despising them." " Such a philosophy, by appealing, as it always does, to the common sense of mankind, is sure of wide popular support." * " Common sense," indeed, is the indispensable foundation; but it is by no means sufficient for these things without a certain intellectual discipline. To mention one point only : philosophy has a terminology of its own: time, space, force, motion, mean one thing for the metaphysician and another for the physicist. Common sense may, however, avail to judge what is the real value of Mr.

* *Science and Thought*, p. 145.

Herbert Spencer's Scientific Agnosticism, as an answer to The Great Enigma wherewith we are concerned in this volume. And so avoiding, as much as possible, all technicalities, but holding fast by the elementary principles of ratiocination, let us now enter upon that inquiry. In conducting it I must take leave to use great plainness of speech—even at the risk of shocking a coterie of fond enthusiasts, who resent as flat blasphemy any questioning of Mr. Spencer's *ipse dixit:* who appear to consider it the noblest occupation of a rational creature " to wonder with a foolish face of praise " when their Master exhibits " the set of visual states which he knows as his umbrella," moving across " the sets of visual states which he knows as the shingle and the sea." * I am unfeignedly sorry to be obliged to offend these little ones who believe in Mr. Spencer. In truth, I may lay claim to some fellow-feeling with them. For, if Mr. Spencer will permit me to say so, I regard him with much admiration, sincere respect, and lively gratitude, profoundly as I differ with him. I admire the fertility and subtlety of his intellect, and his singular power of generalization. I respect the heroic courage and faith unfailing which have sustained him in his colossal task: the sober enthusiasm which has led him to " scorn delights and live laborious days," careless of wealth and indifferent to popularity; intent, with noble singleness of purpose, upon the

* *Principles of Psychology*, second edition, § 462.

severe studies to which he has consecrated his life. I am grateful to him for the abundant light cast by his biological knowledge upon many dark places of psychology, and still more for exhibiting with a power both of analysis and synthesis, not likely to be surpassed, a phase of speculation which I must account vitiated by radical errors. But to point out those errors is a debt which we, who, as we consider, follow a more excellent way, owe to our day and generation. And the obligation is rendered all the more stringent by the fact that Mr. Spencer is unquestionably the most influential teacher of Scientific Agnosticism.

Mr. Spencer has bestowed upon his speculations the name of "The Synthetic Philosophy." The adjective might be challenged. From one point of view, "analytical" would be more accurately descriptive. But without dwelling on this point, let us proceed to Mr. Spencer's definition of philosophy. "Science is partly unified knowledge: philosophy is completely unified knowledge."* "Completely unified knowledge!" Well, unquestionably, a philosophy which completely unified knowledge, would be a perfect philosophy. We may admit that as the ideal. In proportion as it approaches such an ideal, a philosophical system is great: in other words, in proportion as it satisfies

* *First Principles*, fifth edition, § 37.

the intellect, and increases the limits of knowledge. If its principles are objectively true and certain, if they are founded in the order of being and eternal reality, they can be justified on rational grounds. If their root is in the constituent principles of the human intellect, the mind will be bound by its own intrinsic laws to accept them; they will internally cohere; they will be symmetrical, for between all speculative truths there is correspondence or analogy: "natura sibi ubique consentanea est." All philosophy is a search after unity. Hitherto, philosophers have confessed that only an imperfect synthesis rewarded their endeavours. Mr. Spencer claims, apparently, to have been completely successful in the quest. " Je, d'où, où, pour, comment ; l'existence, l'origine, le lieu, la fin et les moyens," he can explain it all: faith and morals, the source of life, the meaning of life, the end of life and the conduct of life. By him, in the fulness of time, the answer to The Great Enigma has been discovered; and has been revealed to this favoured nineteenth century in the five thousand and odd pages of his closely printed volumes. Let us see what it, in substance, is.

The foundation of Mr. Spencer's philosophy is the clear and emphatic distinction drawn in his *First Principles* between the Unknowable and the Knowable. The sentiment of a First Cause, infinite and absolute, is, according to Mr. Spencer, the eternal and secure basis of all religion. This

Deity, whom, hidden more or less under anthropomorphic disguises, the votaries of all creeds ignorantly worship, declares he unto them as "The Unknowable." Next, he bids us turn to the physical sciences, taking as our guide experience. Every persistent impression made upon our consciousness, reveals to us an external reality, a reaction, a resistance, and, consequently, a force. The indecomposable mode of consciousness is force. All ultimate scientific ideas are traceable to experiences of force.* But it is one of the most striking discoveries of the nineteenth century, that forces are intimately connected, are correlated: and this discovery has been largely employed by Mr. Spencer in his theory of the universe. He regards all forces as manifestations of the dynamic energy everywhere diffused, which co-ordinates the whole range of phenomena, past, present, and future: an immanent and eternal energy, at once active and passive, subject to perpetual revolution, and maintaining all things in an ever-changing equilibrium. But what is this dynamic energy? We know not. Whether we analyze what passes within or without ourselves, its essence escapes us. Thus the last word of physical science, as of religion, is that "the Power which the Universe manifests to us is utterly inscrutable." † In this "ultimate truth" of The Unknowable, "this deepest, widest,

* *First Principles*, § 15–21.   † *Ibid.* § 14.

and most certain of all facts," is "the basis of [their] reconciliation." * We can know, then, in the strict sense of knowing, only the phenomenal manifestations of The Unknowable, and these we can know only as purely relative and subjective realities. "Even the highest achievements of science are resolvable into mental relations of co-existence and sequence, so co-ordinated as exactly to tally with certain relations of co-existence and sequence that occur externally." † These manifestations, "called by some impressions and ideas," Mr. Spencer prefers to distinguish as "vivid" and "faint." "Manifestations that occur under the conditions called those of perception" — Mr. Spencer means sensuous perception—"are ordinarily far more distinct than those which occur under the conditions known as those of reflection, or memory, or imagination, or ideation." ‡ "Manifestations of the 'vivid' order precede, in our experience, those of the 'faint' order." § "Those of the one order are 'originals,' while those of the other are copies." ‖ "What is the meaning of this? What is the division equivalent to? Obviously it corresponds to the division between *object* and *subject*. This profoundest of distinctions between the manifestations of The Unknowable, we recognize by grouping them into *self* and *non-self*. These

* *First Principles*, § 14.   † *Ibid.* § 25.   ‡ *Ibid.* § 43.
§ *Ibid.*   ‖ *Ibid.*

faint manifestations, forming a continuous whole, differing from the others in the quantity, quality, cohesion, and condition of existence of its parts, we call the *ego*: and these vivid manifestations indissolubly bound together in relatively immense masses, and having independent conditions of existence, we call the *non-ego*; or rather, and more truly, each order of manifestations carries with it the irresistible implication of some power that manifests itself; and by the words *ego* and *non-ego* respectively, we mean the power that manifests itself in the 'faint' forms, and the power that manifests itself in the vivid forms."* "The totality of my consciousness is divisible into a faint aggregate which I call my mind; a special part of the vivid aggregate cohering with this in various ways, which I call my body; and the rest of the vivid aggregate which has no such connection with the faint aggregate. This special part of the vivid aggregate, which I call my body, proves to be a part through which the rest of the vivid aggregate works changes in the faint, and through which the faint works certain changes in the vivid."† And, "the root-conception of existence, beyond consciousness, becomes that of resistance, *plus* some force which the resistance measures."‡ Mr. Spencer's philosophy then requires as "a primordial proposition,"

* *First Principles*, § 44.
† *Principles of Psychology*, § 462.   ‡ *Ibid.* § 466.

as "a datum," the acceptance of these two separate aggregates, as constituting the world of consciousness, and the world beyond consciousness, and the ascription of both to the action of one single cause, which he terms, The Unknowable. Thus is "the unification of science" "complete," and "philosophy reaches its goal." * That one and the same law everywhere rules, applying alike to organic life, to the individual, to society, to the life of the earth, to the solar system, to the whole of cosmic existence, is a postulate essential to Mr. Spencer's philosophy. The law is identical because the life is identical, for throughout the universe there energizes a Force, "indestructible," "inscrutable," "unknowable," "absolute," "the ultimate of ultimates." Mr. Spencer's theory may be shortly and accurately described as an attempt to find the solution of the problem of the universe in a sole law: the persistence of force under multiform transformations. Physical forces, vital forces, mental forces, social forces, are all only different manifestations of the self-same force. Cosmology, Biology, Psychology, Sociology, Ethics—all are to be explained by the persistence, under various modifications, of that manifestation of The Unknowable. Nature is merely a vast sphere in which it works eternally, bringing to life, bringing to death, integrating and disintegrating, everywhere throughout

* *First Principles*, § 40.

what the Buddhists call "the whirlpool of existence," always repeating the same monotonous, never-ending process. The history of the minutest living organism on earth is precisely the history of a world system. Evolution, equilibrium, dissolution—that is the brief epitome of the career, whether of a star or of a worm. The phenomena of human life, of human history, like the phenomena of astronomy, of geology, of physiology, are, in Mr. Spencer's philosophy, nothing but metamorphoses of the one dynamic principle at different stages of intensity, infinitely varied combinations of the same elements. Such, sketched in the roughest outlines, is the vast philosophical edifice which this bold and patient thinker has reared. What place therein has the race of man? It is an insignificant factor in the sum of things, produced, and, in brief time, to be destroyed by the never-ceasing action of eternal forces. A recent German writer has well put it: "What, in Mr. Spencer's philosophy, is universal life? A succession of beings and of forms expressing the combinations of the same elementary phenomena in a determinate order. What is each individual life? An insignificant moment in the infinite varieties of movement. What is humanity? A collection of those moments. Individual life, all history, are but imperceptible episodes in the immense, eternal work of Nature: accidents without future and without meaning, infinitesimal quantities which the thinker may neglect, in the universal and infinite *processus*." This is the answer which the most popular school of modern philosophy gives to the question, "What is man?" His personality is an illusion. His immortality is a dream. The race will perish like the individual. The earth itself will perish when the sun which vivifies it becomes extinct. Death will assert its reign over the immensity of the world systems which people space. True, the elementary forces which constitute the present order of things will enter into other combinations. Force is eternal, and the only eternal. New universes, peopled by new forms of being, will come into existence, and will in their time disappear. But what is that to *me?* To me, in the presence of this overwhelming vision, the words of Pascal come home with even more appalling meaning than they could have borne for him: "Lost in this little corner of the universe," "plunged in the abyss of those terrible spaces which encompass me," "I am affrighted like a man who, in his sleep, has been carried to some horrible desert island, and there awakes, not knowing where he is, nor how he shall escape." How he shall escape? No: there is no escape.

Now, what are we to say to Mr. Spencer's

gigantic hypothesis? Well, in the first place, I may observe that, notwithstanding its air of novelty, it is a very ancient hypothesis so far as its root idea is concerned. It is substantially the old atomistic theory of self-existent matter, fixed in quantity, indestructible, itself producing all its changes through the antagonistic forces whereof it is composed. I am far from imputing this antiquity as a fault. I am as far from questioning Mr. Spencer's claim to originality. It has been observed by Goethe that the most original authors of this new time are those who have the power of presenting what has been said before as though it had not been said. And certainly in Mr. Spencer's hands the theory of Democritus has assumed quite a fresh aspect; so marvellous is the industry with which he has collected his facts from all departments of the experimental sciences; so singular the ingenuity with which he has systematized them; so consummate the art with which he has employed "the loose abundance of his phraseology" to veil the gaps in his argument. Mr. Spencer's philosophy is, in fact, a vast system of speculative physics. Even his account of the operations of the human consciousness is given in language derived from matter and motion. He appeals to what it is the fashion to call "experience." Does "experience" bear him out? His metaphysic is mechanical, his psychology is biological. We may reasonably ask from him the kind of proof which mechanists and biologists offer. There are three fundamental doctrines upon which his vast edifice rests. If they fail, the whole superstructure falls of necessity into the abysses of time and being above which he has sought to rear it. I mean his doctrines of Causation, of the Relativity of Knowledge, and of The Unknowable. Let us examine each a little in detail; and it will be most convenient to take them in this order.

First, then, what warrant has Mr. Spencer for identifying all the facts of physical and mental causation? Why, even the unity of natural forces is by no means established. Every atom is subject to the action of at least six powers—gravity, chemic attraction, chemic repulsion, polarity, cohesion, elasticity—which are irreducible to one another. Nay, chemistry reckons some seventy simple bodies, of which sixteen form the ultimate elements of the human organism, and each of these sixteen—probably each of the seventy—would seem to have its own proper causative power. "Force," says Dubois-Reymond, "is nothing else than an abortion of the irresistible tendency to personification." To which we may add that Mr. Spencer's great sole law of the Persistence of Force is nothing else than an illegitimate corollary from the unquestionable fact of the conservation of energy. The experimental sciences offer no warrant for his assertion that "the quantity of force always remains the same." The doctrine of the persistence and indestructibility of Force as taught by him is an amalgam of physical dogmatism and metaphysical error. The existence of a *prima materies* is as unproved now as in the days of Berkeley. There is no real oneness known in matter. We can by no means affirm the existence of one primordial physical substance: of one ultimate physical cause. The utmost we can assert is that the ponderable substances are subject to the same laws. Still less are we warranted in affirming that what Mr. Spencer calls, in his question-begging* phraseology, "the vivid aggregates" and "the faint aggregates" are the outcome of the same dynamic energy. Mr. Spencer's "vivid aggregates" are experiences of sensation. His "faint aggregates" are remembered experiences of sensation. Mr. Spencer does not, of course, say that life is merely motion. He knows that it is more than that. Still, if there is any meaning in words, his object

* "Question-begging," and something more indeed. Professor Green has well pointed out, "It is only by a misuse of terms, according to Mr. Spencer's own showing, that this vivid aggregate is called an aggregate at all. The 'states of consciousness, which form it,' have none of them any permanence. Each 'changes from instant to instant.' To speak of such states as 'aggregating' or as 'segregating themselves' is a contradiction in terms."—*Works*, vol. i. p. 393.

is to find the origin of consciousness in the nervous system;* to represent thoughts as generated † from things; to establish the identity of intellectual concepts and material impressions; to exhibit mind as the outcome of the association of sensations. But Mr. Spencer's postulate is open to two fatal objections. In the first place, his doctrine that ideas are only "copies," and "faint copies," of past experience, personal and racial, is untenable. His confusion of psychical with physiological facts, of consciousness with the phenomena of sense, is contrary to observation, which

* " These separate impressions are received by the senses . . . [and are] all brought into relation with one another. . . . But this implies some centre of communication common to them all, through which they severally pass, and as they cannot pass through it simultaneously they must pass through it in succession. So that as the external phenomena responded to become greater in number, and more complicated in kind, the variety and rapidity of the changes to which this common centre of communication is subject, must increase—there must arise an unbroken series of these changes—there must arise a consciousness."—*Principles of Psychology*, § 179.

† I am well aware that Mr. Spencer prefers to speak of coordination. But Professor Green has shown, with unanswerable logic, " On the strength of the admitted determination of subject by object—the converse determination being ignored—things are supposed [by Mr. Spencer] to produce the intelligence which is the condition of their appearance. Through qualities which in truth they only possess as relative to a distinguishing and combining consciousness, and through the 'registration' of these in the sentient organism, they are supposed gradually to generate those forms of synthesis without which in fact they themselves would not be."—*Works*, vol. i. p. 388.

testifies that ideas and impressions differ not in degree but in kind. Of what concrete or physical things, made known to us by sensation, can abstract thoughts be the copy?* Secondly, Mr. Spencer has absolutely failed to show that "the law of metamorphosis which holds among the physical forces holds equally between the mental forces;" that "those modes of the Unknowable which we call motion, heat, light, chemical affinity are alike transformable into each other and into those modes of the Unknowable which we distinguish as sensation, emotion, thought — these, in their turn, being directly or indirectly transformable into their original shapes:" † that life and intellectual energy may be brought under his great formula of the persistence of force. What is his argument? It amounts to this: that mental action is contingent upon the presence of a certain nervous apparatus, the activity of which again depends upon a particular chemical constitution: that the evolution of thought and emotion varies with the supply of blood to the brain, and with the condition of the blood: and that the effete

---

* Take an illustration from St. Augustine: "An vero cum audio tria genera esse quæstionum, an sit, quid sit, quale sit; sonorum quidem quibus hæc verba confecta sunt imagines teneo, et eos per aures cum strepitu transisse ac jam non esse scio. Res vero ipsas quæ illis significantur sonis, neque ullo corporis sensu corporis attigi, neque uspiam vidi præter animum meum." —*Confess.* l. x. c. 10.

† *First Principles*, § 71.

products separated from the blood by the kidneys, vary in character with the amount of cerebral action.* Such are Mr. Spencer's "proofs" of the correlation of mental and physical forces. Proofs! He does not take us within measurable distance of proof. Who doubts that "the proportion of phosphorus, present in the brain, is the smallest in infancy, old age, and idiotcy, and the greatest during the prime of life?"† or that "tea and coffee create gentle exhilaration?"‡ or—if I may present him with a still more striking illustration—that a pinch of snuff clarifies the intellect? The concomitancy, the parallelism between material and mental changes is constant, perhaps invariable. But Mr. Spencer is as well aware as I am, that of the connection between physical motion and psychical change, between the brain and thought, between neurosis and psychosis, we really know nothing. We are almost entirely ignorant of cerebral physiology. Recent discoveries may have traced the nerve fibres of sensation and motion a little further towards the circumference of the brain; but they have entirely failed to reveal to us the properties of the caudate nerve-cells, of the cerebral convolutions. Mr. Spencer,

* *First Principles*, § 71. It is, of course, impossible for me to reproduce the whole of this chapter, which should be carefully read in order to appreciate the strength—or weakness—of Mr. Spencer's argument. I have referred to what appears to be the culminating portion of it.

† *Ibid.* ‡ *Ibid.*

indeed, admits that "how a force existing as motion, heat, or light can become a mode of consciousness, how it is possible for aërial vibrations to generate the sensation which we call sound, or for the forces liberated by chemical changes in the brain to give rise to emotion—these are mysteries which it is impossible to fathom."* He pleads, however, that they are not profounder mysteries than the transformation of certain physical forces into each other. But it is not a question of the relative profundity of mysteries. We know that certain forces of the material world—light, heat, magnetism, electricity—are convertible into one another, and that all appear to be subject to the laws of conservation of energy. But there is no known process of changing ponderable into imponderable substances. Light is not a gas: it is but a mode of motion. And no gas, however attenuated or expanded, turns into light. This is certain, as every schoolboy knows. Equally certain is it that the transformation of a physical force into mental energy is a mere nude hypothesis. There is not a shred of direct evidence to support it. Nor can I admit the validity of the analogy upon which Mr. Spencer relies. In the phenomena of the material world the production and succession of movements take place according to invariable rules. It is perfectly true that here, too, we do not know the how of the causal nexus.

* *First Principles*, § 71.

Still, we can, at all events, follow the various phases of the metamorphosis and ascertain the order of antecedents and consequents. Far other is it in the sphere of vital force. Here there is mechanism, indeed: but there is something more; there is spontaneity, there is consciousness: "apparent diræ facies." In the invisible world of intellect, of spirit, which is properly the domain of the metaphysician, the analogy disappears altogether. Professor Bain admits the "total difference of nature" between "the two extreme and contrasted facts termed Mind and Matter."* There is simply no measurable relation between the intellectual effect and the physical fact alleged as the efficient cause; between—let us say—the vibration of atoms and thrills of gratitude; between the compounding of molecules and the composition of verses. Mr. Spencer is of opinion that "nothing can explain the non-acceptance" of his doctrine except "an overwhelming bias in favour of a preconceived theory."† But in truth nothing save an overwhelming bias in favour of Mr. Spencer's theory can explain its acceptance. The burden of proving it lies upon him. And he has no proof to offer. In fact, the sole ground why he calls upon us to receive it—under pain, as it were, of intellectual reprobation—is that his philosophy cannot get on without it. That is true enough. But it is hardly a sufficient argument why we

* *Mind and Body*, p. 134. † *First Principles*, § 73.

should subordinate reason to faith, and accept descriptions as though they were explanations.

Before I go further, I should like to say one word more on this question of the unity of natural forces. Suppose, for the sake of argument, that all the phenomena known as affinities, or elective attractions, could be reduced to the merely mechanical action of molecules. Well, even then, although in these complex phenomena there were no other elementary principles than mechanical forces, they would still constitute real properties, verifiable by experience. The composition of elementary principles in the world of living beings exhibits not merely simple collocation, but organic arrangement. Vitality, or a vital principle, is indeed, as we all know, peremptorily banished by authoritative persons to the limbo where repose aquosity and other discredited "metaphysical entities." There are, however, savants—Claude Bernard was one of them—who declare that a creative and directive idea (*une idée créatrice et directive*) governs the formation of the organs. Nor is there any immediate prospect of the extinction of this school by the doctrine which explains every organism, all life, all thought, by the simple play of cellular activities. Let us, however, go a step further in our hypothetical concession. Let us suppose that this view were incontestably established. Even then we should be far from the identification of the vital properties of bodies with their chemical or physical properties; very far indeed from the identification of thought with motion. Let me here borrow some pregnant observations from Mr. Romanes:—

"Suppose that physiologists should discover a mechanical equivalent of thought, so that we might estimate the value of a calculation in thermal units, or the 'labour of love' in footpounds: still . . . we should have only cut a twist of flax to find a lock of iron. For by thus assimilating thought with energy, we should in nowise have explained the fundamental antithesis between subject and object. The fact would remain, if possible, more unaccountable than ever that mind should present absolutely no point of real analogy with motion. Involved with the essential idea of motion is the idea of extension: suppress the latter and the former must necessarily vanish; for motion only means transition in space of something itself extended. But thought, as far as we can possibly know it, is known and distinguished by the very peculiarity of not having extension. Therefore, even if we were to find a mechanical equivalent of thought, thought would still not be proved a mode of motion. On the contrary, what would be proved would be that, in becoming transformed into thought, energy had ceased to be energy: in passing out of its relation to space it would cease to exist as energy. . . . Therefore, the proof that thought has a mechanical equivalent would simply amount to the proof, not that thought is energy, but that thought destroys energy. . . . We may, therefore, quit the suggestion that the difficulty experienced by Materialism of showing an equivalency between neurosis and psychosis can ever be met by assuming that some day mental processes may admit of being expressed in terms of physical."*

I venture to hold, then, that Mr. Spencer has no sufficient warrant for identifying all the facts

* "The Fallacy of Materialism:" *Nineteenth Century*, December, 1882, p. 877.

of physical and mental causation: that his theory of the transformation and equivalence of all forces is not reasoned truth, but unproved theory; that his "ultimate of ultimates" is as purely hypothetical as the "chimæra bombinans in vacuo," popularly supposed to be so dear to the medieval schoolmen.

Let us go on to the next postulate of Mr. Spencer's philosophy: his doctrine of the Relativity of Knowledge. I say advisedly *his* doctrine, because there is a doctrine of the relativity of knowledge with which I have no quarrel, and which is by no means his. It is perfectly true that our knowledge is relative to our mental constitution; "quidquid recipitur secundum modum recipientis recipitur." We cannot know things as they are in themselves; we can know them only as they appear to our consciousness and are conditioned by our intellect. And this relative knowledge is imperfect: because to know anything perfectly we must know it in its connection with everything: "Denn jede Strasse führt ans End der Welt." Absolute knowledge is possible only to the Absolute Being. Again, I am quite prepared to admit that mind and matter both proceed from an Infinite Substance, and that knowledge is founded on the discovery by the human intellect of their relations. But when Mr. Spencer teaches the relativity of our knowledge, he means something very different from this. I will show, in his own words, what it is that he means :—

"If," he insists, "Life, in all its manifestations, inclusive of Intelligence in its highest form, consists in the continuous adjustment of internal relations to external relations, the necessarily relative character of our knowledge becomes obvious. The simplest cognition being the establishment of some connection between subjective states answering to some connection * between objective agencies . . . it is clear that the process, no matter how far it be carried, can never bring within the reach of Intelligence either the states themselves or the agencies themselves." † "The general truth . . . is that though internal feeling habitually depends on external agents, yet there is no likeness between them, either in kind or in degree. The connection between objective cause and subjective effect is conditioned in ways extremely complex and variable. . . . The relation between outer agent and inner feeling generated by it depends on the structure of the species.‡ . . . *We are brought to the conclusion that what we are conscious of as properties of matter, even down to its weight and resistance, are but subjective affections produced by objective agencies that are unknown and unknowable.*" §

These last words contain the gist of Mr. Spencer's doctrine of the relativity of our knowledge. He does not deny that the external world exists. On the contrary, he strenuously combats that denial. But he insists that we can know nothing of it beyond the impressions produced by its states

---

* "Some connection"! But the whole question is—What connection?

† *First Principles*, § 25. ‡ *Principles of Pyschology*, § 78.
§ *Ibid.* § 86. The italics are mine.

upon our states of consciousness. From our sense perceptions, which are but subjective modifications of something unknown, we draw certain inferences regarding it: its weight, for example, or its resistance. And that is all the knowledge of it to which we can attain: a knowledge of relations between relations. Ultimate scientific ideas, he maintains, " turn out to be merely symbols of the actual, not cognitions of it." * Is this a valid doctrine?

Now, in the first place, we must of course admit that all our knowledge of the external world is gained through the senses: there is no other channel. But does it follow from this that all our knowledge is merely sensation?—an inference from our sense perceptions? An inference! But that supposes a process of ratiocination. And surely, as a matter of fact, it is not by any such process that our first knowledge of external objects is gained. Consciousness itself testifies that there is in the mind a power to cognize external objects immediately and intuitively. It is the experience of every child as he—

> "—— learns the use of 'I' and ' me,'
> And finds 'I am not what I see,
> And other than the things I touch.'"

The distinction between subject and object is, I say, a primitive fact, or rule of consciousness, and to recognize it is a condition of all sound thinking. And perception is a much more delicate

* *First Principles*, § 21.

and subtle matter than Mr. Spencer imagines. The images presented to our intelligence by the eye, the ear, the touch—Aristotle and the schoolmen after him called them phantasmata—are the *direct* results of sensuous experience. But knowledge means something more than that. We may go on—we do go on—to the reflex act of subjecting those phantasmata to the judging faculty; we reason about them; we compare, we abstract. Passive sensation does not constitute knowledge in the true sense. The instrument of knowledge is thought (*quo cognoscimus*). Knowledge (*quod cognoscitur*) is what is gained by thought. There is a perception of sense, which is concerned with the material, the extended, the corporeal. There is an analytical interpretation of that perception, an intellectual appropriation of it (*das Bewusstwerden*) which has to do with the immaterial, the unextended, the uncorporeal. Mr. Spencer confuses the two. I should like to make this evident, if I can, to the "general reader:" and really, if we put aside sophisms and sophistications, there is no great difficulty in picturing to ourselves the intellect at its actual contact with the presentments of sense. I take into my hands a stone. I am directly conscious of it as an otherness: a non-self. Feeling proper, sensation, reveals to me so much. And I proceed—this is the next step—to interpret the sensation intellectually, to *cognize* the stone as hard and heavy. Thus does the thinking subject respond to the stimulating object, and "convert the feeling into a felt thing." Here is something more than sensation: here is an interior expression of sensation, formulated in words: here is intellection. Surely so much is clear. But we may advance yet a step further. From the cognition of the stone as hard and heavy, we may by comparison, reasoning, abstraction, advance to the general concepts of hardness and weight. These are the three steps in our knowledge which Kant distinguishes as Experience, Understanding, and Reason; and which, under whatever names, are commonly admitted by metaphysicians. It is perfectly true that the weight and resistance of which I am conscious, are "subjective affections." It is not true that they are *but* subjective affections. What is in the intellect, Aristotle observes, is not the stone but the idea of the stone: οὐ γὰρ ὁ λίθος ἐν τῇ ψυχῇ, ἀλλὰ τὸ εἶδος. But the idea of weight, the idea of resistance, has an objective value. The knowledge which the intellect obtains concerning its various objects is not wholly relative.

"The relativity of our knowledge." There is one thing which Mr. Spencer quite ignores in all that he has written upon this theme. And that is that the relations of things are rational. But to say this is to say that those relations possess an element of objectivity. Mr. Spencer excludes the rational element from knowledge. He makes of it merely sensuous experience, compared and synthesized. For him, ideas are merely general abstract relations between phenomena. For him, our intellectual horizon is bounded by the experimental sciences. His method appears to me to be exactly described in the well-known verses of *Faust* :—

> " Wer will was Lebendig's erkennen und beschreiben,
> Sucht erst den Geist herauszutreiben ;
> Dann hat er die Theile in seiner Hand,
> Fehlt, leider ! nur das geistige Band."

"Das geistige Band : " the spiritual *nexus*. Yes. That is exactly what is wanting in Mr. Spencer's philosophy. His synthesis is merely an attempt to generalize the physical sciences: an attempt not judged by the chief masters of those sciences especially successful. It is not rational, intellectual, spiritual. And that is its condemnation. You will never succeed in explaining man and the universe by what is lowest in man and the universe. The physical sciences will never reveal to you the highest form of universal truth. We possess faculties of intuition, of intellection, of sense. Mr. Spencer does not recognize intuition. And intellection he confounds with sensation. He seeks to know mind through matter. Leibnitz truly observes, "It is only by what is within us that we have any knowledge of what is outside." The right starting-point in philosophy is in the natural operations of the intellect.

In the happy words of Coleridge, "Metaphysics are the science which determines what can and cannot be known of being and the laws of being *à priori*—that is, from those necessities of the mind, or laws of being, which though first revealed to us by experience, must yet have pre-existed, in order to make experience itself possible; even as the eye must exist previously to any particular act of seeing, though only by sight can we know that we have eyes."* The object of the intellect is being or truth—*ens vel verum commune*—Aquinas tells us. This idea of being is the root of all our knowledge. Nothing is known save as being. And things are cognizable so far as they participate in being. To this, language itself witnesses, for there is, in strictness, only one verb: the verb *to be*. By all means let us recognize the category of Becoming. But let us not overlook, with Mr. Spencer, the equally real category of Being. Things are related. True. But Mr. Spencer might have learnt from "the old hermit of Prague, who never saw pen and ink, 'That that is, is.'" Yes. Things *are*. They have their separate identity. "Things are what they are." They have their own nature. The *principium individuationis* of the schoolmen is a fact: an ultimate fact: that is a mystery. "Omne individuum ineffabile." "One can only understand what one can make," Aristotle warns us. "Stay," says the Alchemist to his weeping wife, in Balzac's

* *The Friend*, vol. i. p. 253 (Pickering's Edition).

powerful novel: "Stay: I have decomposed tears. Tears contain a little phosphate of lime, some chloride of soda, some mucus, and some water." Is that all that a tear is? "Life," according to Mr. Spencer, "is adequately conceived only when we think of it as the continuous adjustment of internal relations to external relations."* Is life really no more than that? Does this decomposition explain the living man? How is it that I know aught external at all? Without the oneness, continuity, and identity of the thinking subject it would be impossible to unite the elements of sensible knowledge: "to grasp together the manifold of intuition into the unity of apprehension;" as Kant speaks. The very condition of knowledge is the simplicity and persistence of the *ego*. Being is a primitive intuition of the intellect, lying at the basis of each act of cognition, and it is formulated by us under the affirmation, "I am I." † The conscious *ego* reveals self and non-self as entities: as objective realities.

We go on from Mr. Spencer's theory of Knowledge to his doctrine of The Unknowable.

* *Principles of Psychology*, § 131.

† Mr. Spencer admits that "no hypothesis enables us to escape" from "the belief in the reality of self" (*First Principles*, § 20), although elsewhere he assures us that personality is a fiction.

It is an old saying, and a true, that the various questions with which philosophy is occupied are summed up and concentrated in one: the question of the Infinite. Mr. Spencer shall himself state his teaching on this high matter:—

"We are conscious of the Relative as existence under conditions and limits; it is impossible that these conditions and limits can be thought of apart from something to which they give the form: the abstraction of these conditions and limits is, by the hypothesis, the abstraction of them *only*; consequently there must be a residuary consciousness of something which filled up their outlines; and this indefinite something constitutes our consciousness of the Non-relative or Absolute. Impossible though it is to give this consciousness any qualitative or quantitative expression whatever, it is not the less certain that it remains with us as a positive and indestructible element of thought."* "Though the Absolute cannot in any manner or degree be known, in the strict sense of knowing, yet we find that its positive existence is a necessary datum of consciousness: that, so long as consciousness continues, we cannot for an instant rid ourselves of this datum: and that thus the belief which this datum constitutes, has a higher warrant than any other whatever."† "It is alike our highest wisdom and our highest duty to regard that through which all things exist, as The Unknowable." ‡

This is Mr. Spencer's doctrine of the Absolute; and here, as it is sometimes said, is the differentiation of his philosophy from Materialism proper. Certainly he does not teach that external phenomena, *Kraft und Stoff*, are what they seem: that Matter as we know it, or Motion as we know it, is the thing-in-itself. On the contrary, he ex-

* *First Principles*, § 26. † *Ibid.* § 27. ‡ *Ibid.* § 31.

pressly tells us that "Matter and Motion, as we think them, are but symbolic of unknowable forms of existence:" that "Mind also is unknowable," and that "were we compelled to choose between the alternatives of translating mental phenomena into physical phenomena, or of translating physical phenomena into mental phenomena, the latter alternative would seem the more acceptable of the two."* Nay, more, that "it is impossible to interpret inner existence in terms of outer existence." † Elsewhere, however, Mr. Spencer endeavours to accomplish this impossibility. Thus, to cite one instance only—not the strongest, but the most singular—he tells us: "We have good reason to conclude that, at the particular place in a superior nervous centre, where, in some mysterious way, an objective change or nervous action *causes* a subjective change or feeling, *there exists a quantitative equivalence between the two*:" ‡ the "good reason," apparently, being that "nerve centres disintegrated by action are perpetually re-integrating themselves, and again becoming fit for action." This "good reason," I must take leave to say, appears to me "exceeding good senseless." Mr. Spencer does not seem to possess even a rudimentary knowledge of the value of evidence and the nature of proof. Moreover, "a quantitative equivalence!" All physical pheno-

* *Principles of Psychology*, § 63.   † *Ibid.*
‡ *Ibid.* § 47. The italics are mine.

mena, of course, can be expressed in terms of quantity. But what has quantity to do with feeling? This by the way. What I am, at the present moment, concerned to point out is that Mr. Spencer certainly does seek to interpret thought and feeling as manifestations of force. He tells us expressly that mind is "composed of feelings and the relations between feelings." * "They are the materials out of which . . . . Intellect is evolved by structural combination." † But his "feeling" is in truth mere sensation. And thus we pass "without break, from the phenomena of bodily life to the phenomena of mental life." ‡ "It is inferable that all physical relations whatever, from the necessary to fortuitous, *result* from the experiences of the corresponding external relations." § Mr. Spencer teaches, over and over again, that thought and feeling can be interpreted only as manifestations of force. But matter and motion also are "differently conditioned manifestations of force." Whence it would seem that mind and matter are identical. But what is this force in the metamorphoses of which we have the explanation of the wondrous All? Mr. Spencer's doctrine concerning it is not consistent. He regards it as "a relative reality." Body and mind for Mr. Spencer are both relative realities. "Feeling and nervous action are the inner and

---

* *Principles of Psychology*, § 77. † *Ibid.* § 76.
‡ *Ibid.* § 131.   § *Ibid.* § 189. The italics are mine.

outer faces of the *same* change."* They are "the subjective and objective faces of the same thing," but we are "utterly incapable of seeing, and even of imagining, how the two are related."† In the Unknowable Ultimate Reality the two modes of being are one. Dualism has only a relative and phenomenal value. But, on the other hand, "the current belief in objects as external independent entities has a higher guarantee than any other belief whatever: our cognition of existence, considered as noumenal, has a certainty which no cognition of existence, considered as phenomenal, can ever approach."‡ I do not attempt to harmonize these discordant oracles. And I should much like to see the man who can harmonize them. But I do not hesitate to affirm that the very nature of intelligence forbids such a conception of the Absolute as that which Mr. Spencer presents to us under the name of The Unknowable. "What must we say," he asks, "concerning that which transcends knowledge?"§ What indeed! All knowledge, according to Mr. Spencer, is relative. It is rigidly restricted to phenomena. "Thinking being relationing," he tells us in a well-known passage, "no thought can ever express more than relations." ‖ If this is so, if our knowledge is limited to conditioned experience, we

---

* *Principles of Psychology*, § 51. The italics are mine.
† *Ibid.* § 56. ‡ *Ibid.* § 448.
§ *First Principles*, § 26. ‖ *Ibid.* § 25.

cannot possibly know, in any sense of knowing, the unconditioned. But Mr. Spencer tells us, that "besides our consciousness of phenomena, we have a vague consciousness of that which transcends distinct consciousness." * "Vague" consciousness, and "distinct" consciousness! What virtue is there in the adjectives? All consciousness, according to Mr. Spencer, is constituted under forms and limits: it belongs to the order of phenomena. That is for him the one mode of consciousness. If you abolish the limits, you abolish the consciousness. If, as Mr. Spencer insists, our experience is only conditioned, assuredly we are not justified in asserting an unconditioned existence in any form, conceivable or inconceivable. Mr. Spencer himself, indeed, feels this difficulty, and seeks to escape from it. Consciousness of the Unconditioned, or the Absolute, he tells us, "is not and cannot be constituted by any single mental act, but is the produce of many mental acts." †
But if every one of these mental acts has only a relative value, how can a series of them produce the non-relative? Mr. Spencer tells us of "an inscrutable power, manifested through phenomena." "Manifested" and "inscrutable:" "out of relation," and "in relation"! If Mr. Spencer were talking mysticism, this might hold. But he supposes himself to be talking science! Most certainly, if Mr. Spencer's first principles are true,

* *First Principles*, § 26.   † *Ibid.*

we cannot, in any sense, know the Absolute—still less can we have any kind of consciousness of it, for consciousness assumes more than knowledge.*

Mr. Spencer ingenuously confesses, indeed, "the consciousness of something which is yet out of consciousness is mysterious." † The mystery is akin to one of which we read in the history of Baron Münchausen, who is related to have lifted himself out of a river by his own periwig. Upon Mr. Spencer's own showing, only by going out of ourselves, only by transcending what he over and over again lays down dogmatically as the impassable limits of intellect, can we attain to any acquaintance with the Absolute. In no other way can what is out of consciousness be a necessary datum of consciousness. The truth is that Mr. Spencer here darkens counsel by words without knowledge. The Unknowable really means the irrational: the self-contradictory: that is, the non-existent. Everything, in so far as it is, is knowable, though not necessarily to this or that grade of intelligence. *Esse* and *percipi* are synonymous. To affirm that a thing is, and that it is unknowable, is a contradiction in terms. We must know it, and that in the strict sense of knowing, in order to

---

* For a fuller discussion of this subject see the Rev. Dr. William Barry's powerful article, "Mr. Herbert Spencer's Agnosticism," in the *Dublin Review* of April, 1888.

† *Principles of Psychology*, § 448.

assert that it is; in order to bring it into the category of being. I remember hearing, while an undergraduate at Cambridge, of a clergyman of vague theological views, then an ornament of the University, whose duty it was, upon one occasion, to read the Athanasian Creed in his College chapel. When the service was over, a friend said: "Now, do you really believe in the Deity about whom we have so positively asserted so much?" "Well," he replied, "perhaps there may be a Kind of a Something." Mr. Spencer is, of course, at liberty to conjecture, with this cautious divine, that there may be a Kind of a Something out of consciousness. But I demur when he proceeds to erect his surmise into "a datum of philosophy," and to assert dogmatically, "The God that we know, is not; but the God that we know not, is."

I very confidently contend, then, that Mr. Spencer's fundamental doctrine of The Unknowable is as untenable as are his other two fundamental doctrines of Causation and the Relativity of Knowledge. And here, I may remark, that as his erroneous theory of relativity has led him thus to label the Supreme Object of knowledge, so a true theory of relativity would have saved him from the antinomies in which he is hopelessly involved with regard to this high matter. The more the manifold relations of things are examined, the more clearly are they seen to be rational; which is another way of saying that they reveal a law, in the proper metaphysical sense of the word. The world is intelligible. It is Kosmos, not Chaos. That is the postulate with which physical science itself starts upon its triumphant career of investigation. Wordsworth sings of "All thinking things, the objects of all thought." The classification is just. Goethe somewhere tells us that in the subject, the human intellect, there are ideas corresponding with the laws in the object, external nature. The thought in my mind is fitted to grasp the thought in the universe. The reason, wherein we consist, it is, that rules in the microcosm of the leaf and the macrocosm of the fixed stars: "attingens a fine usque ad finem, fortiter suaviterque disponens omnia." The relations of things, I say, themselves testify of Objective Reason. But in truth Mr. Spencer's Scientific Agnosticism is an outrage upon reason. Absorbed in the attempt to make, by physical methods, our higher faculties out of our lower, he puts aside the self-affirmations of the intellect which are the primary sources of all knowledge. I speak of those *a priori* or necessary truths which are laws of thought because they are absolute uniformities, intuitively known as self-evident. Upon such truths physical science itself rests. "The uniformity of Nature," for example, "that what has uniformly been in the past, will be in the future," is one of them. And it is essential to the physicist. He cannot take a step without it. Dr. Bain well calls it "the one ultimate premiss of all induction." But Mr. Spencer does not recognize the faculty of intuition. In truth it is incompatible with his doctrine of The Unknowable. The primordial verities which it reveals to us he explains as lapsed sensations, as experiences of the race transmitted from age to age by heredity in organic form to the individual. He does not appear so much as to understand what metaphysicians mean when they speak of "*a priori*,"* of "ideals," of "laws of thought." He exhibits no acquaintance with the philosophical import of the word "necessity." He refers it, in the last analysis, to quantities of matter, to modes of motion more or less complicated. I contend, on the contrary, that those absolute laws, whether of physics, of mathematics, or of morals, which dominate all experience, which are intuitively discerned by the pure intellect acting *a priori*, are, in truth, independent of the senses. They have their deep foundations in the Infinite Mind, in the Absolute and Eternal. Immutable and transcendant, they are, in the words of Leibnitz, "what God eternally thinks." They are irreversible even by the Omnipotent, for they are grounded in His nature, and "He cannot deny Himself." Here, and not in any integrations and disintegrations of matter, in any collocation and displacement of

---

* For example, Mr. Spencer pronounces the indestructibility of matter "an *a priori* cognition of the highest order." It is not an *a priori* cognition of any order, high or low.

molecules, is the ultimate basis of metaphysics. "Totus ordo metaphysicus," Cardinal Franzelin writes, "constituitur legibus necessariis essentiarum, quæ leges ideo sunt necessariæ, quia divina essentia eas postulat. Unde ipsa essentia divina, non libera voluntate, est ex necessaria sua perfectione, est fons et mensura totius etiam veritatis ordinis metaphysici." *

The truth is, that Mr. Spencer has approached philosophy from the wrong side. His psychology is but physiology thinly disguised in a few metaphysical rags and tatters. Yet, with all his parade of physical science, his system is not really founded upon experience at all. Its three cardinal doctrines, which we have examined, are assumptions, not facts. It is the most conspicuous example of the *a priori* method with which I am acquainted. I do not doubt, but strongly affirm the legitimacy of that method, when rightly used. Hypothesis has, for example, a well-understood place even in the experimental sciences. To give only one instance—What is the undulatory theory of light but an hypothesis? —an excellent working hypothesis: but undemonstrated as yet. Again, great physical discoveries have never been the mere result of laborious

* *De Deo,* p. 316.

analysis, of conscious induction. They are due primarily to the exercise of "the vision and the faculty divine." "Something of the poet's insight," writes Helmholtz, "of that insight which led Goethe and Leonardo da Vinci to great scientific ideas also, must be possessed by the true man of science. Like the artist, he aims at the discovery of new laws, however different their mode of operation."* To invent (*invenire*) means to find. The law is there already. The larger eye of genius discerns it through the veil which hides it. It is perfectly true that the physicist uses the experimental method to test and verify his prophetic anticipation. It is equally true that an idea *a priori*, is his *primum movens*, his point of departure. But Mr. Spencer, while professing to go by experience, starts, like a medieval theorist, with the assumption of those absolute principles, the value of which we have considered, and endeavours to rear upon this problematical conception his theory of the universe. I am far from finding fault with Mr. Spencer's desire for a synthesis which shall unify all knowledge. I suppose we have all, more or less strongly, a sense of the secret solidarity of all truth, of the hidden oneness of all existence. We begin with Dualism. But we cannot rest in it. We thirst "to find the one in the manifold." All philosophy is a search after unity. And in some sense we are all

* *Die Thatsachen der Wahrnemung*, p. 44.

philosophers, even the least metaphysical of us. We seek to bring into harmony our knowledge, our emotions, our wills, as they centre round ourselves and the invisible powers, by whatever name we designate them, in whom, for one reason or another, we believe. Of all hypothetical syntheses none seems to me less successful than Mr. Spencer's. It is surely—to borrow the words of Professor Virchow—"a tyranny of dogmatism, which undertakes to master the whole view of Nature by prematurely generalizing theoretical combinations." I am by no means insensible to the value of the mass of facts which Mr. Spencer has so diligently collected. I admit that some of his generalizations unquestionably hold good, and that others may very likely be satisfactorily established hereafter. His speculative history of the universe undoubtedly contains large elements of truth. But assuredly his system rests upon no sufficient ultimate grounds; his primordial principles lack foundation in the order of being and eternal reality; his ratiocination is not seldom a mass of contradictions, and a plexus of ambiguities.

It appears to me, then, that Mr. Spencer's gigantic hypothesis, which should have been reared upon foundations of adamant, is built upon the sand. But Mr. Spencer's Scientific Agnosticism is not merely speculative. He teaches us not only what to believe, but what to do. He preaches to mankind new morals as well as a new faith. By many of his disciples his ethical doctrine is regarded as his supreme achievement. And, certainly, for practical purposes it is his most important. Mr. Spencer himself, indeed, so accounts it. In his preface to the *Data of Ethics* he tells us that " as far back as 1842," the date of his first essay, his " ultimate purpose, lying behind all proximate purposes," was " that of finding for the principles of right and wrong in conduct at large a scientific basis." This was the "last part of the task "— the colossal task—whereunto he has devoted his life; and to it he regards " all the preceding parts as subsidiary." It was the fear of leaving this purpose unfulfilled which led him to give to the world his *Data of Ethics* out of its proper place in his system—a work, he tells us, which, though it does not exhibit in detail his " specific conclusions," yet " implies them in such wise that definitely to formulate them requires nothing beyond logical deductions." And here let me cite, *in extenso*, the passage which immediately follows, and which it would be unfair to Mr. Spencer to abbreviate.

"I am the more anxious to indicate in outline, if I cannot complete, this final work, because the establishment of rules of right conduct on a scientific basis is a pressing need. Now that moral injunctions are losing the authority given by their supposed sacred origin, the secularization of morals is becoming imperative. Few things can happen more disastrous than the decay and death of a regulative system no longer fit, before another and fitter regulative system has grown up to replace it. Most of those who reject the current creed appear to assume that the controlling agency furnished by it may safely be thrown aside, and the vacancy left unfilled by any other controlling agency. Meanwhile, those who defend the current creed allege that, in the absence of the guidance it yields, no guidance can exist; divine commandments they think the only possible guides. Thus between these extreme opponents there is a certain community. The one holds that the gap left by disappearance of the code of supernatural ethics need not be filled by a code of natural ethics; and the other holds that it cannot be so filled. Both contemplate a vacuum, which the one wishes and the other fears. As the change which promises or threatens to bring about this state, desired or dreaded, is rapidly progressing, those who believe that the vacuum can be filled, and that it must be filled, are called on to do something in pursuance of their belief." *

It has been pointed out, in the first chapter of this work, how greatly Mr. Spencer errs in supposing transcendental moralists to regard " divine commands " as " the only possible guides " in ethics. And his error is the more astonishing since Dean Mansel, with whose writings he is evidently well acquainted, might have preserved him from it. " God," that philosopher well says, " did not *create* absolute morality, it is co-eternal with Himself." † The old *data* of ethics which have guided the civilized world for so many generations are not

* This chapter was written before the publication of Mr. Spencer's book on *Justice*. But nothing in that work leads me to modify the views which I have expressed in the text.

† *Limits of Religious Thought*, p. 146.

"supernatural" although they assuredly are supersensuous. They are, in themselves, independent of religion, although no doubt religion, especially the Christian religion, has invested them with cogent sanctions. And no doubt, also, if, as Mr. Spencer considers, the Christian religion is an out-worn creed, already quite discredited for higher intellects, and gradually, but surely, losing its power over the popular mind, an ethical "vacuum" (to use his somewhat odd phrase) may reasonably be feared. Mr. Spencer applies himself to fill that vacuum. And, whatever we may think of his success, assuredly we must honour him for the endeavour. Mr. Spencer knows well that without morality society cannot hold together. "Few things can happen more disastrous than the decay and death of a regulative system, no longer fit, before another and fitter regulative system has grown up to replace it." True, indeed. The greatest benefactors of mankind have been those who have conducted our race upward on the path of ethical progress. And, certainly, if Mr. Spencer is warranted in his pretensions as a preacher of righteousness, we may well venerate him as not the least among that goodly company of prophets. What more august, what more sacred enterprise is conceivable, than to rescue the ideas of right and wrong from destruction, and to establish them for all time upon the everlasting rock of science? Let us inquire, then, how far these high pretensions are warranted. An examination of the ethics of Scientific Agnosticism is the proper complement to our examination of its theology.

How, then, are we to account for that "fitter regulative system of conduct" which Mr. Spencer invites mankind to accept? The answer is suggested by certain words of Coleridge which occur to my mind. "The sum total of moral philosophy is found in this one question: Is *good* a superfluous word—or a mere lazy synonym for the pleasurable and its causes;—at most a mere modification to express degree and comparative duration of pleasure? Or the question may be more answerably stated, thus: Is good superfluous as a word exponent of a *kind*? If it be, then moral philosophy is but a subdivision of physics."* There are, in truth, two, and only two, great schools in ethics, however much their adherents may differ in details. There is the school which seeks to ascertain morality from the spiritual nature of man by methods purely rational. There is the school which denies the transcendental ground of man's being, and which seeks to derive morality from his animal nature, by methods merely physical. There is the school which finds the real aboriginal principle of morals in pleasure or agreeable feeling. There is the school

* *Table Talk*, p. 157.

which finds it in intuitions of equity, held to be primordial and independent elements of our nature.

Now, there can be no question to which of these schools Mr. Spencer belongs. His philosophy, viewed as a whole, is, as we have seen, an attempt to construct a complete scheme of the universe by means of the persistence, under various transformations, of that manifestation of The Unknowable which he calls Force; to unify knowledge of phenomena, the only knowledge held by him to be possible, and to trace everywhere the one cosmical *processus*. Thus, in his *First Principles*, he applies his one great formula of the Persistence of Force to the evolution of the universe from its primitive gaseous elements to its present stage. In his *Principles of Biology* he seeks, by means of this formula, to account for the structure and functional complexities of plant and animal life: "life" being explained by him as "the continuous adjustment of inner to outer relations," but neither "inner" nor "outer" being defined. In his *Principles of Psychology* the self-same formula unlocks for him all doors. By its aid he exhibits the development of the most complex intellectual processes, from the first indefinite unit of feeling; of consciousness, from the nervous system; of thought, from things. He insists upon the identity of intellectual conceptions and material impressions. He makes of mind the outcome of groups of sensations. Instinct, memory, reason, he represents as all evolved in the mind by its effort to maintain the adjustment with the environment. The faculty of reason receives no real recognition in his psychology—what he calls psychology. True, he tells us that "a rational synthesis must build up" from the "ultimate analysis." But his synthesis is not rational. The facts are not subjected to the judgment of reason. Even when he is not arguing *a priori*, he does not get beyond the sequence which sensible experience reveals. He does not exhibit —he does not allow—the intelligible efficient determining the effect. He sees in the operations of the Will merely the invariable—by which he means inevitable—results of nervous action, of atomic movements of matter.

And in ethics his method is similar. He attempts to construct a science of morals out of physical elements, by means of his one formula.* He lays it down in his *Data of Ethics* that "there is an entire correspondence between moral evolu-

* "Here, then, we have to enter on the consideration of the moral phenomena as phenomena of evolution; being forced to do this by finding that they form a part of the aggregate of phenomena which evolution has wrought out. If the entire visible universe has been evolved—if the solar system as a whole, the earth as a part of it, the life in general which the earth bears, as well as that of each individual organism—if the mental phenomena displayed by all creatures, up to the highest, in common with the phenomena presented by aggregates of these highest— if one and all conform to the laws of evolution; then the necessary implication is that those phenomena of conduct in the highest creatures with which morality is concerned, also conform."—*Data of Ethics*, § 23. But those "laws of evolution" are considered by Mr. Spencer as purely physical. He expressly tells us (§ 29) that "a redistribution of matter and motion *constitutes evolution.*"

tion and evolution as physically defined."* And throughout his *First Principles* and his *Principles of Psychology*, he insists that the physical *produces* the mental evolution. Thus, in the latter work, we read, " Corresponding to absolute external relations, there are established in the structure of the nervous system absolute internal relations, . . . antecedent to, and independent of, individual experiences."† But these are "not independent of experiences in general." "The human brain is an organized register of infinitely numerous experiences, received during the evolution of life, or rather . . . during the evolution of that series of organisms through which the human organism has been reached:" and thus "arise, at length, our Newtons and Shakespeares."‡ Again, he tells us that there is "no impassable chasm"§ between psychology and physiology. He holds that neither the lower nor the higher psychical life is absolutely distinguished from physical life: that intelligence arises out of feeling: and, indeed, generally, that " advance from the simplest to the most complex cognitions is explicable on the principle that the outer relations produce the inner relations." ∥ For him "the problem is to interpret mental evolution in terms of the redistribution of Matter and Motion." ¶ He accounts as " comparatively con-

---

* § 29. † *Principles of Psychology*, § 208.
‡ *Ibid.* § 208. Observe the extreme vagueness of this word "independent." It may mean uncaused by, or unconditioned by.

sistent"* that very remarkable Materialistic dictum "that the activities of the imponderable substance [ether], though far simpler, and in that respect far lower, than the activities we call Mind, are at the same time far higher than those we call Mind in respect of their intensity, their velocity, their subtlety. What has been gained in adaptability has been lost in vivacity."† "Though thought," he observes, "is quick, light is many millions of times quicker,"‡ and the conclusion he reaches is that " we can think of Matter only in terms of Mind : we can think of Mind only in terms of Matter : " but, observe, that in the Spencerian doctrine of evolution, it is Matter that produces Mind.§ "Phenomena"—he makes no

---

* *Data of Ethics*, § 272.   † *Ibid.* § 271.   ‡ *Ibid.*

§ "The progress from these forms of feeling considerably compounded to those highly compounded forms of feeling seen in human beings, equally harmonizes with the general principles of evolution that have been laid down. We saw that advance from the simplest to the most complex cognitions, is explicable on the principle that the outer relations produce the inner relations. We shall see that this same principle supplies an explanation of the advance from the simplest to the most complex feelings. For when the development of Life reaches this repeatedly described stage in which automatic actions merge into actions that are at once conscious, rational, and emotive; what must be the effect of further experiences? The effect must be that if, in connection with a group of impressions and the nascent motor changes resulting from it, there is habitually some other impression or group of impressions, some other motor change or group of motor changes, this will, in process of time, be rendered so coherent to the original group, that it, too, will become nascent when the original group becomes nascent, and will render the original group nascent if it is itself

exception—" are interpretable only as the results of universally co-existent forces of attraction and repulsion:" forces that are, indeed, the complementary aspects of that absolutely persistent Force which is the ultimate datum of consciousness.* "Those modes of the Unknowable which we call motion, heat, light, chemical affinity, etc., are alike transformable into each other, and into those modes of the Unknowable which we distinguish as sensation, emotion, thought: these, in their turns, being directly or indirectly retransformable into the original shapes." † "That no idea or feeling arises, save as a result of some physical force expended in producing it, is fast becoming a commonplace of science." ‡ "If the general law of transformation and equivalence holds of the forces we class as vital and mental, it must hold also of those which we class as social." § Here are both ends of the chain. Attraction and Repulsion transform themselves into the phenomena of Egoism and Altruism, and Ethics results from the Persistence of Force. ‖ "Force being persistent, the transformation which Evolution shows us, necessarily results." ¶ And "the deepest truths we can reach"—in morals as elsewhere—"are simply statements of the widest uniformities in our expe-

---

* *First Principles*, § 176. † *Ibid.* § 71.
‡ *Ibid.* § 71. § *Ibid.* § 72.
‖ See the explicit statement in *First Principles*, § 73.
¶ *First Principles*, § 189.

rience of the relations of Matter, Motion, and Force."*

So much must suffice as to Mr. Spencer's method in moral philosophy. Let us go on to consider his application of it, and see how he manufactures morality from prior conditions that were unmoral. He tells us "Ethics has for its subject-matter that form which universal conduct assumes, during the last stage of its evolution." † And elsewhere he defines it as " Nothing else than a definite account of the forms of conduct that are fitted to the associated state, in such wise that the lives of each and all may be the greatest possible, alike in length and breadth." ‡ By "conduct" he means "acts adjusted to ends, or else the adjustment of acts to ends." § And "always acts are called good or bad, as they are well or ill adjusted to ends." ∥ Thus "the goodness or badness of a pointer or a hunter, of a sheep or an ox, ignoring all other attributes of these creatures, refers, in the one case, to the fitness of their actions for effecting the ends men use them for, and in the other case, to the qualities of their flesh as adapting it to support human life." ¶ Conduct which subserves "the welfare of self, of offspring, and of fellow-citizens" "is regarded as relatively good." ** But

* *First Principles*, § 194.   † *Data of Ethics*, § 7.
‡ *Ibid.* § 48.   § *Ibid.* § 2.   ∥ *Ibid.* § 8.   ¶ *Ibid.*   ** *Ibid.*

"evolution becomes the highest possible when the conduct simultaneously achieves the greatest totality of life in self, in offspring, and in fellow-men." "The conduct called good rises to the conduct conceived as best, when it fulfils all three classes of ends at the same time."* Conduct, in short, is good or bad, according to the Spencerian ethics, as it increases or diminishes the sum total of life. Why? Because life is the highest good. "The final justification for maintaining life can only be the reception from it of a surplus of pleasurable feeling over painful feeling."† "In calling good the conduct which subserves life, and bad the conduct which hinders or destroys it, and in so implying that life is a blessing and not a curse, we are inevitably asserting that conduct is good or bad, according as its total effects are pleasurable or painful."‡ Or, as he elsewhere puts it, "Acts are good or bad, according as their aggregate effects increase men's happiness or increase their misery." § It is impossible to " ignore the ultimate derivations of right and wrong from pleasure and pain." ||

I beg of the reader to ponder this doctrine a little. Mr. Spencer sees in every animal movement what, of course, we all see: an adaptation of means to ends. And he rightly considers that

* *Data of Ethics*, § 8. † *Ibid.* § 10. ‡ *Ibid.* § *Ibid.* § 14.
|| *Ibid.* Observe the vagueness of "derivations." Does it mean cause or condition?

adaptation a good. The evolution of conduct he holds to consist in an ever more perfect adaptation of the most complex means to a totality of ends ever more diversified, and, at the same time, ever more closely linked together in a harmonious unity. And his view embraces not merely individual life, but social life; nay, the universal life of humanity. Every act adapted to its end is good. And the test of goodness in conduct is that it subserves that evolution which is the general and common end of all being. Good conduct is, in short, the conduct relatively the most developed; bad conduct the conduct relatively the least developed. Moral good, then, according to Mr. Spencer, does not differ *essentially* from physical good. "The conduct with which Morality is not concerned, passes into conduct which is moral or unmoral, by small degrees, and in countless ways,"* the "broad distinction" being "a greater coherence among its component motions." † "The ideal goal to the *natural* evolution of conduct . . . we recognize as the ideal standard of conduct *ethically* considered." ‡ The goodness of a hunter and the goodness of a hero, the goodness of a sausage and the goodness of a saint, are for Mr. Spencer, *in kind*, identical. And the test of goodness is always the same: not the character of the agent, not the quality of his intention; no: but the pleasurable

---

* *Data of Ethics*, § 2. † *Ibid.* § 25.
‡ *Ibid.* § 15. The italics are mine.

tendency of his acts. "Beyond the conduct commonly approved of, or reprobated, as right or wrong, there is included all conduct which furthers or hinders, in either direct or indirect ways, the welfare of self or others." "Taking into account the immediate effects on all persons, the good is universally the pleasurable." * Virtue possesses no primordial and independent character. It is whatever, as a means, promotes, on the whole, the supreme end—pleasure.

This is Mr. Spencer's treatment of the fundamental question wherewith ethics is concerned: the nature of moral good: the difference between right and wrong. We will next consider his account of that faculty, witnessing for a moral law, which we have been accustomed to call conscience, and to esteem the endowment in virtue of which man is an ethical being. What is Mr. Spencer's explanation of conscience? of the Categorical Imperative of Duty? Well, conscience is for him merely a nervous structure: duty is only a way of apprehending life, whereby we are led to subordinate proximate to ultimate satisfaction. "The moral motive," he tells us— the true moral motive—"is constituted by representations of consequences which the acts naturally produce. Those representations are not all dis-

* *Data of Ethics,* § 10.

tinct, though some of them are usually present: but they form an assemblage of indistinct representations accumulated from experience of the results of like acts in the life of the individual, superposed on a still more indistinct but voluminous consciousness, due to the inherited effects of such experiences in progenitors: forming a feeling that is, at once, massive and vague." * "The truly moral deterrent from murder" is a representation of "the infliction of death-agony on the victim, the destruction of all his possibilities of happiness, the entailed sufferings to his belongings." The moral check on theft is "the thought of injury to the person robbed, joined with a vague

---

* *Data of Ethics*, § 45. "Corresponding to the fundamental propositions of a developed Moral Science, there have been, and still are, developing in the race, certain fundamental moral intuitions; . . . though these moral intuitions are the results of accumulated experiences of utility, gradually organized and inherited, they have come to be quite independent of conscious experience. Just in the same way that I believe the intuition of space, possessed by any living individual, to have arisen from organized and consolidated experiences of all antecedent individuals who bequeathed to him their slowly developed nervous organizations—just as I believe that this intuition, requiring only to be made definite and complete by personal experiences, has practically become a form of thought, apparently quite independent of experience; so do I believe that the experiences of utility organized and consolidated through all past generations of the human race, have been producing corresponding nervous modifications, which, by continued transmission and accumulation, have become in us certain faculties of moral intuition—certain emotions responding to right and wrong conduct, which have no apparent basis in the individual experiences of utility."

consciousness of the general evils caused by disregard of proprietary rights." "Those who reprobate the adulterer on moral grounds have their minds filled . . . with ideas of unhappiness entailed on the aggrieved wife or husband, the damaged lives of children, and the diffused mischiefs which go along with disregard of the marriage tie."[*] These, according to Mr. Spencer, are "the restraints properly distinguished as moral," and he considers that they are evolved from restraints which are not moral at all: namely, political restraints originating in fear of angering the tribal chief; religious restraints, springing from dread of ghosts; and social restraints, prompted by dislike of being shunned. "These . . . kinds of internal control . . . though, at first, they are practically co-extensive and undistinguished . . . in the course of social evolution differentiate, and eventually the moral control, with its accompanying conceptions and sentiments, emerges as independent,"[†] by a process which Mr. Spencer describes at much length. It may be noted that he claims for this hypothesis of his the merit that "it enables us to reconcile opposed moral theories. For as the doctrine of innate forms of intellectual intuition falls into harmony with the experiential doctrine, when we recognize the production of intellectual faculties by inheritance of effects wrought by experience; so does the doctrine of innate powers of moral perception become con-

[*] *Data of Ethics,* § 45.   [†] *Ibid.* § 44.

gruous with the utilitarian doctrine, when it is seen that preferences and aversions are rendered organic by inheritance of the effects of pleasurable and painful experiences in progenitors."*

It is clear, then, that in Mr. Spencer's ethics, the moral consciousness is wholly a social product, due to the causes which he sets forth: the observed or expected consequences of acts: chief among which are the penalties, real or imaginary, entailed by prohibited forms of conduct. But, as he justly remarks, "one further question has to be answered—How does there arise the feeling of moral obligation?"† (Observe, not the *fact* of moral obligation, but the *feeling*.) He replies, "Since with the restraints thus generated is always joined the thought of external coercion, there arises the notion of obligation:"‡ "a notion," writes Dr. Martineau, "which he afterwards curiously interprets as equivalent to the indispensableness of any means towards a given end,—the means being that which we are obliged to employ, if we would secure the end.§ For instance, if a carnivorous animal is to live, it must eat; if it is to eat, it must kill; if kill, it must catch; if catch, it must chase; and so it is under an obligation to do each of these things. To this generic idea of obligation, the differentia 'Moral' is added on, when it is concerned with the means

* *Data of Ethics,* § 45.
† *Ibid.* § 46. ‡ *Ibid.* § 44. § *Ibid.* § 58.

of avoiding the political, social, and religious penalties attached to certain conduct. The 'moral consciousness' is thus the self-application of a lesson learned *ab extra*."*

In the Spencerian doctrine, then, conscience with its authoritativeness and coerciveness is not the formal principle and rule of ethics, but an adventitious element; nay, a "transitory" element, which "will diminish as fast as moralization increases."† Mr. Spencer considers it "evident" that when the human machine is perfected by evolution, "that element in the moral consciousness which is expressed by the word obligation will disappear. The higher actions required for the harmonious carrying on of life, will be as much matter of course as are those lower actions, which the simple desires prompt: . . . the moral sentiments will guide men just as spontaneously and adequately as now do the sensations."‡ Closely connected with this tenet of the Spencerian gospel is that of the evanescence of evil. "Evolution," Mr. Spencer assures us, "can end only in the establishment of the greatest perfection and the most complete happiness." §

I have now put before my readers the funda-

* *Types of Ethical Theory*, vol. ii. p. 26.
† *Data of Ethics*, § 46.   ‡ *Ibid.*
§ *First Principles*, § 176. Mr. Spencer has pursued this subject at greater length in his *Social Statics*.

mental positions of that "fitter regulative system" which Scientific Agnosticism proposes to us in the place of the rule of right and wrong hitherto received. What are we to think of it? In reply to that question I shall make four observations, which although, of course, not unfolding in detail my conclusions, yet—to use Mr. Spencer's own words—"imply them in such wise that definitely to formulate them requires nothing beyond logical deductions."

And first, I would remark, that Mr. Spencer's ethical doctrine is at variance with the primary principle upon which his whole system rests. "I do not ask," said Talleyrand, upon one occasion, "that my opponent should be of my opinion; but I may fairly expect him to be of his own." This is precisely what Mr. Spencer is not. There is an absolute contradiction between his hedonistic morality and his account of the great law of evolution: the law of all living beings from the most rudimentary, to the most highly specialized. Evolution does not demand as its starting-point any degree of sensibility, any capacity for pleasure and pain. It is essentially the advance from an inferior to a superior state. But agreeable feeling is by no means necessarily attached to that advance. Even among the higher vertebrates, in which consciousness and emotional sensibility are largely developed, agreeable feeling is not the sole form of life, the sole subject of evolution.

Health, physical strength, the due proportion of limbs, the harmonious working of the physical organs, are real goods, of which one may be more, or less, sensible, but which exist in their entirety, irrespective of the agreeable feeling received from them. We may assuredly say the like of the intellectual powers. And, as assuredly, we must include among the goods of life the orderly interaction, the rhythmical balance, of all the component parts of our being. Sensibility develops with the rest; and the agreeable feeling resulting from it has place in the total perfection issuing from the concordant development of all our faculties. But—this is the point on which I am insisting—agreeable feeling, where it is found, is merely an *accompaniment*. Mr. Spencer allows that, as evolution progresses, pleasure and pain do no more than *accompany* actions, which are, in themselves, advantageous or hurtful. How, then, can it be the sole end, the supreme ideal? Again, nothing is more certain than the variations of sensibility, depending, as it does, upon individual character and environment. Mr. Spencer shows this, at length, in his chapter on "The Relativity of Pleasures and Pains." The fact is that there is no sort of correspondence between the degree of perfection and the satisfaction of sensibility; and therefore pleasure cannot possibly be the measure of good. But further. The operative principle of evolution is the struggle for existence; which means that the pleasure of one being is obtained by the pain of another; or, as Mr. Spencer euphemistically expresses it, that "very generally a successful adjustment made by one creation involves an unsuccessful adjustment made by another creation, either of the same kind or a different kind."* But this principle Mr. Spencer completely abandons in the ultimate form of human society whereof he prophesies. "Pleasure," he assures us, "will eventually accompany every mode of action demanded by social conditions." As we saw just now, Mr. Spencer pronounces this "evident." How is it evident? There is no kind of evidence for it. And it is as far as possible from being self-evident, for the more automatic an act is, the less pleasurable is it. There is no reason whatever, beyond Mr. Spencer's *ipse dixit*, for believing that "the form which universal conduct assumes during the last stage of evolution"—such, it will be remembered, is Mr. Spencer's definition of ethics—will be in direct opposition to the fundamental principle of evolution. Mr. Spencer, indeed, does not speak of opposition. He masks his *volte-face* by the word antithesis. "Imperfectly involved conduct," he writes, "introduces us, by antithesis, to conduct that is perfectly involved."† Antithesis! indeed. It is really a complete abandonment of the evolutionary hypothesis.

* *Data of Ethics*, § 6. † *Ibid.*

But—to go on to my second observation—Mr. Spencer's whole teaching essentially depends upon arbitrary assumptions of this kind. I know of no speculator who makes more violent demands upon our credulity; who so liberally indulges in a licence of dogmatism. At the very points in his system where proof—such proof, of course, as the nature of the case admits of—should be forthcoming, he has nothing to offer but a nude assertion. Take, for example, his doctrine of one ultimate form of matter, as expounded in his *Principles of Psychology*. His object is to elucidate the nature of Mind by comparing it with the nature of Matter,* or rather, to justify his conjecture representing Mind by a parallelism " with that which chemists have established respecting Matter." It is a curious and characteristic endeavour. Let us see how he sets about it. We might reasonably look, in the first place, for a clear and precise account of what chemists have *established* about Matter. We should look in vain. Mr. Spencer begins by remarking, generally, " Multitudinous substances that seem to be homogeneous and simple prove to be really heterogeneous and compound; and many that appear wholly unrelated are shown by analysis to be near akin." He then proceeds as follows:—

"There is reason to *suspect* that . . . there is but one ultimate form of Matter, out of which the successively-more complex

* *Data of Ethics*, § 61.

forms of Matter are built up. By the different grouping of units, and by the combination of the unlike groups each with its own kind, and each with other kinds, it is *supposed* that there have been produced the kinds of matter we call elementary; just as, by further compositions similarly carried on, these produce further varieties and complexities. And this supposition the phenomena of allotropism go far to justify, by showing us that the same mass of molecules assumes quite different properties when the mode of aggregation is changed. If, then, *we see* that by unlike arrangements of like units, all the forms of Matter, apparently so diverse in nature, may be produced—if, even without assuming that the so-called elements are compound, we remember how from a few of these there may arise by transformation and by combination numerous seemingly-simple substances, strongly contrasted with their constituents and with one another—we shall the better conceive the possibility that the multitudinous forms of Mind known as different feelings, may be composed of simpler units of feeling, and even of units fundamentally of one kind." *

I beg the reader's attention to the words which I have put in italics. He will observe that Mr. Spencer begins with a suspicion; which is presently magnified to a supposition; and a few lines further on to a fact: "we see." But in truth the "suspicion" on which this wordy edifice is reared is a mere hypothesis. We may if we please "suspect"—what is to hinder us?—"that there is but one ultimate form of Matter." We have no right to make our suspicion the corner-stone of a philosophical system.

Again. It is essential to Mr. Spencer's speculations that the origin of consciousness should be

* *Principles of Psychology*, § 61.

found in the nervous system. This is how he finds it:—

"Those abilities which an intelligent creature possesses, of recognizing diverse external objects and of adjusting its actions to composite phenomena of various kinds, imply a power of combining many separate impressions. These separate impressions are received by the senses . . . [and] must be all brought into relation with one another. But this implies some centre of communication common to them all, through which they severally pass; and as they cannot pass through it simultaneously, they must pass through it in succession. So that as the external phenomena responded to become greater in number and more complicated in kind, the variety and rapidity of the changes to which this common centre of communication is subject must increase—there must result an unbroken series of these changes—there *must* arise a consciousness."*

Must! Comment upon this "must" is surely superfluous. And such is Mr. Spencer's method throughout his *Psychology*. As Professor Green has observed, with entire accuracy, "he first triumphantly explains, through three-fourths of the book, the genesis of 'thought' from 'things,' on the strength of the *assumed* priority and independence of the latter, and defers the considerations likely to raise the question whether this assumption is correct—he never directly raises it himself—till he can approach them with the prestige of a system already proved adequate and successful."†

* *Principles of Psychology*, § 179. The italics are mine.
† *Works*, vol. i. p. 389.

Once more. In his account of "the genesis of the moral consciousness," or, as he prefers to call it, "the feeling of moral obligation," Mr. Spencer is equally dogmatic. "Accumulated experiences," he tells us, "*have* produced the consciousness that guidance by feelings which refer to remote and general results is usually more conducive to welfare than guidance by feelings to be immediately gratified." "The idea of authoritativeness *has,* therefore, come to be connected with" "complex re-representative feelings." "Fears of the political and social penalties (to which, I think, the religious must be added) *have* generated that sense of coerciveness which goes along with the thought of postponing present to future, and personal desires to the claim for others."* Mr. Spencer's whole moral doctrine rests upon these three propositions. Are they self-evident? No. Are they proved? Assuredly not. Experience by no means warrants them. Introspection and analysis alike fail to support them. Here again we have no other foundation for Mr. Spencer's dogma than Mr. Spencer's *ipse dixit*. He does indeed offer us in support of it an analogy. "The sentiment of duty," he tells us, "is an abstract sentiment generated in a manner analogous to that in which abstract ideas are generated:" and by way of example he adduces the abstract idea of colour. Unfortunately for Mr. Spencer, the analogy is a

* *Data of Ethics,* § 46. The italics are mine.

false one, as I have had occasion to point out elsewhere. "Colour, in general, no doubt is known by abstraction from colours in particular. But moral obligation in general cannot by any possibility be abstracted from a representation 'of the natural consequences' in particular, for the very simple reason that it is not contained in them. 'Moral' is one genus; 'natural consequences,' meaning pains or pleasures, another. And in abstracting, as in syllogizing, we are forbidden to pass from this genus to that genus. This is elementary metaphysics; or, if Mr. Spencer prefers my so putting it, elementary common-sense. If the specific thing called morality is not in the particular actions under the form of 'authority' and 'coerciveness,' it cannot be got from them by abstraction. If it is, the genesis of it remains to be investigated, and cannot be explained by an abstraction which has not yet taken place. The sophism—really Mr. Spencer must pardon me the word—is glaring. From particular colours, colour in general. *Concedo.* From particular pleasures and pains, pleasure and pain in general. By all means. But from the representation of (future) pleasures and pains, morality in general! Why not, then, sunbeams from cucumbers, or the sense of ethical justice from the varieties of the triangle?"*

My third observation is, that Mr. Spencer's

* *On Right and Wrong*, p. 87.

moral philosophy is hopelessly vitiated by his misapprehension of the subject wherewith such philosophy is concerned. Ethics is the science of our moral nature, and the question which lies at the root of that science is this: What is the difference between virtue and vice, between right and wrong, between a good action and a bad? Mr. Spencer, as we have seen, holds that virtue and vice can be calculated in terms of pleasure and pain; that "agreeable feeling" supplies a definite standard of moral rectitude; that the difference between a good and a bad deed is in the results. It is true that in terms he repudiates the expediency morality, whether in the raw Benthamite form, or as cooked by Mr. Mill.* But that he is really involved in it is absolutely clear from his own words: "I conceive it to be the business of Moral Science to deduce, from the laws of life, what kinds of action necessarily tend to produce happiness, and what kinds to produce unhappiness."† For such is, *totidem verbis*, the utilitarian or expediency account of morals. It reduces ethics to eudæmonism. "Happiness, our being's end and aim"—that is one view, and Mr. Spencer holds it, interpreting

* See the introduction to his *Social Statics*.

† *Data of Ethics*, § 21. So in § 37. "The purpose of ethical inquiry is to establish rules of right living; and . . . the rules of right living are those of which the total results, individual and general, direct and indirect, are most conducive to human happiness."

happiness as "agreeable feeling." "Fiat justitia, pereat mundus" expresses quite another view, into which happiness does not enter as an element, nor are its laws determined by considerations of the eudæmonistic order at all. Mr. Spencer's morality is *ego-altruistic*, limited by the idea of the social organism. The transcendental morality rests upon a natural and permanent revelation of the reason, and social ethics is but a subordinate chapter of it. There is a whole universe between Mr. Spencer and genuine *a priori* moralists. But the difference between Mr. Spencer and the elder schools of utilitarianism is unessential. "Its deductions," he says of his ethical "science," "are to be recognized as laws of conduct, and are to be conformed to, irrespective of a direct estimation of happiness or misery."* "Direct." The word indicates the differentiation of Mr. Spencer's method from Bentham's. The estimate, according to Mr. Spencer, will be indirect, because it has been performed for me by the tribe, and I have a ready reckoner in the brain. Again, Mr. Spencer lays down that happiness ought not to be the object of direct pursuit, because, if it is, we shall probably miss it:† a statement which I find it hard to reconcile with his fundamental proposition that we never can, or do, pursue anything but our own happiness. For either we seek virtue because it is pleasant, or not because it is pleasant. In the

* *Data of Ethics,* § 21.   † *Ibid.* § 91.

first case, we seek happiness alone. In the second, we do not seek happiness alone. But, finally,* he conciliates individual and general interests by means of "a higher egoistic satisfaction," exemplified in the case of the love of parents for their children. Thus we come to happiness and agreeable feeling, after all, as the formal constituent of virtue.

Now this resolution of the idea of good into the idea of pleasure, I take leave to call Mr. Spencer's master-error. I will explain why I so call it. In the first place, Mr. Spencer's account of the meaning of the words "good" and "bad," is quite unphilosophical and wholly inadequate. I am far from denying that pleasure is a good. But it is a good of an entirely different nature from virtue. Good—*bonum*—according to the schoolmen, to whose precise thought it is a relief to turn, if but for a moment, means that at which the human will can aim. And they allow of two † kinds of good: *bonum delectabile*—pleasure, which may be either physical or mental; and *bonum honestum*—virtue. Both are legitimate objects of pursuit. To return, however, to Mr. Spencer.

---

* *Data of Ethics*, § 92.

† They speak also of *bonum utile*. We act *propter bonum utile* when we act for the sake of some object which is useful as a means towards pleasure or virtue. Our absolute end will always be either *bonum honestum* or *bonum delectabile*. Our relative or intermediate end will be *bonum utile*.

Goodness, generally, means for him, as we have seen, adjustment of means to ends. And, in human life, in particular, the word means, for him, conduct that promotes the welfare of a man's self, of his offspring, and of his fellows: actions which subserve life: which further "complete living:" which produce, on the whole, a balance of pleasure over pain. Now Mr. Spencer is here the victim of a fallacy, so obvious that it is difficult to understand how he can have fallen into it. The good is pleasurable. True. But it is a curious logic which concludes, *ergo* pleasure is the test of goodness. Pain ensues upon bad actions. True again; and in a far profounder sense than Mr. Spencer supposes. But how does it follow that "what some call the badness of actions is ascribed to them solely for the reason that they entail pain, immediate or remote"?* A conclusion which, Mr. Spencer judges, "no one can deny," but which, as I venture to think, no consecutive reasoner can maintain. And can Mr. Spencer have really weighed his doctrine that the goodness of mutton and the goodness of man are essentially the same? that the one test of virtue always is adjustment to the end of promoting human life? Surely a little more consideration would have shown him that not all acts adapted to promote that end are ethically good; that the distinction drawn by metaphysicians between material and

* *Data of Ethics*, § 11.

formal goodness is well warranted. A case occurs to me, as I write, which may illustrate this simple proposition, if indeed illustration be necessary. An old man disinherited his son and left his fortune to a hospital in order to punish the young man for marrying a young woman, with whom his septuagenarian parent had fallen in love. Undoubtedly, the irate testator did much, by this disposition of his property, to improve the living of his fellow-men: undoubtedly he produced by it, on the whole, a balance of pleasure over pain. But will Mr. Spencer maintain that his deed of jealous vengeance was moral? Again, a man who gives to a crowded neighbourhood, in which he resides, a public park or garden, performs an act adjusted to achieve " totality of life in self, in offspring, and in fellow-men "—Mr. Spencer's criterion of most highly evolved conduct. But if the donor be a fraudulent speculator, who so invests his money, by way of advertisement, in order to procure a character for public spirit, and thereby to ensnare more victims in his financial cobwebs, is his act ethical? Agreeable feeling the source and rule of right? But surely, as a matter of fact, nothing memorable in the moral order has ever been accomplished by men in whom the spring of action has been desire of agreeable feeling. It seems a well-nigh universal law that suffering, not pleasure, is not only the condition and the reward of goodness, but the most masterful incentive to it.* Evil that which causes pain to sentient beings? But surely many acts are evil which cause no pain at all, but only pleasure—and that of an intense kind—to sentient beings. That virtue, in our earthly experience—his only test—is a happiness producing conduct, is an assumption which Mr. Spencer, of all people, has no right to make. Evolution, he teaches us, is a struggle for existence. Will he maintain that the morally good always survive in that struggle, and so are the fittest? What shall we say of those "who loved, who suffered countless things, who battled for the true, the just"—and failed? Of the lost causes, with their martyrs and prophets, which make up so much of history? Is it clear that after apparent failure they triumphed, or will some day triumph, if they were morally good? How will Mr. Spencer show the necessary connection? *A priori?* He is debarred by his own principles. And experience—to say the least—gives an uncertain sound.

Let us, however, suppose that such a connection as Mr. Spencer postulates does, in truth, exist between virtue and agreeable feeling. I ask, why must virtue be only the means and that feeling

* So Mr. Carlyle, in words as true as noble: "It is a calumny on men to say that they are roused to heroic action by ease, hope of pleasure, recompense—sugar plums of any kind in this world or the next. In the meanest mortal there lies something nobler. Difficulty, abnegation, martyrdom are the *allurements* that act on the heart of man."—*Lectures on Heroes*, lect. ii.

the end? Why not consider virtue as the cause and happiness as the effect? Virtue, the final cause for which happiness exists, and the efficient cause which can alone produce it in perfection? Grant that in the long run they are inseparable. Still, we must ask, which is for the sake of the other? This is a point of capital importance. Mr. Spencer leaves it out altogether. We, who found ourselves on conscience, maintain that the motive determines the nature of conduct, and must be moral; whereas, the motive of pleasure, taken by itself, is neither moral nor immoral, but indifferent. Granting that the state of goodness is necessarily the state of perfect felicity, we maintain that the pursuit of such felicity not only does not constitute goodness, but does not even enter into its meaning. Granting that "Honesty is the best policy," we maintain that he who pursues it, merely as the best policy, is not honest. Granting that pleasure, of one kind or another, may be the consequence of well-doing, we maintain that to make pleasure an end in itself, exclusive of the entirely different aspect of things which we call "moral," is not well-doing: that so long as we pursue pleasure absolutely because it is pleasant, and not because it is, under the circumstances, *right* to choose pleasure, we cannot be acting ethically: nay, that virtue, sought for the sake of pleasure, ceases to be virtue. Mr. Spencer agrees with us so far as to reject the Benthamite calculation of pains and pleasures, while substituting for it, chiefly, certain innate emotions due to associations of feelings in the remote past. He explains "the moral sentiment" by evolution. But the point is not as to the history of "the moral sentiment"—there I might, very likely, agree largely with him—but as to its essence, its nature. I say it is, here and now, a faculty, *sui generis*, having nothing to do with pleasures and pains, but only with right and wrong. If, however, the history is looked into, we shall find that Mr. Spencer, instead of explaining right and wrong, will be found to have degraded virtue into mechanism, and to have made of ethics a corollary from the Persistence of Force. That he likewise makes it impossible for us to think of ethics as such a corollary, I am well aware. But this is merely one of his many self-contradictions. My argument, however, is, that the concepts of morality and mechanism are irreducible, and that Mr. Spencer's purely mechanical explanation of good leaves out its essential element. Τὴν ἡδονὴν προλαμβάνοντες ὑστεροῦμεν τἀγαθοῦ.

My last observation upon Mr. Spencer's ethical doctrine is this: that it is no less fatal to the concept of moral obligation than it is to the concept of moral goodness. The first question in ethics is, What formally constitutes virtue? The second, Why should I practise virtue? Mr. Spencer's reply to the second of these questions is of a piece

iv.] *THE DESIRABLE AND THE OBLIGATORY.* 191

with his reply to the first. The good, he tells us, is the pleasurable. And then, recurring to his favourite method, he assumes that men must and will follow the greatest happiness known to them. Nay, more, to help them in this excellent way, he instructs them, at some length, how the finest Altruism may be turned into the coarsest Egoism.* But really this assumption is quite as unwarrantable as are those other primary assumptions of Mr. Spencer's, at which we have already glanced. When you have demonstrated to others that such and such things will yield them agreeable feeling, neither you nor they, in truth, suppose for one minute, that you have laid upon them the *obligation* of pursuing those things. A convicted thief in a London police-court, not long ago, after receiving from the magistrate a homily, and a sentence, turned to his "pals," and addressed them on this wise. "Be virtuous, and, as his Worship says, you'll be happy: but you'll have devilish little fun." It is a truer reading of human nature than Mr. Spencer's. His "morality" can but counsel. It cannot command. Its highest appeal is a prudential recommendation. But the desirable is one thing. The obligatory is another. It is the distinction between "may" and "must:" or rather, to put it more accurately, between "mögen" and "sollen." To say that men are *bound* to follow pleasure, is—I must be pardoned

* See chap. xiv. of his *Data of Ethics*.

the word—nonsense. It is double distilled nonsense in Mr. Spencer's system of physiological fatality, where power of choice—"arbitrement," Milton calls it—does not really come in at all, where our volitions are accounted as merely facts of a certain order, absolutely governed by certain physical laws, which we cannot help obeying. Evolution, as expounded by Mr. Spencer, effaces all difference of nature between beings, and distinguishes them only according to the degree of their development and complexity. It is absolutely fatal to the idea of the moral person, endowed, consciously endowed, with the power of freely choosing a better or a worse, both equally possible, and responsible for his choice. But without personality, liberty, and responsibility there can be no ethical obligation. And, in truth, in Mr. Spencer's ethics, duty is merely a name for profit, advantage, pleasure.

But whose profit, advantage, pleasure? Mr. Spencer thinks he can point to "certain principles, in the nature of things, which causally determine welfare."* The science of these is what he means by ethics. He confesses, however—as of course he must—that individual welfare does not always coincide with social welfare. "The two ends," he tells us, euphemistically, "are not harmonious at the outset:"† though he promises their conciliation in his Millennium. At present, however,

* *Data of Ethics*, § 60.   † *Ibid.* § 49.

"the life of the social organism must, as an end, rank above the lives of its units;"* "the welfare of the society, as a whole," must be "put in the foreground."† But why the "must"? Why *ought* the individual to sacrifice himself to the organism? It may be profitable, advantageous, pleasurable for the organism that he should do so. It is assuredly most unprofitable, disadvantageous, and unpleasurable for the man himself. No principle causally determining his welfare can be cited here. And self-sacrifice is outside the sphere of Spencerian ethics. Here, again, Mr. Spencer has nothing to fall back upon but his own *ipse dixit*. He tells us that the "deductions" of his ethical science "*are* to be recognized as laws of conduct, and *are* to be conformed to, irrespective of a direct estimate of pleasures and pains."‡ "Are"? Why? Why must I conform to Mr. Spencer's "deductions"? They have to be confronted with the struggle for existence. They may, possibly, point to what is advantageous for the tribe. But, if I follow them, *I* may not survive. Why, then, should I follow them? What is meant by saying it is *wrong* not to follow them? Wrong, in the old sense, does not come in at all. With Mr. Spencer it merely means, inexpedient for the tribe. But why should I consider the tribe? Assuredly, in the struggle for existence, the tribe will not

---

* *Data of Ethics*, § 49.
† *Ibid.* ‡ *Ibid.* § 21. The italics are mine.

consider me. "Nay, nay," Mr. Spencer insists, "in subordinating your own immediate advantage to the future advantage of the tribe, you gratify certain emotions the result of organized experiences within you." But the facts do not bear out this assertion. How many men are there in whom such emotions are not felt at all?—in whom neither introspection, nor analysis, discloses their existence? And even if they do exist, where is the obligation to postpone to them other emotions, certainly, as a rule, much more masterful? But, in truth, the discussion of this question with Mr. Spencer is idle as the fighting of those who beat the air. Declaring, as he does in terms, that we have no real power of choice, that free-will is an objective and subjective delusion,* he does but mock us, when he calls upon us to elect this or that course of action. In fact, liberty of volition is absolutely irreconcilable with the physical fatalism which is of the essence of his doctrine: or, as he prefers to express it, "with the beneficent necessity displayed in the evolution of the correspondence between the organism and the environment."†

The truth is, that to the whole Utilitarian school, in which Mr. Spencer must assuredly be classed, the facts of our moral consciousness present quite insuperable difficulties. Bentham proposed to get rid of those difficulties by the simple

* *Principles of Psychology*, §§ 219, 220.   † *Ibid.* § 220.

method of banishing the word "ought" from the vocabulary of morals: and by ceasing to talk about duties.* Mr. Spencer, less boldly, endeavours to explain away the ethical sense by deriving it from the instincts of selfishness, sympathy, imitation, disciplined by the experiences of the countless generations who have bequeathed to us their slowly developed nervous organization. Such are the unmoral factors from which he seeks to evolve the commanding sanctity of Right, the stern benignity of Duty. One cannot help wondering whether Mr. Spencer, absorbed as he has been in the spinning of his hypotheses, has ever found time seriously to reflect upon the real significance of the moral "ought." Unqualified obligation is a *fact* of the world of consciousness. From conscience we receive dictates. From sense, impressions. The Imperative of Duty is Categorical: that is primary and unconditioned. How, then, can it spring from the conditioned? How can it be derivative? Mr. Spencer's account of it is wholly inadequate. He leaves out the chief facts which call for explanation. Mr. Spencer, apparently, sees no difference between the counsel of prudence and the mandate of conscience: between regret for a lost opportunity, and remorse for a violated duty. "Here stand I," said Luther at the Diet of Worms: "I can do no other." There is a whole universe between the feeling of the indis-

* *Deontology*, vol. i. pp. 32, 40.

pensableness of the means, if we would attain the end, and the feeling that obedience to the voice within is itself the end, to be followed "in the scorn of consequence." You may as reasonably explain the ethical "ought" by the mechanism of the common pump, as by the mechanism of man's nervous structure.

It appears to me, then, that "the fitter regulative system," which Mr. Spencer proposes to substitute for the old data of ethics, is a mere abortion of moral philosophy; just as his doctrine of The Unknowable is a mere abortion of natural theology. I do not deny Mr. Spencer's speculative ingenuity. I am far from questioning his positions that animated nature, in general, has risen from a lower to a higher stage: that, in particular, man's whole being has been derived from the universe, as a whole, in an orderly and natural manner. But the question is as to the cause of this progress. Again I do not doubt—who does?—that a nervous structure may give rise to tendencies which become hereditary. But this is a very different thing from saying that the primary principles of reason are the product of brain or nervous action. Once more. I have nothing to except against Mr. Spencer's doctrine that the subjective organ of ethical knowledge, and the objective formula of the moral idea, are both in a permanent state of becoming. But that does not deprive conscience, or the moral law, of their imperative character, for each act recognized by me as obligatory: it does not, in the least, imply the destruction of ethical liberty, properly understood. The idea of duty is one thing: the nomenclature of duties is quite another. When Mr. Spencer advocates a "scientific morality" he means not a morality independent of dogmatic theology — for that independence, as has been seen, I strenuously contend—but a morality independent of metaphysics. And such a morality is impossible, for the science of Doing rests on the science of Being. What Mr. Spencer means by scientific morality is a morality based on the experimental sciences. His object, in that department of his philosophy which we have last considered, is to find a justification in physics for utilitarian ethics: to discover the rules of human action in the properties of matter. It appears to me that the result at which he arrives is the annihilation of the moral idea: while, the more closely we examine his argument, the more abundantly shall we find his reasoning nonsequacious, his terminology shifting, his inductions superficial and hazardous, his assumptions colossal, and his explanations mere descriptions. Mr. Spencer is a realist who affects to deal with the whole range of human knowledge: to give us " a comprehensive view of truth in all its branches." But even within the province of physics he falls into grave error: while in the methods of metaphysics he is obviously unversed. "Given," he tells us, "the Persistence of Force, and given the various derivative laws of Force, and there has to be shown . . . how there necessarily result the more numerous and involved traits exhibited by organic and superorganic existences: how an organism is evolved? what is the genesis of human intelligence? whence social progress arises?"* This has to be shown. Yes. But Mr. Spencer, with all his perseverance and energy, has not shown it, in all his vast volumes. He has not solved a single one of these problems.

Let us, however, suppose that he has, in truth, exhibited the simplest elements of the universe, the ultimate principles of things: that he has reduced all of which we have knowledge to his one law—the Persistence of Force, under various transformations: that he has demonstrated our nescience of everything but our sensations, and has established our duty—"our highest duty"—of believing in The Unknowable, as the objective cause of our sensations. Does this Scientific Agnosticism, after all, constitute a real explanation of The Great Enigma—"Je, d'où, où, pour, comment?" The problem of individuation would remain the same. "Pourquoi y a-t-il quelque chose?" asked d'Alembert. And he could only

* *First Principles*, § 193.

answer "Terrible question." Does Mr. Spencer even so much as pretend to tell us why anything exists? Why it is itself, and not something else? Does he bring us any nearer to a constituent explanation of things? It is in vain that he seeks, by grocer's scales and carpenter's plummet-line, to reduce them to averages and mechanism. His portentous generalities, with their integrations and disintegrations, leave the mystery of "the immeasurable world" precisely where they found it. "We live by Admiration, Hope, and Love." Can any one live by Mr. Spencer's philosophy? Its inadequacy to life is its condemnation.

"Lass das nur stehn! Dabei wird's niemand wohl.
Es ist ein Zauberbild, ist leblos, ein Idol."

The key to the problem of existence is not sensation, but personality. And it is to be sought, not in the charnel-house of Physics, but in the spiritual temple of Reason.

CHAPTER V.

RATIONAL THEISM.

WE have now examined the substitutes for Theism offered by Atheism and Agnosticism. The next step in our inquiry is, whether Theism is, in fact, so hopelessly discredited as is frequently and confidently alleged. It will be remembered that in this volume I am addressing myself not to those who believe in God, but to those who do not: an exceeding great multitude, as I fear, who have been infected by the intellectual epidemic of the age. The great majority of them, perhaps, could give no coherent account of their scepticism. M. Renan has somewhere truly observed that " few people have a right to reject Christianity." Such rejection is, most frequently, the result of indulgence in what George Eliot called " the unlimited right of private haziness," which many people, apparently, consider the most precious portion of their intellectual heritage. It is a sort of mental *morbidezza*, and has become the fashion. At the beginning of the century Rivarol pronounced impiety the greatest of indiscretions. Now "society" not only tolerates, but even relishes, its most full-flavoured manifestations. Fifty years ago, Emerson noted "polite bows to God in the newspapers" as an English trait. Now, the one thing which our journals, delivering their "brawling judgments unashamed, on all things, all day long," are agreed upon, is to ignore "the Judge of all the earth." Sir Robert Peel said, upon a well-known occasion, "Take my word for it, it is not prudent to trust yourself to a man who does not believe in God and in a future life after death." What would Mr. Gladstone now say to such a sentiment? Nay, how many members are there of either House of Parliament, who would endorse it? But I need not dwell further upon what must be plain to every competent observer. Let me rather go on to inquire what is the special cause of this movement of contemporary thought.

It seems to me largely due to the stupendous advance of the experimental sciences, usually and justly reckoned a distinctive glory of the nineteenth century, and to the absorbing devotion to them so generally displayed. And this is natural enough. For those sciences dwell in the sphere of physical uniformity. They are nothing but a knowledge of the relative. Hence the tendency of professors of physics—the faculty of thought being, like the dyer's hand, subdued to what it works in—to shut out the idea of a First Cause;

a tendency described with equal vigour and accuracy by the great English poet of the last century, in words breathing true prophetic inspiration:

> "Make Nature still encroach upon His plan,
> And shove Him off as far as e'er we can,
> Thrust some mechanic cause into His place,
> Or bind in matter and diffuse in space,
> Or, at one bound, o'erleaping all His laws,
> Make God man's image: man the final cause."

Existence presents two problems—the how and the why. To explain the how of things, we must discover those uniformities of sequence or co-ordination which we call their laws. That is the province of physics. And with all beyond that, physical science, as such, is not concerned. It traces for us links—more or fewer—in the chain of phenomena. But it cannot go farther than that uniform succession of antecedents and consequents. It cannot reach the innermost foundation of things, nor confer upon us a knowledge of their essence, or of their origin. It can no more reveal to us the source of the movement innate in the molecule, than it can explain the dialectic evolution of thought. These problems belong to a different order. They lie within the domain, not of experimental physics, but of pure reason.

That everything which happens must have a cause, and that there is not an infinity of secondary causes, are the two indispensable postulates of all philosophy. The category of causality is the *sine qua non* of all ratiocination : we cannot think without it. And the idea of cause is entirely metaphysical. To employ the word merely to denote antecedents, to define it as the relation of objects to objects, of impressions to impressions, of phenomena to phenomena, is simply to empty it of its real meaning, which is the dynamical. " Cause," Dr. Martineau has well observed, "is not the relation of phenomena to one another : " it is " the relation of phenomena to something which is not phenomenal but real." As a matter of fact, it is from our own energy, as personal agents, that we gain the idea of cause. The only type of causation known to us is volitional. To this one type "we are absolutely limited ; . . . and so, behind every event, whatever its seat and whatever its form, must post, near or far, the same idea taken from our own voluntary activity. This, it is plain, is tantamount to saying that all which happens in nature has One kind of cause, and that cause a Will like ours ; "* *causa ultima, sola vera causa.*† |It appears to me most necessary at the present day to insist upon this, for, as I had occasion to show at length, some time ago,

* *A Study of Religion*, vol. i. p. 230.

† Aristotle, in the Twelfth Book of his *Metaphysics*, argues from the law, order, and progress visible in the phenomenal universe that the First Cause must be ἐνέργεια, and this simply and purely. The Latin scholastics translate " Energy " by *Actus Purus*.

in controversy with Professor Huxley,* contemporary masters of physical science often display a desire, and more than a desire, to bring everything within its boundaries. Perhaps no one has exhibited this characteristic more signally than Mr. Herbert Spencer, who excludes free spontaneity from all spheres of life, and imposes everywhere the same mechanical "necessity"—what he is pleased to call necessity—which rules in the domain of physical or chemical forces. No one acquainted with my writings will suppose me likely to contravene the authority of experimental science within its proper department. But I feel deeply that one of the most crying needs of our time is to repel the aggressions of its professors upon provinces of thought absolutely beyond their jurisdiction; to resist their restriction of our ideas to generalizations of phenomena: their erection of experimental observation into the sole criterion of certitude. Most fruitful is this method in the interpretation of organic and inorganic nature: how fruitful the wonderful growth of the physical sciences during the present century sufficiently shows. But what are we to say of the application of that method to the intellect and its operations? "Oh! psychology, be upon thy guard against physics!" exclaimed Maine de Biran fifty years ago. But psychology has been quite unable to repel the rude assault. By how many writers of

* See *On Right and Wrong*, p. 243.

great repute is the soul now quietly assumed to be a group of phenomena—what they call phenomena—which may be assimilated to purely material facts, depending upon one another by an unbroken chain? I am far from denying that there is a true, a close analogy, between physical and intellectual laws, both being, as I judge, manifestations of the same Reason. What I am now speaking of is the application—misapplication—of the physiological method to the mental and moral order: the claim that purely metaphysical questions shall be determined by the laws of matter. In every department of thought we see the same tendency. Thus, in history, first principles are quite abandoned by an influential school. The business of the historian, they tell us, is not to judge, but to understand: "to seize the reason of each thing in its necessity." And so history is severed from philosophy, and becomes a mere branch of physics. Nay, the physiological method is applied even to divinity, and we have "scientific" theology, with Strauss, Bauer, and Ewald as its professors. The mental habit of which I am writing is curiously and unconsciously illustrated by the prevailing custom of using the word "science" as a synonym for physics. Professor Huxley, as I have pointed out,[*] expressly identifies the growth of "science" with the extension of "natural causation," and fully ac-

[*] *On Right and Wrong*, p. 256.

quiesces in the tendency to reduce " all scientific problems," except those which are purely mathematical, to questions of molecular physics. "*Of course*," Mr. Mill has observed, "we can never know anything but phenomena." If this is so, then, equally of course, there is an end of metaphysics. Then is the prediction of Pope verified:

> "Philosophy, that leaned on heaven before,
> Sinks to her second cause, and is no more."

Yes; that is precisely how it fares with philosophy in the hands of these thinkers, whose philosophical culture is usually not very profound. They refuse to acknowledge that anything which has physical effects can have a hyperphysical source. Their main position is the rejection of the supersensuous. In what I am now about to write I shall keep specially in view this special character of the antitheistic current of thought in our days, for in its various forms, I think, will be found to work one and the selfsame spirit. It would be mere waste of my time and of my readers' for me to go over ground already trodden by thinkers —undervalued only by such as from defect of will or intelligence have not mastered them—who, in former days, have vindicated the Divine concept. But the old-world answers may suffice for old-world objections, and yet be quite inadequate to meet that contemporary mode of thinking which especially militates against the theistic idea. Let us see, then, first, what are the grounds now specially urged why we, the heirs of all the ages, should abandon the Theism which we have been wont to esteem the most precious portion of our inheritance. I shall afterwards proceed to inquire what Reason, freely exercised according to the methods specially prized in these days, and without any reference to systems of religion professing to be revealed, makes evident, unless we stultify its teaching, concerning the existence and character of the Supreme Reality.

Now, the last considerable contribution made in this country to antitheistic literature is, I suppose, Mr. Cotter Morison's work, *The Service of Man*. Great and general was the jubilation wherewith its appearance was hailed by those who shared its gifted author's opinions. Mr. John Morley, in particular, unless my memory is at fault, solemnly blessed and approved it as "an epoch-making book." Let us then turn to its pages to learn what are the latest reasons given to the world why men ought not to believe in God. Mr. Morison did not, indeed, bring out of his treasure-house anything absolutely new. I find no vestige of original thought in his volume. His object appears to have been to exhibit, in their most persuasive form, the most formidable arguments of the antitheistic Rabbis at whose feet he had himself sat. The special value of his performance lies in the ability with which he acquitted himself of this task. No one can be insensible to the lucidity and vigour of his style. No one can deny to his pages the higher merit of transparent candour and unfeigned earnestness. With much of his work I am not here concerned. I confine myself entirely to his case against Theism in general. He expressly tells us that if men will go on believing in God, it is "in spite of science and the laws of consciousness."* Let us see, then, what reasons in support of the antitheistic argument "science and the laws of consciousness" supply.

And first as to science—by which Mr. Morison, of course, meant physics. What arguments against Theism do the latest developments of physical science present? After diligent search I find only one set forth by Mr. Morison in any definite and precise shape. Let me give it in his own words. "The early glimpses of the marvels of Nature afforded by modern science," he writes, "undoubtedly were favourable to natural theology in the first instance. Knowledge revealed so many wonders which had not been suspected by ignorance, that a general increase of reverence and

* Page 52.

awe for the Creator was the natural though not very logical consequence. But a deeper philosophy, or rather biology, has disturbed the satisfaction with which 'the wisest and most exquisite ends' were once regarded. It is now known that for one case of successful adaptation of means to ends in the animal world, there are hundreds of failures. If organs which serve an obvious end justify the assumption of an intelligent designer, what are we to say of organs which serve no ends at all, but are quite useless or meaningless?"* Now this is very moderately put. I confess if I had been in Mr. Morison's place I should have stated it much more strongly. The argument from the apparent waste, failure, nay, blundering, in Nature would seem at first sight to disprove the old notion of finality much relied upon by Theistic apologists in former times. I do not speak of the doctrine of final causes so inimitably expounded by Dr. Pangloss: "Observe that noses have been made to wear spectacles, and so we have spectacles. Legs have been manifestly framed to be clad in stockings, wherefore we have stockings. Stones have been formed to be hewn and made into *châteaux*, and so monseigneur has a very fine *château*; and pigs having been made to be eaten, we eat pork all the year round." I speak not of this teleology, but of that which Voltaire himself considered to be absolutely evident. "It seems to me," he

---

* Page 21.

writes, "that one must be mad [*forcené*] to deny that stomachs are made to digest, eyes to see, ears to hear.... When effects are invariably the same in every place and at every period, when these uniform effects are independent of the beings to which they belong, then there is visibly a final cause."* But now we are told that the notion of finality is banished by contemporary science as a relic of superstition. Functions are pronounced to be a result, not an end. As M. de Candolle will have it, "The birds fly because they have wings; but a true naturalist will never say, 'The birds have wings to fly with.'" Nature, we are assured, always acts without prevision of an end. It is mere monotonous mechanism elaborating all organisms after one plan—often unsuccessfully—the variations being merely the result of environment. Not intelligence, not design, but fortuitousness or fatality, is the real explanation. Where former generations saw divine wisdom—"God geometrises," said Plato—we, whose eyes have been opened, see only blind groping. That is, indeed, the message delivered to the world by *Physicus* in his well-known work. What is the substance of his book but this?—I believed in God

---

* The whole of the article, "Causes Finales," in the *Dictionnaire Philosophique*, from which I am quoting, is well worth reading. It is a model of lucidity and masculine commonsense. To say that it is excessively amusing also, is merely to say that it is Voltaire's.

on account of the argument from design—all other proofs seemed worthless—until I read Darwin, and then that broke down too. Well, upon this matter I shall express myself with absolute candour. If any man can still argue, solely from the phenomena of the physical world, to an absolutely wise and all-powerful First Cause, by all means let him. I cannot. But to affirm that the progress of physical science has disproved, or tends to disprove, thought, order, finality in the universe, is quite unintelligible to me. I find Mr. Darwin's books teeming with evidence of plan, adaptation, that is, purpose in nature. But purpose, according to Kant's masterly analysis, implies an intelligent will, in possession of principles or rules of conduct, and directed to a specific end. The argument from design may have been pressed to absurd lengths. The argument from failure is in itself absurd. In strictness, it must be said that there is no such thing as failure known to us, because there may be always ends which are hidden from our eyes. We can affirm order, because that is a thing positive. But to affirm disorder, absolute and final, is like attempting to prove a negative. Moreover, there is this weighty fact telling for the divine induction: that, as our knowledge of nature advances, more purpose appears. Take one familiar instance only. Where could waste apparently more utterly senseless have been discovered than in those vast buried forests in which solar rays have been imprisoned since the Secondary Epoch? For two millions of years this profuse and seemingly purposeless growth has lain in the earth, entombed and idle. It is now the fuel which gladdens us with light and heat, and which is the chief factor in our material civilization. Again, a rudimentary organ may be useless now, but destined to use in after ages; a dwarfed survival, useless now, may have had its use in bygone times. But I decline to take theories borrowed from the economical schools of the day as the measure of finality in the universe. I cannot accept the standard supplied by utilitarianism, or " pig philosophy," as the rule of all things in heaven and earth. Utility? The word requires definition. Useful for what? Beauty is surely a sufficient justification for the works of " Nature's own sweet and cunning hand." Wisely does the poet speak of the " liberal applications " which lie in her bosom, as in the soul of the artist. Of how many of her productions does his caution hold good:—

> "So 'twere to cramp its use if I
> Should hook it to some useful end."

Once more. The doctrine of organic evolution, which, taken by itself, is an admirable revelation —so I must account it—of an universal law, does not in the least conduct us to the necessity of modern phenomenists as the true explanation of the universe. Everywhere reigns one law: a law of progress, of development, of perpetual becoming;

therefore there is no First Cause whence that law issues: there is only necessity. An admirable argument indeed, issuing, fitly in an *équivoque*. Necessity is a question-begging word. Is blind necessity meant? Such necessity assuredly could not produce the diversity, the succession, the return of phenomena. But if necessity is not blind it is merely another name for law: and law implies an abiding and unchanging self, a spiritual principle. The truth is that evolution is a modal, not a causal theory of creation, and it is quite compatible with the hypothesis of divine finality while it is quite incompatible with the old mechanical theory of nature. But further: The question of a First Cause is one with which the physicist, as such, is not concerned. His domain is the sphere of sense perception. The science with which he has to do explains to us the materials of the inorganic world. It unfolds to us the movements which succeed one another there in a definite series. But that is all it can reveal to us of the elements of life. Physical science, as I have already insisted, knows nothing of the cause which formed the first cell, which developed therefrom the organism and which rules its evolution. Physicists may, if they will, call that cause force; but they are unable to tell you what force is. This has been frankly confessed by one whose words, upon such subjects, carry great and deserved weight. "If you ask," writes Professor Tyndall, in his

Fragments of Science, "whence is this matter of which we have been discoursing, who or what divided it into molecules, who or what impressed upon them the necessity of running into organic forms [the physicist] has no answer. Science"—the Professor means, of course, physical science—"is mute in reply to these questions." Yes. We must go elsewhere if we want an answer to them. Physical science is not concerned with them. They lie outside her domain.

So much upon the antitheistic argument from the latest developments of physical science. But "tarry a little, there is something else," Mr. Morison admonishes us. Consider the argument from the laws of consciousness. Has not Mr. Herbert Spencer laid it down that they present a quite insurmountable obstacle to Theistic belief? Well, it must be admitted that he has. It is a favourite, not to say a well-worn thesis with that master. Thus in his *Principles of Psychology* he writes, "The antithesis of subject and object, never to be transcended while consciousness lasts, renders impossible all knowledge of the Ultimate Reality in which subject and object are united." *
Thus in his *Essays* he argues, "Mental analysis shows that the product of thought is, in all cases,

* § 272.

a relation identified as such or such"—a singular statement upon which I shall have something to say later on—"and that therefore Being, in itself, out of relation, is unthinkable."* And in an article contributed by him in 1885 to one of the Magazines, he has abounded in the same sense. Mr. Morison quotes, with much satisfaction, a few pages of it,† which he evidently regarded as unanswerable. The gist of them is that we can believe in a divine consciousness only by refraining from thinking what is meant by consciousness, and that the condition of believing in a divine will is similar. "Whoever conceives of any other will than his own," Mr. Spencer urges, "must do so in terms of his own will, which is the sole will directly known to him, all other wills being only inferred. But will, as such, is conscious, if it presupposes a motive, a prompting desire of some kind; absolute indifference excludes the conception of will. Moreover, will, as implying a prompting desire, connotes some end contemplated as one to be achieved, and ceases with the achievement of it; some other will referring to some other end taking its place. That is to say, will, like emotion, necessarily supposes a series of states of consciousness. The conception of a divine will, derived from the human will, involves like it, localization in space

* Vol. iii. p. 258.
† See *The Service of Man*, p. 44.

and time; the willing of each end excluding from consciousness, for an interval, the willing of other ends, and therefore being inconsistent with that omnipresent activity which simultaneously works out an infinity of ends. It is the same with the ascription of intelligence. Not to dwell on the seriality and limitation implied as before, we may note that intelligence, as alone conceivable by us, presupposes existence independent of it and objective to it. It is carried on in terms of changes primarily wrought by alien activities—the impressions generated by things beyond consciousness, and the ideas derived from such impressions. To speak of an intelligence which exists in the absence of all such alien activities is to use a meaningless word." When I read these and similar pronouncements of Mr. Herbert Spencer, I am reminded of the wise admonition of Dale the Quaker to his son-in-law, Robert Owen. "Thee should be very right, Robert, for thee's very positive." But is this eminent person very right? I venture to think, on the contrary, that he is very wrong. Mr. Spencer's argument, as set out in the passage which I have quoted from him, and which I believe presents it very completely, appears to me to be vitiated radically and hopelessly, first, by his utter misconception of what is meant by the faculty of abstraction; secondly, by his failure to apprehend the essential nature of intellect; and lastly, by his assumptions of the most arbitrary *a priori* description, concerning the Ultimate Reality, whose existence and attributes reason seeks in some degree to know.

Let us take the last point first. Who, I would ask Mr. Spencer, asserts that subject and object are transcended in the Ultimate Reality? Why should they be? Does transcending mean identifying one with the other? Again, what is there to hinder an ideal distinction of subject and object in the Eternal Being? Such distinction is all that intellect requires for its existence. And, as a matter of fact, so far from being denied, or transcended, by theists, it has supplied the philosophical foundation of the Christian doctrine of the Trinity since the later Platonists. Again, ought we to begin by defining the Ultimate Reality as that in which subject and object are transcended? Must we not take for our proper starting-point in theology—the science of God—as in every other science, facts, viewed in the light of first principles? And do not these compel us to infer, not all at once, an Ultimate Reality, but a superhuman intelligence? I do not think Mr. Spencer will deny such an intelligence to be possible, to be conceivable—nay, to be admissible. Well, then, let me ask him to consider the consequences of admitting it. What we are seeking is an Ultimate Reality, which shall be Eternal Consciousness; not a reality which has no attributes. No, no, Mr. Spencer objects; the Ultimate

Reality *can* have no attributes. Why? I will ask him. Because, he replies—this is what his argument strictly amounts to—because the Ultimate Reality is merely Being, and indifferent to attributes. Now, here I beg the reader's most careful attention. The Being of which Mr. Spencer speaks is in truth only the notion of Being; it is a pure abstraction arrived at by taking no account of attributes; not by denying them, but by prescinding from them; and, as such, it does not exist, nor can exist. Pure Being, in Mr. Spencer's sense, is an idol of the den; a logical abstraction; or, as they would say in the schools, an *ens rationis*: and no abstraction exists as an abstraction. It exists in the concrete, and therefore with what we call attributes. Nor are these attributes—as Mr. Spencer seems to imagine—things added to it, and detractable from it; they are the thing itself, which, viewed in different lights, has now this predicated of it, now that. Mr. Spencer's Being is a mere notion, founded indeed upon any and every reality, but not itself real. It is *ens abstractissimum*; the most abstract of abstractions. But what we are seeking as the foundation of things is the Ultimate Reality, and that must be *ens realissimum*, independent, self-existent, of which endless attributes, or aspects — that is to say imperfect representations of the whole—may be predicated. Mr. Spencer might have learnt all this from the first book of Spinoza's *Ethics*, where it is irrefragably established. I note in passing that Hegel, too, came very near this verity on which I have been insisting, when he identified Being and Nothing, although by a singular aberration, he turned aside from it to wanderings long and devious as those of Ulysses. He should have said that Being in the abstract is nothing in the concrete, or that Being in general is nothing in particular. So much must serve as to the first and third points. Lastly, as to the essential nature of intellect, what is it, I would ask Mr. Spencer, but to distinguish between the accidents and the substance of a thing or notion, and to arrive at the substance? Hence in reflecting on itself it perceives that while an object, or *terminus in quo*, is necessary to its operations, the succession of objects, or the reception of them from without, is not. Hence, too, it perceives that the higher the intellect, the wider become its intuitions, the fewer its reasonings, and the larger its affirmations. Thence we conclude by an unimpeachable logical process to the nature of an eternal, self-dependent intellect. And there Mr. Spencer will find the answer to his long-drawn argument. Mr. Spencer tells us, " My intellect is dependent on time, space, and succession." I reply, Yes, truly, it is so dependent, not, however, as intellect, but as *your* intellect: by accident, so to speak. Mr. Spencer must pardon me if I observe parenthetically that his ratiocination reminds me irresistibly of a certain cowherd, mentioned by Voltaire. The good peasant had never in his life seen any other beasts than those which he tended; and he confidently affirmed that if God chose to create any other they must have horns and ruminate. A similar answer may be given to what Mr. Spencer says of the will. It needs an end, I grant. But I maintain that the end may be in itself, or outside. So far as this argument is concerned, the universe may be either a necessary end of the divine activity— which I personally do not hold—or contingent. But that it should be an end, derogates nothing from the perfection of the Absolute. Mr. Spencer's logical puzzles are, I admit, fatal to idolatries. They leave Rational Theism absolutely untouched.

And now having, I trust, sufficiently cleared away the objections to Theism, urged from the latest developments of physical science, and from the laws of consciousness, let us go on to my next point, and inquire what grounds for belief in God are afforded by reason freely exercised, according to the methods specially prized in these days. And here I must frankly admit that the strongest grounds for such belief are inexpressible, because they transcend the logical understanding. To those with whom the Divine Noumenon is no tradition of the schools or of the nursery, no shibboleth of a sect, no war-cry of a party, but an object, and the Supreme Object, an experience, and the most intimate experience, the very source and fount of their whole moral life—to such, I say, it is always distasteful, and something more, to engage in controversy concerning what is so personal and so sacred. If they do so, it is as a matter of duty, and not because it makes any difference to them how the argument goes. But apart from this, they may surely claim to have done enough in satisfaction of the debt which they owe to all men, if they show that their faith, so far from being unreasonable, does, in fact, sum up the conclusions to which reason points; that the language wherein they clothe it, although infinitely inadequate, is the nearest approximation to the truth which is possible to us. Let us start, then, from the way of thinking just now so much in credit. The popular philosophy of the day is a philosophy of relativity, employing as its most valued instrument comparative analysis. I am not going to say one word against this philosophy considered in itself. I know well how many provinces of intellectual activity are full of its labour, and how fruitful that labour has been. I admit that to reduce the complex to the simple, the phenomenon to the law, the special law to the general law, is, so far as it goes, an explanation. I do not deny that if universal being were merely monotonous and inflexible mechanism, such would be the whole explanation. But universal being is not merely that. It is also organic. It seems to me self-evident that the tendency of lower forms to pass into higher, implies something else than mechanism, that a system of definite directions is merely a synonym for finality. To say that "all things are *essentially* constituted by the sum of their relations" is surely a contradiction in terms. I cannot understand how any one with the slightest tincture of philosophical discipline could have committed himself to so surprising a proposition. All things are related. True. But how can correlation be essence? It is like saying that the outside of a thing is its inside. I take leave to hold as absolutely clear and irrefragable truth that it is a logical impossibility for the Relative to exist alone. It pre-supposes the Absolute. To the Absolute the whole series of relative realities tends. I venture very confidently to affirm that, however hard we try, it is a psychological impossibility for us to rid ourselves of the idea that finite phenomena, apprehensible by the senses, veil an Infinite Reality. To that Reality comparison cannot apply; "nec viget quidquam simile aut secundum." Analysis cannot reach it, for to analyze the Infinite is a contradiction in terms. So far Mr. Spencer is with me, and it is always a pleasure to find myself in accord with that patient and candid thinker. He regards "the consciousness of an Inscrutable Power, manifested to us through all phenomena," "the Ultimate Cause of things," "the Absolute" as a certainty.* And here Mr. Spencer is but echoing, perhaps unwittingly, the words of Kant, although that philosopher, in his old-fashioned style, speaks not of "an Inscrutable Power," but of God. It is God, as he judges, "whose existence we are compelled to conceive as the idea of something upon which the supreme and necessary unity of all experience is based," something, he adds, "which we represent to ourselves as standing in a relation to the whole system of phenomena analogous to that in which phenomena stand to each other." I hold that there is something in the human mind—and no fork of Positivism will ever succeed in expelling it—which compels us to take account, not only of the external universe, but of the mysterious principle behind it, the last term upon which hang all nature and all thought. Nay, more, I hold it the necessary conclusion of the human understanding that phenomena, apprehensible by the senses, must have a reason which is not a phenomenon, and which therefore is "beyond the probe of chemic test." And here I may be told, You have appealed to Kant: to Kant shall you go. Are you not doing precisely what that master has shown to be wholly inadmissible: venturing with

* *First Principles*, § 31.

the speculative reason beyond the limits of sensible experience, forgetting that the principle of causality is of purely subjective value? Certainly I should be the last person in the world to shut my eyes to the great philosophical revolution wrought by Kant. Unquestionably his system enshrines much eternal truth. But in philosophy it is well to risk, if so it must be, the reproach of eclecticism, and to call no man, Rabbi. Adequately to discuss the Kantian doctrine of causality would demand a volume. I must content myself with here indicating, in the fewest words, how the argument seems to me to lie. I admit, then, that the subject imposes its own form on knowledge and makes it subjective. I deny that subjectivism necessarily follows from this. The phenomena of the external world are not merely abstract signs, like algebraic symbols. They are instinct with life: they obey law: they are disposed in a wonderful order. The life, the law, the order demand explanation. And for this explanation the principle of causality is necessary. It has been admirably pointed out by Dr. Martineau that "we ourselves are the only cause of whose mode of action we have immediate knowledge, through inner intuition," and that "it is . . . by an *a priori* axiom of the understanding, that we apply the causal relation to the external world." * The idea of cause is both subjective

* *A Study of Religion*, vol. i. p. 200.

and objective: subjective so far as this, that the intellect actually possesses the idea; objective in that the idea is founded upon something which is not our reason. Deny this objective foundation and you are necessarily landed in Nihilism. And will any one who takes Kant's teaching as a whole affirm that such is its issue? I do not for one moment believe that Kant himself held the law of causation to be wholly subjective. We might, indeed, have been compelled so to think if he had given us only *The Critique of Pure Reason.* But it appears to me that, in the light of his other writings, this view of his doctrine is quite untenable. I will merely add the caution—which recent philosophical literature in this country shows to be not unnecessary—that to Kant transcendental means true, not false. Nor is there any way out of Nihilism for his disciples, save to take the Supreme Principle which is beyond sensible experience, and to build on that.

Now what can we know about this Supreme Principle? this Ultimate Reality? As we saw in the last chapter, Mr. Spencer, the most eminent spokesman of Scientific Agnosticism, answers Nothing. "The Absolute cannot in any manner or degree be known, in the strict sense of knowing."* "The forms of our consciousness are such that the Absolute cannot in any manner or degree be brought within them."† Mr. Spencer's argument from the laws of consciousness I have already dealt with. Here I may remark that he is not quite consistent. But I will not make it matter of reproach to Mr. Spencer that, in the same breath, he declares our utter inability to know anything of the Ultimate Reality, and tells us several important particulars regarding it. Surely to know that anything exists, is to know something considerable about it. And Mr. Spencer predicates of the Ultimate Reality not only being, but causal energy, eternity, omnipotence; more, he recognizes it as " the basis of our intelligence."‡ Of all this we have certitude, Mr. Spencer thinks. I quite agree. I equally agree when he lays it down that the "nature" of this Power " transcends intuition and is beyond imagination," § and that it may be called, nay, must be called, so far as its essence is concerned, "unknown and unknowable." Indeed, I would myself put it even more strongly, and would say with Pascal, "If there is a God, He must be infinitely incomprehensible." ‖ I go on to assent

---

* *First Principles*, § 27. † *Ibid.* § 31.
‡ *Ibid.* § 32. § *Ibid.* § 31.
‖ So St. Augustine: "De Deo loquimur: quid mirum si non comprehendis? si enim comprehendis non est Deus."—*Serm.* cxvii.

as unreservedly when Mr. Spencer tells us that this Power—*Deus absconditus*, as I hold it to be—is "manifested" "through phenomena" to our "consciousness." I should like here to point out the exception which ought to be taken to Mr. Spencer's employment of these words "phenomena" and "consciousness," if the occasion permitted. But it does not; so I will follow his terminology, and will ask him to consider what the manifestations of the Ultimate Reality through phenomena to consciousness do, in fact, amount to.

First consider the phenomena of the external universe. Every sensible outcome of intelligence, every work, for example, of plastic or constructive art, is in some sort a revelation of its cause.* It is not only a thing, but a thought. Now what does the external universe manifest to our consciousness of the Power which, as Mr. Spencer tells us, "persists unchanging under these sensible appearances," and which he would not object, I think, to call "their great Original"? If we look around us and above us, we find everywhere what we term mind and matter: "mens agitat molem." Shall we say then that the Ultimate Reality is both mind and matter? No. That would be to make it in our likeness, to fall into the anthropomorphism from which Mr. Spencer so earnestly beseeches us to abstain. Surely, however, we may say with Fénelon that the Ultimate Reality "is

---

* Ἐνεργείᾳ δὴ ὁ ποιήσας τὸ ἔργον ἐστί πως.—*Aris. Eth.*, l. ix. c. 7.

neither mind nor matter, but is all that is essential in mind and matter." Now what is essential in mind is reason. And if there is any lesson taught more clearly than another by the recent researches of physicists, it is the intelligibility of the universe. Reason everywhere, in the microcosm of the leaf as in the macrocosm of the fixed stars; in the lowest protozoa as in the highest mammals. Such is the lesson which we see writ large in Nature. Its laws, as Hegel has irrefutably shown, are identical with the laws of the human intellect. Reason is the constituent element of reality. Mr. Spencer happily speaks of "the veritable revelation of the external universe"* made to us by physical science. The more fully that revelation discloses it to us, the more completely its grand title of Kosmos is seen to be justified. "In contemplating the structure of the universe," said Goethe, "we cannot resist the conclusion that the whole is founded upon a distinct idea." I need not dwell upon what is so familiar. And does not this point to the Supreme Cause as Objective Reason? Does not the intelligibility of the world imply an intelligent Author of the world? We are often told that Nature is an infinite virtuality, potentially containing all: that the universe is self-caused, is at once cause and effect: that its activity is immanent and necessary, and also instinctive, until it attains consciousness in man:

* *First Principles*, § 7.

that intellect is not the starting-point but the goal: not a principle but a resultant. Now, what does all this mean but that from brute force you may get intelligence; from matter, mind; from mechanism, will? Surely that is an irrational doctrine. Surely it is against reason to believe that the unintelligible is the primary source of the intelligible. "He that formed the eye shall He not see?" asked the Hebrew poet. But now we are told that the eye formed itself; that this most exquisite piece of mechanism has insensibly developed from a sensitive membrane. Natural selection, we are assured, has transformed a simple apparatus, formed of an optic nerve, clothed with pigment, and covered with a transparent tissue, to that admirable instrument of vision called the eye. Well, let us suppose that this is so, as I, for my part, have no difficulty in believing. And pray, how does it tell against the Divine induction? May we not rather apply to it the words which Geoffroy St.-Hilaire used of the succession of species, and see in it "one of the most glorious manifestations of creative power and a fresh motive for admiration and love"? Is not this a more reasonable hypothesis than that which explains so marvellous a development by chance or blind necessity?

Natural selection! Let me say another word upon that topic before I pass on. Who that has given attention to the great question of evolution, so much discussed of late years, does not remember the unbounded confidence with which the mechanical theory of species was advanced by ultra-Darwinians? I mean the theory which explained the type as a sort of mosaic put together by the hazard of external circumstances, as a fortuitous aggregation of characteristics, produced in isolation, one after another, by selection or habit. But it was pointed out that the very facts —experience itself—force us to recognize the regular correlation of the characteristics appertaining to the type of a species, and that this is absolutely fatal to the mechanical principle of explanation. Recognize—and you cannot help recognizing, unless you are theory-blind—recognize the law of correlation, and you must also recognize the fact that every individual modification of importance is directly linked to a system of correlative modifications. And such recognition makes an end of that hypothesis of indeterminate variability, resting upon purely fortuitous influences, which furnishes a basis for the merely mechanical concept of the two forms of selection. Is it reasonable to ask us to regard as fortuitous a totality of correlative modifications producing themselves in the most different parts of the organism and preserving among themselves the same relation? It is unreasonable. The only rational explanation is to be found in Objective Reason.

Reason, then, the essence of mind, is what

sensible phenomena disclose to us, ever more clearly. And what is essential in matter? Of matter in itself we of course know nothing; we know only its qualities, to some extent, through sensation. Make abstraction of its qualities, and what remains of it? It is given us, Kant has well observed, only as the union of two forces—the force of expansion and the force of attraction. It is the visibility of force. Shall we say, then, that the Ultimate Reality is force? As the Christian poet sang long centuries ago, "Deus, rerum tenax vigor immotus in Te permanet." But force is only a resultant; nor, as I have already had occasion to observe, if we go by experience, have we knowledge of any other primary cause of force than volition. It seems to me that the logical following of Mr. Spencer's own method leads us to the conclusion that what we call the laws of nature are the unchanging visible expression of volition; that this is the only possible name under which we can gather up the mighty forces ever energizing throughout the boundless universe; that matter, therefore, is merely a manifestation of Will. But what of space? it may be asked. Well, if space be wholly subjective, it is, as the French would say, a negligible quantity. If it have any objective reality, we may account of it, with Kant and Boscovitch, as a result of force. Abundant grounds, then, seem to exist in support of Hartmann's dictum, "The whole world-process is, in its content, only a logical process, but in its existence a continued act of will." That is what physical law means. Reason and Will are inseparably united in the universe, as they are in idea. If we will anything, it is for some reason. Hence Aristotle's definition of will, ὄρεξις μετὰ λόγου: *appetitus rationalis*, as the Schoolmen render it. Abstract intelligence from will, and *pace* Schopenhauer, it is will no longer. But this union of reason and will, this *appetitus rationalis* it is which constitutes what we call personality.* I shall have to touch upon that point again shortly. Here I observe that I think this is as far as external nature enables us to go. I do not understand how we can argue from a scheme of things, apparently so imperfect, to a perfect First Cause. I do not understand how it can be maintained that Nature reveals to us the creative God of theology or the perfect God of metaphysics.

But the phenomena of the external world are not the only channels through which the Ultimate Existence is manifested to consciousness. We must also take into account the lessons of what the somewhat slipshod language of the day calls "mental phenomena." "Unde arripuisti mentem tuam?" asks Cicero. Mr. Spencer answers the question. He tells us that the Ultimate Existence is "the basis of our intelligence." What then

---

* The theological definition of personality is "naturæ rationalis individua substantia."

does our intelligence tell us concerning its basis? Let us go by experience, we are cautioned, on every hand. By all means. But let us take the totality of experience. Let us recognize internal as well as external facts. "Nihil est in intellectu quod non prius fuerit in sensu," Locke insisted. "Nisi ipse intellectus," added Leibnitz. The dictum, so completed, seems to me the only foundation of all philosophy worthy of the name. The sages of old explained "intellectus" as "intus legens," and the etymology, whatever we may think of it, expresses a great truth. It is intellect that interprets for us the phenomena of the external world. It is intellect that provides for us the explanation of what Faust calls the deep mysterious miracles—" geheime, tiefe Wunder "— in the depths of our own consciousness. Mr. Spencer in his *Psychology* has committed himself to the surprising proposition, "To be conscious is to think: to think is to put together impressions and ideas." But surely the first step in cognition is direct perception. And as surely reflection is the second. Aristotle has drawn this out with much clearness at the beginning of his *Physics*. We first view the thing as a whole, passively, involuntarily. We then proceed to consider it in parts: to divide it, to analyze it, to define it; in other words, to reason about it. And indeed Mr. Spencer himself elsewhere seems to recognize this. "Disjunction," he tells us, "is the primordial form of all reasoning." What, then, is the primary fact which the intellect reveals to us, as soon as the act of thinking takes place in our own consciousness? Unquestionably it is the distinction of self and non-self. And, as unquestionably, it is mere matter of fact, which not even the most strenuous professor of what is called "autonomous morality" will deny, that this distinction is *accompanied*—I beg the reader to note the word—by the idea of moral obligation. It is also matter of fact that the source of that obligation has ever been felt to lie in a mysterious and hyperphysical Entity whereon man depends. Dr. Martineau does not express himself too strongly when he insists that "the constitution of our moral nature is unintelligible except as living in response to an objective Perfection, pervading the universe with Holy Law."* "The one substance with many names," sings Æschylus. Nay, and unnamed, as among the Buddhists, who in the moral order of the universe recognize the inexorable law of righteousness, ruling in the three worlds: the one Power, supreme over gods and men and all things. This is the common factor of all creeds. They all proclaim, however rude or refined, grotesque or sublime their symbolism, the absolute dominion of the moral law, as a perpetual obligation binding upon all possible intelligent beings, and therefore, as a Transcendental Reality, a manifestation of

* *A Study of Religion*, vol. ii. p. 30.

the Eternal under the condition of time. The word religion signifies as much. It imports, to use the words of Kant, "the recognition of all our duties as divine commands." All religions, I say, witness to the concept of duty as a primary intellectual fact: a concept the essence of which, Mr. Darwin tells us, is "appreciation of justice, independently of any pain or pleasure felt at the moment;" they point to the Ultimate Reality which is "the basis of our intelligence" as law moral.

But Mr. Spencer will have it that the concept of duty is merely an altruistic tendency developed by the survival of the fittest; that the moral sense is only the past experience of countless generations commanding what is useful for the tribe; that conscience is nothing but the gradual transference of an external to an internal relation. It appears to me that this overweening dogmatism collapses at the touch of comparison or of analysis. Take first, comparison. I account it absolutely certain that we find among the animals called lower, not, indeed, an ethical sense, but what we may term the analogon of that sense; nay that we sometimes find it in a high state of development; while there exist vast multitudes of men in whom the fundamental ideas of right and wrong are most dim and inchoate. The South African Bushmen, whom the Rev. Mr. Richerer, a missionary, describes as "lower than the beasts around them in moral qualities," are fair specimens of the most abject varieties of savage humanity. He is but one out of a great cloud of witnesses, for the evidence on this matter is overwhelming. But, indeed, we need not go so far afield as South Africa. Our great cities swarm with veritable Yahoos, who would seem almost—

> "Unfettered by the sense of crime;
> To whom a conscience never wakes."

On the other hand, no one who has lived much with dogs, and has candidly and closely studied them, can doubt their possessing a quasi-ethical standard, by which, as they know well, their actions should be governed: their thoughts accusing or else excusing one another, according as they fall short of it or conform to it. I quite grant that the canine analogon of conscience is really the dog's sense of the obligation, under penalties, to bring his will into harmony with a higher will; which, indeed, is precisely the true account of the human conscience too. I quite deny that you can explain it as an ultimate tendency developed by the survival of the fittest dogs, or as the result of the past experience of countless generations of dogs, commanding what is useful to the tribe; or as the transference of an external to an internal relation of doghood. Comparison is fatal to Mr. Spencer's view. So is analysis. Take conscience as we find it in its fullest development—the conscience of a virtuous man or woman—and analyze it as you would analyze any other human instinct, and you will find that it includes a sense of right and wrong in motives, an absolute obligation to follow the right, and a sanction in the shame and remorse and fear which attend upon a violation of this obligation. These are its essential elements, and you will in no way get them out of the tribal utilitarian feeling by evolution, unless you put them into it, previously, by hypothesis. I am far from denying that the course of the evolution of the moral sense may have been pretty much what Mr. Darwin supposes. But I repeat that evolution is a modal and not a causal theory. We do not really explain a thing by tracing it back to rudimentary forms and by exhibiting its growth.

It appears to me, then, that as external phenomena manifest to our consciousness the Ultimate Reality as Law, which is another name for the union of Reason and Will, wherein consists Personality, so do "mental phenomena" also, adding this further revelation first of all, that the Law is just, the Reason right, the Will ethical, the Person holy. I should like to go on, were it not for the inexorable limits of space, to show, after the manner of Plato, how the intellect testifies that the ideas of Truth, Goodness, Beauty, as of Justice, dimly reflected in itself, belong to an order of absolute principles anterior and superior to man; how by an architectonic law of its being it is compelled to refer the complete realization of these ideas to the Ultimate Reality, which it therefore contemplates as τὸ Ἐρώμενον, the Object of all desire. I should especially like to dwell upon the manifestation of that Ultimate Reality made to our consciousness by necessary truths, such as the axioms of ethics; truths self-evident, universal, unchangeable. Are we told that these are so many generalizations of the experience of the race? The answer has been given by the late Professor Green with great plainness of speech: "People who think that the development of habits, through hereditary transmission, will account for the necessity of necessary truths, show that they do not know what is meant by such necessity." These verities are those of which the noblest heroine of Hellenic tragedy spoke: "Not of to-day nor of yesterday, but timeless." They are revelations of the noumenal, gleams of the Eternal Truth which is their source, for there is only one Eternal: μέγας ἐν τούτοις θεὸς οὐδὲ γηράσκει. But I hasten on to the point especially necessary for the elucidation of my argument. I have said, and I suppose no one will deny, that the primary fact revealed to us by reason, as soon as the act of thinking takes place in our consciousness, is the distinction of self and non-self. Intellect, then, manifests to me myself. The perception of selfhood is the very fundamental interior fact of which I am conscious. If any one can really believe that this self is merely a succession of states of consciousness, of thoughts, volitions, hopes, fears, without any underlying unity—well, I suppose he must. It is an old saw, and a wise one, "No absurdity is so great that it does not find favour with some philosophers." The *credo quia incredibile* appears to have passed from theologians to physicists. The whole matter has been summed up by Lotze in a well-known chapter of his *Microcosmos* with a terseness and cogency too rare in his writings. "Our belief in the unity of the *ego* rests not upon our appearing to ourselves such a unity, but upon our being able to appear to ourselves at all. What a being appears to itself is not the important point. If, anyhow, it can appear to itself, or other things to it, capable must it be of unifying manifold phenomena in the absolute indivisibility of its own nature." Until Mr. Spencer sees his way to answering this argument, I shall take leave to hold as a self-evident truth that I am not a mere succession of states of consciousness; that the *ego*, upon its own self-testimony, is a something which is one, identical, permanent, rational, volitional, and free—not, of course, absolutely, but relatively free—a something which is the principle and the cause of our acts.* All this, as it appears to me, we must admit, if we will not shut our eyes to self-evident facts of our intellect, known by us more certainly than any other facts.† But these facts are "manifesta-

* Mr. Spencer insists—and it is a fair specimen of what I have called his logical puzzles:—"It may readily be shown that a cognition of self, properly so called, is absolutely negatived by the laws of thought. The fundamental condition to all consciousness is the antithesis of subject and object. . . . What is the corollary from this doctrine as bearing on the consciousness of self? The mental act, in which self is known, implies, like every other mental act, a perceiving subject and a perceived object. If, then, the object perceived is self, what is the subject that perceives it? or, if it is the true self which thinks, what other self can it be that is thought of? Clearly, a true cognition of self implies a state in which the knowing and the known are one—in which subject and object are identified: and this, Mr. Mansel rightly holds to be the annihilation of both" (*First Principles*, p. 65). The simple answer to this argument is that all being, by virtue of being, is in itself knowable, though not necessarily to this or that grade of intellect. Being—*Ens*—has certain so-called transcendental notes (transcendental in the genuine school-sense, because they transcend, or are not peculiar to any one category of experience). These are *unum, verum, bonum*. *Verum* means knowable. Being, which is not knowable, is not—being. Nor does the act of knowledge abolish the distinction between subject and object either *in ordine essendi*, or *in ordine cognoscendi*. The truth is, that, as I have already pointed out at p. 218, Mr. Spencer does not understand the meaning of the word abstraction. He appears to have entered upon the vast task to which he has so patiently devoted his great powers, without even an elementary knowledge of metaphysics.

† Dr. Martineau has well observed, "Till we accept the '*faiths*' which our faculties postulate, we can never *know* even the sensible world: and when we accept them, we shall know much more."—*Contemporary Review*, March, 1876, p. 547.

tions" to our "consciousness" of the Ultimate Reality, which is "the basis of our intelligence." And they manifest that Reality as possessing—I quite grant, or rather insist, in some transcendent and incomprehensible way—those qualities which are the self-affirmations of the intellect:* Substance, Causality, Being, and all else included in the metaphysical conception of Personality. Are we here met with the objection which Mr. Spencer adopts from Dean Mansel that "there is a contradiction in conceiving the Absolute as Personal," or, as Hegel puts it, that "it is absurd to predicate personality, selfhood of the Infinite, which, by its very nature is the negation of personality, of selfhood, the Infinite being that which combines and contains all, and which therefore excludes nothing"? Utterly inconsistent with the idea of the Absolute, would Personality, of course, be, if it were a limitation. But it is not. In the proper sense of the word, Personality—Für-sich-sein—can be predicated only of the Infinite. "Ipse suum esse est." Perfect selfhood means immediate self-existence. What we call personality, selfhood, in man, is but the dimmest

* Spinoza says that there is no more in common between the Divine intelligence and the human, than there is between the puppy lying on the hearthrug and the constellation which we call the Dog. Surely this view is no longer tenable. All analogy points to the conclusion that mind, like matter, is objectively similar throughout the universe; that it extends in an unbroken line from the lowest monad to the Infinite and Eternal.

shadow, the faintest effluence from the source and fount of Being, in whom alone is perfect Reason, perfect Will. "Signatum est super nos lumen vultus tui Domine." The Ultimate Reality contains within itself the conditions of its existence. Man does not; for he needs the stimulus of non-self to be conscious of his selfhood. He does not need that stimulus to become a person, for the non-self does not create consciousness; it merely manifests it; it is an occasion, not a cause. The idea of Personality, like all ideas, is realized only in that Self-Existent—the original of all existence —which transcends those ideas, indeed, but in transcending, includes them. There is a true sense in the fine saying of Schelling, "That in God alone is being, and that therefore all being is only the Being of God—this thought neither reason nor feeling can take away; it is the supreme thought, in unison with which all hearts vibrate." This is the incommunicable attribute of the Ultimate Reality which we name God— self-existence. He alone, in the highest sense, is. But, as Leibnitz has conclusively shown, the concept of being, when analyzed, implies the concept of cause, and finds in that concept its explanation.

So much, as it seems to me, we *know* concerning the Ultimate Reality. And surely it is enough to warrant us, after the manner of our fathers, in calling that Reality God. I say that Reality is manifested to our consciousness as the Original of the law physical, which rules in the phenomenal world, and of the law moral written on the fleshly tables of the heart; as the Supreme Good, in whom all ideas are realised; as the First Cause and Final End of the universe, where all is causation and finality; as the Self-Existent, and therefore a Person, or rather let us say, with the *Mundaka-Upanishad*, "The Person," from whom all personality is an effluence; as the "basis of our intelligence," of all intelligence; for "as the spokes in the nave of a wheel, so all worlds and souls are fastened in the One Soul."* Such are the conclusions which we must accept upon the testimony of intellect. The only logical alternative is to deny the validity of intellect altogether. And that, I take leave to say, is what is done by the school of which Mr. Spencer is so accomplished a representative. His philosophy is nothing but a gigantic attempt to explain the real, the living, by mechanism.† And it fails for the reason which I have indicated in a previous portion of this chapter: mechanics being nothing but an abstract science, and its properties mere abstractions. If the intellect is valid, the true conclusion can never be Atheism or Agnosticism, but

* *Prasna-Upanishad*, ii. 6.

† It is hardly too much to say that Mr. Spencer makes of consciousness nothing more than a simple accompaniment of merely nervous functions.

must be either Theism or some higher form of Pantheism, which is really, in good logic, a kind of Theism.

But, it may be said, the conception of God involves us in invincible antinomies. I am far from denying it. Whenever we approach too near to ultimate questions, there are those dread forms to drive us back with that flaming sword which turns every way to keep the way of the tree of life. We should remember, however, that while in the finite, contradictories are in opposition, in the Absolute they find their union. Still antinomies, like miracles, are not to be needlessly multiplied. They are needlessly multiplied by many writers in great credit at the present day; by those, to give one example, who tell us that a cause cannot be absolute because it exists in relation to its effects. It is a mere verbal puzzle. The idea of the Absolute is not incompatible with the idea of relation, although with the idea of necessary relation to the finite it is incompatible. This, by the way. I should here enter a *caveat*, which current literature shows to be abundantly necessary. Let me not, for a moment, be supposed to hold that our human and relative notions are the measure of the Absolute and Divine. The Infinite and Eternal is not " a magnified, non-natural man;" nor can our speech do more than most dimly adumbrate Him. " Pour dire ce qu'il est, il faut etre Lui-même." How predicate ratiocination of Him to whom all things are manifest, or free action of Him who cannot swerve from the law of righteousness which Himself is? Reason and liberty are indeed in Him, in essence and in truth, but under a form quite unknown to us, inconceivable by us, "beyond the reaches of our souls." All our words, essentially phenomenal and relative, are but sensuous symbols of the great Noumenal Fact, concealing while they express; "broken lights," distorting while they reveal. "The best in this kind are but shadows." Professor Huxley, in one of his most interesting essays, denounces as "senseless babble" "the demonstrations of those philosophers who undertake to tell us *all about the nature of God.*"* If such philosophers there be—I confess I have not met with them in the course of my own reading †— I cheerfully say Amen to this anathema. But surely there is some mean between knowing all about a thing and knowing nothing about it. Surely there is a dogged dogmatism of negation as irrational as the most daring dogmatism of assertion. I feel sure Professor Huxley would assent

* *On the Hypothesis that Animals are Automata*, published originally in the *Fortnightly Review*, November, 1874. The italics are mine. To the like effect Professor Tyndall somewhere writes: "We have as little fellowship with the Atheist who says that there is no God as we have with those Theists who profess to know what is in the mind of God."

† Spinoza, at the end of the first book of his *Ethics*, does, indeed, write, "I have now explained the nature of God and its properties." But it is not, probably, Spinoza whom Professor Huxley had in view—if, indeed, he had any one in view.

to this. Nor can I refrain from cherishing the charitable hope that when he and many other eminent men make profession of Agnosticism, they really mean to deny, not what I have called Rational Theism, but what Mr. Tyndall has termed "the more grotesque forms of the theological." * I am surprised that they should think this worth their while. The popular god, in all religions, is a thing of shreds and patches, a vice of gods, and cannot possibly be other. Comte has well spoken of that primary tendency in man to import the sense of his own nature in the radical explanation of all phenomena whatever. Nor is this tendency peculiar to man. We find it in other animals, very clearly marked. Deep down in the most secret recesses of sentient existence are the roots of the religious consciousness.

We may safely admit, then, that anthropomorphic conception based upon analogy is the simplest element in religion. And how little beyond that simplest element can the great mass of men soar? They are, in Swift's trenchant phrase, as incapable of thinking as they are of flying. While the sage is on the mount, in rapt

* Professor Huxley is himself my warrant for this hope. In replying to an article of mine, he cites the well-known words of Spinoza: "Per Deum intelligo ens absolute infinitum, hoc est substantiam constantem infinitis attributis," and pronounces "The God so conceived is one that only a very great fool would deny, even in his heart."—*Fortnightly Review*, December, 1886, p. 799.

communion with the Highest, they demand a golden calf as a present deity. And if Aaron consents, it is not only, nor chiefly, for the personal reason "il faut vivre"—although here, too, I suppose the law of supply and demand prevails—but out of good nature; nay, out of piety, lest the people be godless altogether. Surely to such as, rightly or wrongly, account themselves to have attained "a purer air," the proper attitude to what they deem popular superstition is that of indulgent toleration, whereof Plato has left us so conspicuous an example. Mr. Herbert Spencer well writes, "Through the gross body of dogmas, traditions and rites, a soul of truth is always visible—dimly or clearly, as the case may be. . . . Though from higher perceptions they hide the abstract verity within them; yet to lower perceptions they render this verity more appreciable than it would otherwise be. They serve to make real and influential over men that which would otherwise be unreal and uninfluential. Or we may call them the protective envelopes, without which the contained truth would die; . . . modes of manifestation of The Unknowable; and as having this for their warrant."* Zeal against superstition! Good, if usually a trifle ridiculous. But superstition is not the worst of errors. Take care that while you root up the tares, you do not root up the wheat also; that in trying to purify the

* *First Principles*, § 33.

popular belief you do not destroy it. There is in the *Mesnevî Sherif* of Jelâlu-d'-Dîn, the illustrious Saint and Doctor of Islâm, a striking and pathetic story in which this great lesson, so little apprehended by the sectaries, whether of Puritanism or of physics, is powerfully inculcated. "Moses," we read, "in his wanderings in the wilderness, came upon a shepherd, who was praying to God in the fervour of his soul, and saying, 'Oh, my Master, my Lord, would that I knew where I might find Thee, and become Thy servant. Would that I might tie Thy shoelatchet, and comb Thy hair, and wash Thy robes, and kiss Thy beautiful feet, and sweep Thy chamber, and serve the milk of my goats to Thee, for whom my heart crieth out.' And the anger of Moses was kindled, and he said to the shepherd, 'Thou blasphemest. The Most High has no body, and no need of clothing, nor of nourishment, nor of a chamber, nor of a domestic; thou art an infidel.' And the heart of the shepherd was darkened, for he could make to himself no image of one without bodily form and corporal wants; and he gave himself up to despair and ceased to serve God. And God spake unto Moses and said, 'Why hast thou driven my servant away from me? Every man has received from me his mode of being, his way of speech. What is evil in thee is good in another. What is poison to thee is honey to him. Words are nothing to me. I regard the heart. The compass serves only to direct the prayers of those who are without the Kêbeh. Within, no one knows the use of it.'" Such is the apologue of the great Sûfi, and surely it is well worth pondering. We are too apt to undervalue that exceeding great multitude of people who are simply good and religious-minded, wholly undisturbed by the anxious questionings which shake the world. They are not intellectually considerable; mostly fools, perhaps. Yes. But diviner lips than Carlyle's have said, "Take heed that ye despise not one of these little ones." "Babes and sucklings." I grant it. But to them are ofttimes revealed things hidden from the wise and prudent. The difficulties, the doubts which, like evil spirits that no exorcism can banish, haunt our philosophic and scientific schools, trouble them not—

"In den heitern Regionen
Wo die reinen Formen wohnen."

Unconsciously, passively, they, it may well be, have attained the higher synthesis withheld from us: and the problems which darken our horizon have melted into floating clouds for them, in the ampler æther, the diviner air, of a nearer heaven.

Unquestionably, of all those problems the most terrible is the existence, not of the Absolute, but of the Perfect Being. Hard is it to conceive how the Supreme Self, in whose unmoved and immoveable calm all ideals are realized, could have become an active cause. It is infinitely harder to conciliate the existence of a Perfect Creator or First Cause with the existence of such a world as this. No doubt those Pessimist philosophers who pronounce it the worst of possible worlds, carry their sad doctrine to an unwarrantable length: we do not know what is possible. But certainly it must, if viewed by itself, appear to any one who has not closed the eyes of his understanding, to be at the best the work of a very narrowly restricted or of a very imperfect goodness. "That was the door to which I found no key." Resignation is the last word of philosophy as of religion; of Goethe as of St. Augustine. Conscience alone helps us by its testimony, "God is a righteous Judge." There is a powerful passage in Schopenhauer, where he formulates the stern doctrine that the condition of "the purblind race of miserable men" cannot be other than it is, because justice reigns in the universe. "Do we desire," asks that profound and bitter thinker, "to know what men, morally considered, are worth as a whole and in general? We have only to consider their fate as a whole and in general. That is want, wretchedness, affliction, misery, and death. Eternal justice reigns. If men were not, as a whole, worthless, their fate would not be so sad. In this sense we may say the world itself is the judgment of the world. If we could lay all the misery of the world in one balance, and all the guilt of the world in another, the needle would certainly point to the centre." What an overwhelming, what a piercing thought is this! And yet, if we consider the rest of sentient existence, groaning and travailing in pain together with us, it is but as a flash of lightning illuminating an unfathomable abyss. "Behold the spectacle of brute nature; of impulses, feelings, propensities, passions, which in us are ruled, or repressed, by a superintending reason, but from which, when ungovernable, we shrink, as fearful and hateful. . . . Millions of irrational creatures surround us, and it would seem as if the Creator had left part of His work in its original chaos, so monstrous are these beings, which move, and feel, and act without reflection and without principle. . . . [They] pass to and fro, in their wildness and isolation, no yoke on their neck, or 'bit in their lips,' the enemies of all they meet, yet without the capacity of self-love. They live on one another's flesh by an original necessity of their being; their eyes, their teeth, their claws, their muscles, their voice, their walk, their structure within, all speak of violence and blood. They seem made to inflict pain; they rush on their prey with fierceness, and devour it with greediness. There is scarcely a passion or a feeling which is sin in man, but is found brute and irresponsible in them." * Well might Dr. Arnold say, "The whole subject of the brute creation is one of such painful mystery that I dare not approach it." The curse which justly lies on

* Cardinal Newman's *Discourses to Mixed Congregations*, p. 273. It is worth while to compare the following striking passage of Schopenhauer: " In this respect the condition of the animal world, left to itself, in uninhabited countries, is especially instructive. A fine picture of it and of the sufferings which, without the co-operation of man, nature herself prepares, is given by Humboldt in his *Ansichten der Natur*, nor does he omit to cast a glance at the analogous suffering of the human race, always and everywhere at variance with itself. However, in the simple, easily viewed life of the beasts the nothingness and vanity of the striving of the whole phenomenon becomes more clearly apprehensible. The multiplicity of the organization, the artistic skill of the means whereby each is fitted to its element and its prey, here clearly contrasts with the want of any one permanent final end: instead of it is exhibited only momentary pleasure, fleeting enjoyment conditioned by want, much and long suffering, constant war—bellum omnium—each in turn hunter and hunted, oppressions, want, need, and anguish, crying and howling; and so it goes on in secula seculorum until the crust of the planet breaks again. Junghuhn relates that in Java he saw a vast area entirely covered with skeletons, and took it for a battle-field. They were, however, merely skeletons of great turtles, five feet long, three feet broad, and of the same height, which, in order to lay their eggs, came this way from the sea, and then were set upon by wild dogs (*canis rutilans*), who, with their united strength, lay them on their backs, tear open the lower armour, that is the little shells of the belly, and so devour them alive. But it often happens that a tiger falls on the dogs when so engaged. All this suffering repeats itself thousands of times, year after year. For what were these turtles born? For what crime must they endure this torment? For what end this horrible scene?"—*Die Welt als Wille*, etc., Ergänzungen zum zweiten Buch Kap. 28.

us, extends to them guiltless. Such is "the burden and the mystery of all this unintelligible world." Nor is there any alleviation of it save in the testimony of the inner oracle: "Thou hast made us: Thou art just." This is the one anchor of the soul, sure and steadfast; the primary, the deepest of our certitudes—that justice rules the world, and that in loving justice and hating iniquity we are fellow-workers with the Highest. I wrote just now that resignation is the last word. And yet, not quite the last; happily for us. There is that other word of the indestructibility of our doing, common to all the great religions of the world, and so strangely and vividly pronounced by the one of them which has been embraced by the largest number of our race, I mean the Buddhist: that our personality is impressed upon our acts, and raises them from the phenomenal order, and seals them for eternity. Mere dreams of shadows as we are, we *can* follow the law within, we *can* do good. That is certain. And in that certitude the wisest and best of mankind have ever found "amid the encircling gloom," "a light unto their feet," guiding them from the phenomenal to the noumenal world. "Exortum est in tenebris lumen rectis." We will speak of this in the next chapter.

CHAPTER VI.

THE INNER LIGHT.

" LET us consider what happens in conversation, in reveries, in remorse, in times of passion, in surprises, in the instruction of dreams wherein often we see ourselves in masquerade—the droll disguises only magnifying and enhancing a real element, and forcing it on our distinct notice—we shall catch many hints that will broaden and lighten into knowledge of the Secret of Nature. All goes to show that the soul in man is not an organ, but animates and exercises all the organs; is not a function like the power of memory, of calculation, of comparison, but uses these as hands and feet; is not a faculty, but a light; is not the intellect or will, but the master of the intellect and the will; is the background of the being in which they lie, an immensity not possessed, and that cannot be possessed. . . . Of this pure nature every man is, at some time, sensible. Language cannot paint it with his colours. It is too subtile. It is indefinable, immeasurable, but we know that it pervades and contains us. . . . The sovereignty of this nature whereof we speak is made known by its independency of those limitations which circumscribe us on every hand. . . . Before the revelations of the soul, Time, Space, and Nature shrink away. . . . With each divine impulse the mind reads the thin rinds of the visible and finite, and comes out into eternity, and inspires and expires its air. . . . By the necessity of our constitution, a certain enthusiasm attends the individual's consciousness of that divine presence. The character and duration of this influence vary with the state of the individual from an ecstasy and trance and prophetic inspiration—which is its rare appearance—to the faintest glow of virtuous emotion in which it warms, like our household fires, all the families and associations of men, and make society possible."* So Emerson, in one of the most striking and suggestive of his *Essays*. Does the reader exclaim, "But this is mysticism!"? Certainly it is. And mysticism is the proper complement of that Rational Theism which we considered in the last chapter; its office to point from the phenomenal to the noumenal, from that which seems to that which is. It is based upon what I take leave to call the indubitable fact, that the spirit of man comes in contact with a Higher Spirit whose manifestations carry with them their own proof, and are moral in their nature, are out of time and place, are enlightening,

* Pages 221-231, Macmillan's edition.

purifying, and are therefore, in a true sense, ascetic. Here is that core of nature—"der Kern der Nature"—which, as Goethe says, must be looked for in men's hearts. The mystic is one who knows divine things otherwise than by hearsay, who sees them by an inner light; one to whom the Infinite and Eternal is no mere article of belief, but an experience. The mystical doctrine, in its essence, is that the highest in man can hold immediate intercourse with the Highest in the universe, that the human soul can enjoy direct communion with the Supreme Object, to which neither the senses nor the logical understanding can attain. I shall proceed briefly to survey the chief systems in which that doctrine has been clothed. And I shall then consider the especial significance of the expression which it has found in modern philosophy.

First, then, let us go back three or four thousand years in the history of our race and look at the primitive wisdom stored up for us in the *Upanishads*, and particularly in the *Katha Upanishad*, the most perfect specimen of mystic Hindu philosophy. The Brahmin Vêgasravasa, desirous of heavenly rewards, surrendered at a sacrifice all that he possessed. Faith entered into the heart of his son Nakiketas and he said, " Dear father, to whom wilt thou give me?" He said it a second and a third time. The father angrily replied, "I shall give thee unto death." The rash promise had to be kept, like Jephthah's. Nakiketas goes to the abode of Yama, the Regent of the Dead, and finds there none to receive him. After three days Yama returns, and by way of reparation for his want of hospitality to "a venerable guest, a Brahmin," promises to grant him three boons, whatever he may choose. The third boon which Nakiketas demands is "a knowledge of what there is in the great Hereafter." Yama begs him to ask for something else. "On this point even the Gods have formerly doubted. It is not easy to understand. The subject is subtle. Choose sons and grandsons who shall live a hundred years; choose the wide abode of earth, abundant harvests, fair maidens with their chariots and musical instruments." "No," says Nakiketas, "these things last but till to-morrow, for they wear out the vigour of the senses. Keep thou thy horses: keep dance and song for thyself. No man can be made happy by wealth. Shall we possess wealth when we see thee? What mortal, slowly decaying here below, would delight in long life after he has duly weighed the pleasures which arise from beauty and love?" So he presses for his boon. And at last Yama unfolds in mystic language the supreme secret. "The good is one thing: the pleasant is another. The wise prefer the good to the pleasant. The fool chooses the pleasant through greed and avarice. This is the world, he thinks; there is no other. Thus he falls again and again under my sway."* And then Yama expounds the doctrine of the Self—*Âtman*—infinite, invisible, divine, life of the world and life of our life; of whom many are not able to hear, whom many, even when they hear of Him, do not comprehend. This Self is not born, it dies not; it sprang from nothing, nothing sprang from it. It is not killed though the body is killed. If the slayer thinks that he slays, if the slain thinks that he is slain, they do not understand: for this does not slay, neither is that slain. Lesser than the least and greater than the greatest, this Self is seated in the breast of every living thing. This the passionless sage beholds and his sorrows are left behind. The sage that finds in his heart the infinite all-pervading Self no longer sorrows. There is, then, as the great teacher, Death, unfolds the mystery, one Reality and only one; and the highest wisdom is for a man to see that he is one with this one Reality, this characterless thought, which like the ether is everywhere, in a continuous plenitude of being. It is *Mâya*, the self-feigning world fiction, which has feigned itself from everlasting, that presents the variety of experience, the duality of subject and object, and

---

* He is subject to perpetual rebirth and death.

these melt away into unity in the light of the ecstatic vision.

But how may a man thus put aside the veil of *Mâya*, transcend the illusion of phenomena, and attain to this intuition of the Self? "Not by the *Veda*," Yama teaches, "nor by understanding, nor by much learning; neither he that has not ceased from evil, nor he that is not concentrated, nor he whose mind is not quiescent, can reach this Self by spiritual insight."

I have dwelt thus much upon this *Upanishad* because here we have the substance of Aryan mysticism in its most ancient expression: the dominant idea, however variously developed, of all the schools of Hindu theosophy, including the Buddhist. And if from India we turn to Greece, we find the same thought gradually unfolded. Pythagoras is little more to us than a name. Certain, however, it is that he lived chiefly in the memory of his countrymen as the founder of a mystical system, derived probably from the East, of which "Know thyself" was the cardinal precept. And what shall we say of Socrates, "the religious missionary doing the work of a philosopher," to use Mr. Grote's happy phrase? That, Daimon, or Deity,* of his, an internal guide, not

---

* I am following Kühner. See his *In Xenophontis Commentarios Prologomena*, § 5, "De Socratis Demonio," the best account of the matter with which I am acquainted, and one of the briefest.

peculiar to him, but, as he taught, apprehensible by all men who piously and holily worship the Gods and preserve their bodies pure and chaste, what is it but the light spoken of in the *Brihadâranyaka Upanishad*; the light within the heart, which when the sun has sunk, and the moon has set, and all sounds are hushed, still illumines man, the light of the Self, which is other than the body and the senses? This was the kernel of the teaching for which he witnessed a good confession. It was his great achievement to recall philosophy from the beggarly elements of the physical world to the study of human nature: to maintain, in opposition to the sophists, that the true point of departure is to be sought not in the senses, but in thought, in the mind. And this is the keynote of the whole doctrine of Plato, who, in the striking words of Mr. Maurice, enfranchised men from systems, and sent them to seek for wisdom in the quiet of their own hearts. There can be no question at all that in the Platonic *Dialogues* we have the seeds of the mysticism which attained its full growth in the great school of Alexandria, seeds fated to develop according to the necessary laws which govern the growth of ideas. Plato seeks out, in the multitude of individual, variable, contingent things, their principles, to which they owe what they possess of general, of durable, that is to say, their ideas. These he reaches by stripping finite things of their limitations, their individuality. And above the hierarchy of ideas—the first of them—is the Sovereign Principle, the Supreme Unity, Absolute Beauty, Absolute Truth, Absolute Good, the life of our life and the light of spirits. The Neo-Platonists, going beyond their master, but following logically his method, deny to this Divine principle diversity of attributes, they divest it wholly of finite conditions. They make it uncharacterized, abstract, innominate, a simple undetermined essence—for they agree with Spinoza, "Omnis determinatio negatio est"—transcending existence and not cognizable by reason. It is in the soul's intuition of this Supreme Reality, in apprehension of unity with it, that Plotinus,* the greatest of his school—"magnus ille Platonicus," St. Augustine calls him—places the *summum bonum*. Half dust, half deity, he deems, is man, but the soul, divine in its nature, a portion of the Divinity imprisoned

---

* For some exceedingly interesting and acute remarks on Plotinus, see Schopenhauer's *Fragmente zur Geschichte der Philosophie*, § 7. Schopenhauer holds—and gives weighty reasons for holding—that the doctrine taught by this very considerable thinker, and by the Neo-Platonists generally, was essentially Indo-Egyptian, the Platonic philosophy merely serving as a vehicle wherein to convey it. "Plotinos ... und die Neuplatoniker überhaupt, nicht eigentliche Philosophen, nicht ... Selbstdenker sind; sondern was sie vortragen ist eine fremde, überkommene, jedoch von ihnen meistens wohl verdauete und assimilirte Lehre. Es ist nämlich Indo-Aegyptische Weisheit, die sie der Griechischen Philosophie haben einverleiben wollen und als hiezu passendes Verbindungslied, oder Uebergangsmittel, oder menstruum, die Platonische Philosophie, namentlich ihrem in's Mystische hinüberspielenden Theile nach, gebrauchen."

in this house of clay (just as, according to the similitude of the *Upanishads*, the light shining in many houses is one with the sun) is the real Self. To deliver it from the prison where it languishes, expiating the sins committed in former existences, is the one true end. And the way to attain thereto is a *Via Purgativa*, a way of purification from earthly desires, of complete abstraction from phenomenal things, which leads to annihilation of self, to abolition of consciousness, until in the transcendent state of ecstasy (ἔκστασις) the distinction between the intelligent subject and the intelligible object ceases: the Supreme Perfection is seen, not without—ὡς ἐν ἄλλῳ—but within, and unity is gained. This is precisely the ecstatic vision of Vedic theosophy, and they who enjoy it lose themselves in the one and only Self, as rivers lose themselves in the sea. It is not substantially different from that attainment of perfect indetermination, utter impersonality, called by the Buddhists *Nirvâna*, a bliss, we must remember, which according to the *Book of the Great Decease*, a man "while yet in this visible world may bring himself to the knowledge of, and continue to realize, and see face to face." Death does but set the seal to this union with the Supreme Reality. "I go," said the dying Plotinus, "to bear the Divine within me to the Divine in the universe."

These words of Plotinus might no less fitly have been uttered by a Moslem mystic than by a Vedic theosophist or a follower of Gotama. The late Professor Palmer * held Sûfism to be really the development of the primeval religion of the Aryan race. Certain it is that its root idea is identical with the root idea of the *Upanishads*. The spiritual life is usually described by the Sûfite writers under the allegory of a journey, the goal of which is union with God. But at the outset, we meet with a paradox. It is one of their maxims that there is no road from man to God, because the nature of God is illimitable and infinite, without beginning or end or even direction, whereas the perception of man's understanding, "the intelligence of life," as the Prophet calls it, is restricted to the finite. It is by a Divine light, "the light in the heart," in Mohammed's phrase ("the light of God," the Sûfite writers commonly term it), that the Divine proximity is revealed: that mysterious proximity spoken of in the *Qu'rân*, "He is with you wherever you are," and hidden from man by the illusion of the senses. And so Jelâl, the great Sûfite saint and poet, in the *Mesnevî*:

"Beyond our senses lies the world of unity.
Desir'st thou unity? Beyond the senses fly."

The first stage in the journey is the purification of the heart from worldly impressions and desires, from the animal, the brutal, the fiendish, by the

* See his *Oriental Mysticism*, Pref. p. xi. In what follows regarding Moslem mysticism I have largely availed myself of this work.

study of the *Qu'rân*, and the practice of its precepts and the discipline of asceticism. Thus does a man attain to self-knowledge, and thus does he soon arrive at the Divine light. Now this light is the nature of God, and hence the verse of the *Mesnevî* :

"I am not I : the breath I breathe is God's own breath."

Similar sayings are common in the Sûfite books. When the traveller acknowledges in his heart, they tell us, that God only always was, that God only always will be, his eyes are opened to the inner meaning of the formula, "There is no God but God," and he has closed the door upon existence and non-existence. He who has reached thus far has performed what is called the journey to God. It remains that he journey *in* God, drawn on to ever closer union by the splendour and sweetness of the Divine perfections, until he is lost in the ocean of the Divine love,* reabsorbed in the Divine intelligence—the true end and purpose of his existence.

Professor Palmer describes the system of the Sûfis, which he considers to steer a mid-course between the Pantheism of India and the Deism of the *Qu'rân*, as an attempt to reconcile philosophy with the Moslem revelation, by assigning a mystical and allegorical interpretation to all religious doctrines and precepts. For myself,

* Compare Keble—
"Till in the ocean of Thy love
We lose ourselves in heaven above."

I must say that I see no great difference between the Indian and the Sûfite mystics in respect of their Pantheistic tendencies. Indeed, what I have written will, I think, sufficiently show that the mysticism of the *Upanishads*, the Neo-Platonists, and the Sûfites is substantially identical. Let us come now to the fourth great mystical school, the Christian, which although largely influenced by Plotinus and his followers, through the writings of St. Augustine and still more of Dionysius, the so-called Areopagite, is clearly marked off from all other schools by its doctrines of the Trinity and creation. In Catholic theology, the three Persons of the Godhead are conceived of under the similitude of a Divine circle having no necessary relations save those which unite them; self-sufficient and not implying any other existence. Moreover, the universe is regarded not as engendered by God, nor as emanating from the Divine substance, but as freely created out of nothing. A great gulf, an infinite abyss, is held to separate the Creator even from the highest and most perfect of creatures; a difference not of degree but of essence, to divide the human personality from the Divine. Still, Christian, like all other mysticism, aims at grasping the Ultimate Reality, at direct communion with the Highest, and professes to open a way of escape from the blinding tyranny of sense, to transcend the veil of illusory phenomena, and to set free its votaries by an inward vision. The fundamental thought of the Christian religion is that there are two orders, commonly called nature and grace; the one discernible by sense and understanding, the other by a spiritual sight. From the first until now the mystic light of Tabor, before which the phenomenal world fades away into nothingness, has ever burned at the inner shrine of Christianity. Thence has come the illumination of those who, age after age, have entered most fully into the secret of Jesus; thence are the bright beams which stream from the pages of *St. John's Gospel*, *St. Augustine's Confessions*, *The Imitation of Christ*, *The Divine Comedy*, *The Pilgrim's Progress*. The supreme blessedness of man, as all Christian teaching insists, is the vision, in the great Hereafter, of Him who is the substance of substances, the life of life, who alone, in the highest sense, is—"I am," His incommunicable name—and who, even in this world, is seen by the pure in heart. "External nature," St. Bernard writes, "is but the shadow of God, the soul is His image. The chief, the special mirror in which to see Him is the rational soul finding itself." And he continues, "If the invisible things of God are understood and clearly seen by the things which have been made, where, I ask, rather than in His image (within us) can be found more deeply imprinted the traces of the knowledge of Him? Whosoever therefore thirsteth to see his God, let him cleanse from every stain his mirror, let him purify his heart by faith."* The substance of Christian mysticism is presented in this passage of St. Bernard. The allegories used by spiritual writers to expound it are various. St. Bonaventura treats of the *Journey of the Soul to God*, St. John Climacus of the *Ladder of Paradise*, St. Teresa of the *Interior Castle*. But their doctrine is ever that which, as we have seen, is so emphatically enforced by the great non-Christian schools of mysticism, that the Being of Beings is cognizable only by the purified mind. At first the Supreme Reality appears to the inner eye as darkness, whence Dionysius the Carthusian tells us, "Mystica theologia est ardentissima divini caliginis intuitio." This apparent darkness is, however, in itself light, dazzling and blinding in its splendour, and it gradually becomes visible as such, when the spiritual vision is purged and strengthened and renewed by the stripping off of all love for the relative, the dependent, the phenomenal, and by the assiduous practice of all moral virtues. The reader who will consult the books of mystical theology—for example, the great treatise of St. John of the Cross, called *The Dark Night of the Soul*—will find all details of this process. It is an active process at first, but by-and-by changes into a passive, wherein the soul undergoes search-

* *De Domo Interiori*, c. 6. This tractate is sometimes attributed to Hugh of St. Victor.

ing torture. There are pages in the writings of St. Catherine of Sienna and in those of Angela da Foligno, to mention no others, which I can only describe as appalling. To the Purgative succeeds the Illuminative, and to this the Unitive Way, and silence is accounted an indispensable help for walking in these paths of holiness. "Sacrum silentium," St. Bonaventura calls it, and he reckons two stages; the first in speech, the second in thought. "The perfection of recollection," he says, "is for a man to be so absorbed in God as to forget all else and himself also, and sweetly to rest in God, every sound of mutable thoughts and affections being hushed."* Thus does the soul attain to that union with its Supreme Object which is brought about by the love of God, and which Gerson terms "transformation." "Amor," says this Doctor Christianissimus, "rapit ad amatum et ecstasim facit;" and ecstasy he describes as a state of the mind which not only weakens, but, for the time, annihilates all the inferior powers. It is a state in which a man passes out of himself, and the ordinary cognitive faculty is transcended; the body seems as dead and the senses are hushed, but the will, retaining full vigour, is absorbed in God.

Enough has perhaps been said to indicate,

* *De Profectu Religiosorum*, c. 1.

if but in outline, and as by a few strokes of a pencil, the main features of the four chief systems of mysticism which the history of the world exhibits to us. It is hardly necessary to remark upon the dangers which, in greater or less degree, are incident to them all. A pregnant saying of the *Upanishads* declares the Path of Release to be "fine as the edge of a razor." On one side of it lie the deep gulfs of madness: on the other the abysses of sensuality. The perpetual analysis of motives and brooding over circumstances, the heightened self-consciousness which cannot but arise in a life of contemplation, the shock caused to this frail tenement of clay by perpetual converse with the supersensible, are masterful incentives of insanity: ἔνθεος καὶ ἔκφρων the Greeks truly said. Again, mysticism delights in imagery, and, indeed, can no otherwise be expressed or taught, and its images have ever been borrowed from the strongest of human emotions, the passion of love. Thus the favourite text-book of Christian mystics is the *Cantica Canticorum*, and with them this Hebrew epithalamium is interpreted as a song of Divine love celebrating the nuptials of the soul with God. Hence it is said, "Deus osculatur, amplectitur animam:" and again, "Anima fruitur Verbo sponso." But in spite of the high and sacred meaning which has been shadowed forth by such similitudes, and although millions have proved that innocence and wisdom are combined in them, there are only too many sad and terrible examples justifying the melancholy dictum, "Qui veut faire l'ange fait la bête." It is, however, a very palpable fact, worthy of being deeply pondered, that in the Catholic Church mysticism has been incomparably more healthy, more sober, more beautiful, than anywhere else. How could it be otherwise when the eye of the mystic is ever turned, not upon some vague abstraction of the Absolute, but upon "God manifest in the flesh," upon the glorious figure of Jesus Christ, full of grace and truth? It can hardly be from prejudice, certainly it is not from any conscious undervaluing of other religions, but nowhere else can I discern such perfect specimens of spiritual excellence as Christianity affords, as St. Bernard, St. Francis of Assisi, St. Philip Neri, St. Francis de Sales, St. Catherine of Sienna, and St. Teresa. And it is the doctrine and discipline of the Catholic Church that have made and fashioned them; it is her symbolism, historical, social, visible, that has provided for their highest aspirations congruous expression, and restrained them within the bounds that may not be passed in this phenomenal world. While as the type of Christian mysticism, practically exhibited "for human nature's daily food," it is enough to point to *The Imitation of Christ*. Most noteworthy, too, is it that when the paramount authority of dogmatic theology has been lost sight of, the speculations of medieval and modern transcendentalists have usually issued in Nihilistic Pessimism. Even in mystical writers whose orthodoxy is not impugned, we come upon statements such as these: that God not only is, but also is not, the Infinite Spirit; that He transcends both finity and infinity; that He is more truly not-Being than Being, and may, not improperly, be called Nothing. The reader might suppose me to be citing Hegel, but he will find all this, and much more to the same effect, in the books of medieval mysticism. The theologians do not deny that there may be sound sense underlying these transcendent speculations, so long as the Arachne clue of authoritative dogma is held fast in the labyrinth. Once lose it, and you will be compelled to assert either that God is unknowable, or that the inmost essence of the Divinity is the clean opposite of what Christianity declares it to be. And then God will appear as the Supreme Evil, striving to redeem and raise itself by evolving the universe: a doctrine which was eloquently preached in the Middle Ages by the celebrated Dominican Meister Eckhart, and which has received its most complete and powerful statement from that stupendous genius, Jacob Böhmen. But if the mystic transcends time and space, the writer on mysticism enjoys no such privilege, and I must no longer dwell upon this curious and fascinating subject. My present concern is with what I may call the normal aspects of mysticism. I have, of course, chiefly spoken of it as manifested in clearest relief and fullest development by its great lights and philosophical teachers. But we must not forget that it has ever been the kernel of the religion of the common people, whose instincts are, usually, as true as their reasonings are false. It is a fact of human nature, and is, therefore, exhibited, at all times, in history: it is a fact which confronts us to-day. And, in my judgment, contemporary mysticism possesses a peculiar significance when viewed in the light—or darkness—of modern philosophical speculation. What that significance is I shall now endeavour to indicate.

And first let me set down briefly where, as it seems to me, the age is in respect of its metaphysics. One of the most hopeful of its characteristics is that the license of affirmation, indulged by system-mongers, is becoming daily more and more discredited. The chief philosophical achievement of the last two hundred years has been of a kind to check such license; and European thought, after a century of not very fruitful wanderings, is going back to Kant. His *Critique of Pure Reason* deals precisely with the question, What are the limits of sane affirmation? and we may confidently say that none who have not read, marked, learned, and inwardly digested it, are competent even to discuss metaphysical problems as they present themselves to the modern mind. But it is not my purpose here to enter upon an examination of that great work. My present inquiry is this; taking it as it stands, assuming, for the sake of argument, that its theory of cognition is substantially correct, where are we in regard to The Great Enigma of which man ever seeks the solution? that momentous question which, by a law of his nature, he cannot keep from asking—the question which Nakiketas put to Yama about the Self and that which dwells in the great hereafter? Such, and no other, is the scope of the *argumentum ad hominem* with which I shall be occupied in the remainder of this chapter.

The *Critique of Pure Reason*, then, is essentially a doctrine of nescience. Our first view of the world discloses to us phenomena which we take for realities. Kant purges our intellectual vision, and shows them to us for mere phantasmagoria of sense. And to these phantasmagoria he restricts our perception. The human understanding, he insists, is shut up within the circle of our sensations and conceptions; these reveal to it merely phenomena, and beyond the sphere of phenomena all is a void for it. Time and space are mere mental forms; they have no reality, that is, no noumenal externality. The categories—conceptions which exhibit laws *a priori* to phenomena—are indeed ours; they are the moulds in which the materials presented by sense perception are arranged, and by means of them it is that synthetic judgments *a priori* are possible. But no faculty of the speculative reason has any objective worth, for the subject imposes its own forms on knowledge, and so makes it subjective. Even what is called "the law of causality" is subjective, a regulative principle. Again, what are termed "laws of nature" are in truth the forms of our intelligence which we apply to phenomena. And, more than this, the understanding cannot affirm anything about noumena—real things, things in themselves. The word finds place in the *Critique of Pure Reason* merely as the antithesis of phenomena. It expresses, Kant says, a limitary conception, and is therefore only of negative use. Noumena may exist, or they may not exist. All that is certain is that no faculty of the human understanding can discover anything about them. Such, in few words, and those as untechnical as the subject permits, are the main outlines of the *Critique of Pure Reason*. Its issue clearly is to annihilate dogmatism, affirmative or negative, and to warn us against venturing with the speculative reason beyond the limits of experience. Its practical operation will be evident at once, and may be held to warrant the title of *Der Alleszer-*

malmender, the Universal Crusher, which the Germans have given to its author. Take, for example, its effect upon the ordinary "proofs of the existence of God." The argument from causality is impugned, for if "the law of cause and effect" apply only to the world of the senses, no reasoning can be founded upon it which touches the conception of a world beyond sense. The other well-known Deistic demonstrations fare as badly. Kant insists that no unity of thought and being is knowable save the unity of experience, and that this is the sole realization, cognizable by the speculative reason, of the ideal to which men have ascribed the name of God. "If," he urges, "the Supreme Being forms a link in the chain of empirical conditions, it must be a member of the empirical series, and, like the lower members which it precedes, have an origin in some higher member of the series. If, on the other hand, we disengage it from the chain, and cogitate it as an intelligible being apart from this series of natural causes, how shall reason bridge the abyss that separates the latter from the former?"

Thus does Kant lead us into what may well be called "the dark night of the soul." The *Critique of Pure Reason* presents a striking parallel to the *Via Purgativa* of the mystics. The illusoriness of the phenomenal world, the impotency of the mere understanding to penetrate beyond it to the vision of a Reality transcending sense—these are its main lessons. It opens the disciples' eyes—Schopenhauer describes its effect as very like that of the operation for cataract upon a blind man—but it opens them to behold the great darkness. I said just now that it does not enable us even to assert the existence of the noumenal. And this is true, but it is a half-truth. Kant's language on this subject is not superficially consistent, although it is consistent, I think, in a deeper sense. He employs the word noumenal to express a limitary conception. He gives it a negative use. But it is worthy of notice that this is pretty much the sum of the knowledge of God to which, as the mystics of all schools teach, we can attain by means of the phenomenal order. They, in effect, allow to the human understanding rather a negative than a positive ideal of that transcendent Reality beyond appearances which eye hath not seen, nor ear heard, nor the heart of man conceived. And so St. Augustine, in the *De Ordine*:* "Of whom there is no knowledge in the human soul, save to know how it knows Him not;" or as we read in the *Upanishads*: "Words turn back from it, with the mind not reaching it." And hence the phrase common to them all: "The Divine Darkness." Is there any way in which this darkness may be made light for the disciple of Kant?

* "Cujus nulla scientia est in anima nisi scire quomodo eum nesciat" (ii. 18).

The master has answered that question in the *Critique of Practical Reason*, a work the true position of which is very little understood, even by some who undertake most confidently to expound his teaching. I suppose Heine has done more than any one else to mislead the world in general about it by the well-known passage in the *Ueber Deutschland*—inimitably witty it is, although one could wish that this bitter mocker had spared us his flouts and gibes upon so momentous a subject —the passage in which he represents the consternation that ensued when the sage of Königsberg had stormed the heavenly citadel and put the garrison to the sword. All the time-honoured proofs—the bodyguards—of the Divine Existence destroyed and the Deity Himself deprived of demonstration and laid low: supreme mercy, infinite goodness, the great hopes of the hereafter all gone, and the immortality of the soul in its last agony: on all sides the groans and rattle of death. Old Lampe, the philosopher's faithful servant, is in terror and tears at the catastrophe, and lets fall the umbrella, with which—a living image of Providence—he had followed his master for so many years. Kant's heart is softened, for he is not only a great metaphysician, but also a good-natured man. "No, this will never do," he reflects. "Poor old Lampe must have his God, or there will be no happiness for him: and man ought to be happy in this world: that is the dictate of the

Practical Reason. Very well: let the Practical Reason guarantee the existence of God." And so, with a wave of the magic wand of the Practical Reason, he resuscitates what the Speculative Reason had slain. Old Lampe is consoled, and the police cease from turning upon the philosopher the eyes of suspicion.

This excellent fooling of Heine's represents with sufficient accuracy the account of the *Critique of Practical Reason* generally current. But in truth it is mere fooling. Kant himself, who may surely be accepted as a tolerably good authority on the subject, tells us that the second *Critique* is the necessary complement of the first: another storey of the same edifice. He knew well that there is far more in the human consciousness than is explicable by "the pure forms of intuition," the concepts of the understanding, the ideas of reason; he knew well that the understanding is not the whole man, and that to confine us within the phantasmal circle of sense conception, and to shut us off from the intelligible world, is to doom us to moral and spiritual death. And the opening into this transcendent region, the revealing agency of supersensual realities he finds in the concept of Duty; a concept marked off from the notions of space, of time, of substance, and the like, by vast differences which prove its objective character. Here is the creative principle of morality, of religion; more sublime to Kant than the starry heavens, and rightly; for what are the starry heavens, in his philosophy, but a creation of sense, the product of the innate forms of time and space? But the Categorical Imperative is independent of time and space. "Cogita Deum, invenies Est, ubi Fuit et Erit esse non possunt. Ut ergo et tu sis, transcende tempus."* It is the precept of St. Augustine, and the *Critique of Practical Reason* is but an effort to accomplish it. To find the true Self, Kant transcends time and space and the vain shadows of the phenomenal world, and reaches *that perception of right and wrong in motives, and of the supreme claims of right upon our allegiance*, which testifies to him of God, Freewill, Immortality. "We recognize," he says, "in our moral being, the presence of a power that is supernatural." Now this recognition is a direct intuition of self-evident truth, pointing to that Supreme Reality of whom the Hebrew poet sang, "Clouds and darkness are round about Him, righteousness and judgment are the establishment of His throne." Thus does our darkness become light. It is the Kantian equivalent of the Illuminative Way of theology: and here the rigid analytical philosopher is in accord with all that is most mystical in modern literature. When Wordsworth testifies of conscience—

"As God's most intimate presence in the soul;
And His most perfect image in the world;"

---

* In *Joann. Evan. Tract.*, xxxviii. 10.

when Lord Tennyson declares—

> "If e'er when faith had fall'n asleep,
> I heard a voice, 'Believe no more,'
> And heard an ever-breaking shore,
> That tumbled in the Godless deep;
>
> "A warmth within the heart would melt
> The freezing reason's colder part,
> And like a man in wrath the heart
> Stood up and answer'd, 'I have felt;'"

when George Eliot proclaims that

> "In conscious triumph of the good within,
> Making us worship goodness that rebukes,
> Even our failures are a prophecy,
> Even our yearnings and our bitter tears,
> After that fair and true we cannot grasp;"

they all, in their varying moods, teach Kant's doctrine of the Categorical Imperative; and are at one with the mystics of every age in pointing to the light guiding from the phenomenal to the noumenal world,

> "Letting us pent-up creatures through
> Into eternity—our due."

But though in this doctrine of the Categorical Imperative we have the essence of all mysticism, it must, I think, be allowed that Hartmann is well warranted when he says, "Unfortunately, Kant did not attain the same depth of insight in reference to *a priori* forms of intuition, as in the case of the forms of thought." The intuition of duty is but one of many faculties independent of sense perception which, as a matter of fact, exist in human nature. Or, to put the matter more accurately, that power within us which discerns the axioms of eternal righteousness is the very same, in root and substance, which grasps the facts and interprets the laws of a world beyond appearances. Unquestionably, there is in man an αἴσθησις τῆς ψυχῆς, a faculty of spiritual perception. Take the sense of personality, whereby we know the self of ours which is no phenomenon, but something more, abiding amid change, and so making experience possible: take the sense of force, possessing a permanence and reality not belonging to the phenomena by means of which we apprehend it, or the sense of power, of will—surely all these give us a glimpse into the noumenal world, an intuition of things in themselves. But again, consider the vast region—most real, however dim and ill-explored and infested by fools and knaves—the region of prescient instinct, of spiritual sight and hearing and contact, of abnormal psychical states, of seemingly miraculous powers. Nothing is easier than for the gainsayer to suspend upon his upturned nose the mass of evidence available regarding these things, and to take refuge in a stupid *a priori;* but nothing is more "unscientific," if science proceed upon observation and experience. I decline, indeed, to follow " Esoteric Buddhists " to the cloudy regions of Thibet. I hope I do not wrong them, but I frankly confess that their stock-in-trade appears to me to consist of fragments of a great religion wholly misinterpreted, and of tricks of jugglery imperfectly acquired. Their "Esoteric Buddhism" seems to me but a shoddy system, the worn-out linen of venerable sanctuaries ground down with non-adhesive Yankee glue. Still, where there is smoke—especially so thick a smother—there may be fire. And if the "Esoteric Buddhists" will show me the smallest scintilla of fact I will respect it, if not them. But let us go to a very different teacher, who, whatever we may think of his system, is assuredly in some respects the sanest of recent Teutonic philosophers. I am at a loss to conceive how any candid mind can read the section in Hartmann's great work, wherein he discourses of the manifestation of the Unconscious in bodily life, and resist the cogency of the data gathered by that most careful and critical observer from so many departments of physical science. If any fact is clear it is this, that not only in man, but in all animate existence, down to its lowest forms, we find a perceptive power transcending sense and reflection, and far more trustworthy. The subject is too large for me to enter upon. I can only refer those of my readers who would follow it out, to Hartmann's masterly treatment of it, merely observing here that the evidence for the facts of second sight, of presentiment, of presage, is so various, so abundant, and so overwhelmingly corroborated, that in the words of this clear and judicial writer, "for impartial judges, the absolute denial of such phenomena is consistent only with ignorance of the accounts of them." And these phenomena, he justly observes, are essentially mystical. Well warranted, too, must I account him when he reckons as mystics all great artists, for they do but body forth, according to their diverse gifts, what they have intuitively discerned in the high reason of their fancies; and all philosophers, so far as they are truly original, both because their greatest thoughts have never been the result of laborious effort, nay, nor of conscious induction, but have been apprehended by the lightning flash of genius, and also because their essential theme is connected with the one feeling only to be mystically apprehended, namely the relation of the individual to the Absolute. Of religion I need not speak. Every great faith of the world has originated in mysticism and by mysticism it lives; for mysticism is what John Wesley called "heart religion." When this dies out of any creed, that creed inevitably falls into the moribund decrepitude of mere formalism or superstition.

So much must suffice to indicate the transcendent importance which mysticism seems to me to possess in these days, when so many a fair philosophy lies in ruins, and time-honoured theologies are threatened with swift extinction, as mere collections of meaningless words about unintelligible chimæras. Founded as it is in that highest faculty which St. Bonaventura calls "apex mentis," mysticism is the impregnable citadel of the supersensible, a citadel which no *Zermalmender* shall ever overthrow, though he crush all else. But there are two objections to which, in concluding this chapter, I must briefly reply. First, it is said by an exceeding great multitude—Mr. Mill may serve as their spokesman—that "whether in the Vedas, the Platonists or the Hegelians, mysticism is nothing more nor less than ascribing objective existence to the subjective creation of our own faculties, to mere ideas of the intellect." * Surely this is a tyrannous *ipse dixit*, if ever utterance deserved to be so called. Why should I believe, upon the authority of those who confessedly do not speak as experts, that the choice specimens of human wisdom and virtue in all ages have been wrong, when they thought themselves to be holding communion with supersensible Realities? Is not their own account of the matter as credible as the hypothesis that they were given over to a strong delusion to believe a lie, that their highest vision was but a turning about in their own thoughts, as in the void inane? No;

* *System of Logic*, bk. v. chap. iii. § 4.

when the spirit is perfectly master of itself, when passion and interest are stilled for the moment, when there is a combined ease and energy of thinking which cannot be mistaken for vacancy of mind, I defy a man to believe that the intuitions of which he is conscious are illusory or merely subjective. He may say so when the hour is past, and he has been disobedient to the heavenly calling; but he did not think so when it was present. And here I would point to one most unquestionable and most significant fact. However strange, it is no less certain, that the farther we recede from mathematics and the formal teaching of logic— or, in other words, the nearer we approach to life and its perfections—the more delicate, subtle, and easily overlooked are the truths we come upon. The surest and most sacred verities are precisely those which appear the most fantastic illusions to such as have no real, no personal apprehension of them, who know them but as notions, and at second hand. Thus, who that has not experienced the tender passion, can endure the extravagances, the unreason, the madness—so he deems—which characterize it? But let Benedick fall in love, and he will be as insane as the rest of us. The true doctrine is that only those are verily and indeed out of their minds, out of harmony with life and nature, who do not confess the sway of the gentle goddess: "Alma Venus, quæ rerum naturam sola gubernas!" Birth, life, family, the state, the world's great order are all carried on by means of a passion which laughs at syllogisms, yet has a higher reason than all logic, which defies analysis, yet has "its deep foundation set under the grave of things." Now this has a direct bearing upon that highest kind of love and knowledge which makes the universe of the mystics. It is precisely in proportion as they do not argue that they are convincing; the secret of persuasion is theirs in a transcendent degree which no analytical philosopher has ever possessed. It is the easiest thing in the world to hold up their imaginations, their ecstasies, their visions and revelations to scorn as intellectual intoxication or mental disease. The hard, the impossible thing for one who has held high converse with the sages of the *Upanishads*, with Plotinus, with Jelâl, with St. Teresa, is to believe that what those great souls accounted the prime and only Reality was wholly unreal.

I say "*wholly* unreal." And this brings me to that second objection which is based upon the discrepancies and contradictions of mysticism. It is an objection that seems to fade away, when it is fairly considered. The primary position of the mystics is that highest truth is not so much intellectually known as spiritually felt: "cognoscendo ignoratur et ignorando cognoscitur." Theirs is a doctrine of divine nescience, or, in the words of the Areopagite, of negative theology. In the higher moods of spiritual exaltation the understanding is hushed and the light of sense goes out, paled before the splendour of the invisible world. Thus was it when St. Paul was rapt in ecstasy and—whether in the body or out of the body he could not tell—heard *arcana verba*, unspeakable words which it is not given to man to utter. Thus when St. Augustine and St. Monica held that memorable converse at Ostia, and passing in contemplation beyond the world of phenomena came to their own minds, and transcending self reached the Very Self (*Idipsum*) and were ravished and absorbed in the ineffable sweetness of the vision. Thus when St. Teresa in the fruition of that intimate union with her Divine Spouse, "in the centre of the soul, where illusion is impossible" was instructed by the light which is the life of men, without words or the use of any corporal faculty, in mysteries "too sublime to be spoken of in earthly speech, for they are figureless and formless." The feeling of the greatest saints has always been "Sacramentum regis abscondere bonum est;" it is good to conceal the secret of the King. And one reason why this is good is because that Divine Secret cannot be congruously conveyed in the language of sense perception: "transumanar significar *per verba* non si poria," sings Dante in the *Paradiso*. To attempt to render the noumenal in phenomenal symbols is, of necessity, to refract it, for the laws of the mind impose their own form upon ideas. The straight staff must seem bent when we view it in the pool. In our cognition divine things are discerned " per speculum et in ænigmate." The looking-glass of the human understanding cannot but reflect sensuous images. The accounts of the mystics are necessarily discrepant, and the discrepancy is due to the varying symbolisms used by them : symbolisms, for the most part traditional, inherited from the nation or school to which they belong. The very incongruity of human words as a vehicle of transcendental truth, accounts sufficiently for defects in its presentation. It has been well said that the speech of angels is music. And who can translate music? In the rendering of that celestial language into the tongues of men, it is much if any trace of its divine perfection remain. Certain it is that in the more popular, the more vulgar manifestations of religion, that is to say in the religion of the great majority, the mystical element, which is its life, will assume the most unlovely forms, until for the harmony of the spheres you have the howls of the Salvationists. True, too, is the saying, that the common people like to mix water with the wine of their belief. They usually mix a great deal : sometimes so much as to drown the precious drop from the " calix inebrians," " the chalice of the grapes of God." But it is still there, potent in its divine virtue to slake the thirst of human nature for a good transcending sense; to lift eyes, dim with tears and dull with pain, towards the Beatific Vision; to heal and strengthen feet, sore and weary from the rough ways of earth, for the steep ascent of Heaven.

CHAPTER VII.

THE CHRISTIAN SYNTHESIS.

SHALL we say, then, that the solution of The Great Enigma is given by what is called Theism of the natural order? A Theism at once rational and mystical, revealed by the world without us, and by the world within us, exhibiting the Absolute and Eternal as the First Cause and Final End of an universe where all is causation and finality, and as a Present Deity, whose temple is the purified heart, whose voice is the enlightened conscience? Assuredly we may say this. But is this all we can say? Or is there, among the world's religions, any to which, without making our reason blind, or our conscience dumb, we may join ourselves, as filling up the revelation of the external and internal universe, as corresponding with those religious instincts which we may assuredly trust, for they are part and parcel of our nature, as exhibiting the realities of which our sentiments are symbols?

It is held, as we all know, by many excellent and distinguished persons that this last question must receive a negative answer. They make of religion merely an emotion, an aspiration, and of religions merely temporary and fluxional hypotheses which have served to render the ideal accessible to the multitude. Professor Tyndall may serve, as well as another, for their spokesman:

"The error of the priests is this: that they are mechanics, not poets; and that they claim objective validity for that which springs from the innermost need and nature of man. It is against this objective rendering of the essentially ideal and poetic, that science, consciously, or unconsciously, wages war. Religion is as much a verity of human consciousness as any other of its facts, and against it, on its subjective side, the waves of science beat in vain. But when, manipulated by sacerdotal constructiveness, and mixed with imperfect or inaccurate historical data, and moulded by misapplied logic, it makes claims which traverse our knowledge of nature, then science, as in duty bound, stands as a hostile power in its path. Sooner or later, among thinking people, the temporary and fluxional rendering of religious mysteries will be abandoned, and the ideal will be universally recognized as capable only of ideal approach." *

---

* A widely read novelist translates this doctrine *ad populum* into the following profession of faith, put into the mouth of her hero. "My friends, the man who is addressing you to-night believes in God and in *Conscience*, which is God's witness in the soul, and in *Experience*, which is at once the record and the instrument of man's education at God's hands. He puts his whole trust, for life and death, *in God the Father Almighty:* in that force at the root of things which is revealed whenever a man helps his neighbour or a mother denies herself for her child: whenever a soldier dies without a murmur, or a sailor puts out into the darkness to rescue the perishing: whenever a workman throws mind and conscience into his work, or a

Now what are we to say of this pronouncement? I really must be permitted to say, plainly, that it seems to me a medley of commonplace and sophism. I am as ready as Professor Tyndall to reject "imperfect or inaccurate historical data," "misapplied logic," and "claims which traverse our knowledge of nature." But when, in the name of "science," he declares war against the "objective rendering of the essentially ideal and poetic," when he denies the claim to "objective validity" of "that which springs from the innermost need and nature of man," when he pronounces that the ideal is "capable only of ideal approach," he appears to me, *pace tanti viri*, to be talking grandiloquent nonsense. He might just as reasonably say that because the principle of life is spiritual and immaterial, we ought to support life only by spiritual and immaterial means, and not by anything so grossly material as meat and drink. The dweller in Cloud-Cuckoo Town may be able to live on mere abstractions. But assuredly they are not sufficient "for human nature's daily food." The subjective and unhistorical religion, or rather religiosity, which Professor Tyndall preaches, makes God into an impersonal force, with no objective character at all, or, at all events, undis-

statesman labours not for his own end, but for that of the State. He believes in an Eternal Goodness, and an Eternal Mind, of which nature and man are the continuous and only revelation."
—*Robert Elsmere*, c. xl.

tinguishable from human impulse. To speak of Christianity alone, it will be found impossible, in fact, to separate the idea of Christ from the person of Jesus, and to live by the one without believing in the other. If we would drink wine, there must needs be a vessel from which to imbibe it. We cannot have the contents and no container. The starting point of the Christian faith, which itself, is, no doubt, spiritual and internal, must always be "the sinless years that breathed beneath the Syrian blue:" the Word that "wrought with human hands the creed of creeds." It is to the very combination of eternal truth with the details of the evangelical history, that we must ascribe the influence of Christianity over the hearts and lives of men. A plausible thing it has often seemed to say, "Let the facts be as though they were not." But here, if anywhere, Bishop Butler's dictum applies: "Things *are* what they are, and their consequences will be what they will be." The facts contain the revelation: the idea without the Person is empty. "A present God." Yes, surely. It is just because Christians believe in a present God, that they recognize Him as having spoken, at sundry times and in divers manners, in times past unto the fathers by the prophets, and in these last days unto us by His Son. Reject historical Christianity, and in the course of a very few years how much definite Christianity will be left? Of course, I do not say that the assent to a bare intellectual proposition is religious faith. No; that is but *fides demoniorum*. But faith, if it is to be anything more than a blind instinct, must involve assent to propositions. And that it should likewise involve assent to historical truths, is simply of a piece with the laws by which man lives, and moves, and has his being. He never is abstract self-consciousness: he belongs to the world of time; he is individual, concrete— *hic et nunc*, the schoolmen say. And the religious faith which binds him to a present Deity must have the same character. As the Italians say, "l'uomo é cosi fatto." Such is the nature of man and of the religious instinct in man. And precisely because it is such, is man led to form religious associations. Solidarity is the law of our race. No man liveth to himself in any sphere or department of his life. If he experiences a want, he seeks help from others. If he realizes a truth, he desires to communicate it. And this holds good of his moral life as of his physical; and of his religious life, as of his moral. A common cult is a natural necessity. It is also a great human bond. There is a true meaning in the word "religio." Public worship is to the soul what an oath is to speech; a tie, an obligation. The personal and conscious relation of the individual with his Creator no more hinders that communion with his fellows which we call the Church, or is a bar to his receiving light and strength by means of it, than the fact that every man is born of his parents can make it untrue that he came from the Almighty.* The spirit of religion? Yes. "But the Church must provide the body in which that spirit is to be lodged. ... We may as well expect that the spirits of men might be seen by us without the intervention of their bodies, as suppose that the Object of faith can be realized in a world of sense and excitement, without the instrumentality of an outward form to arrest and fix attention, to stimulate the careless and to encourage the desponding. ... Religion must be realized in particular acts in order to its continuing alive. There is no such thing as abstract religion. When people attempt to worship in this (what they call) more spiritual manner, they end, in fact, in not worshipping at all. ... In these times, especially, this is why the

* Compare the fine lines of Schiller:

"Nicht allein genug ist sich
Das Herz; ein irdisch Pfand bedarf der Glaube,
Das hohe Himmlische sich zu-zueignen.
Drum ward der Gott zum Menschen, und verschloss
Die unsichtbaren himmlischen Geschenke
Geheimnissvoll in einem sichtbarn Leib.
Die Kirche ist's, die heilige, die hohe,
Die zu dem Himmel uns die Leiter baut;
Die allgemeine, die Katol'sche heisst sie;
Denn nur der Glaube aller stärkt den Glauben.
Wo Tausende anbeten und verehren,
Da wird die Glut zur Flamme, und beflügelt
Schwingt sich der Geist in alle Himmel auf."

Church itself is attacked, because it is the living form, the visible body of religion, and shrewd men know that, when it goes, religion will go too." *

In what I have just been writing, I have had Christianity specially in view. And surely it is enough, for our present very practical purpose, to confine ourselves to Christianity. True it is that, although this religion has been in the world for well-nigh two thousand years, it has not as yet, in all its various forms, received the allegiance of a majority of the human race. Still none of my readers, probably, would seriously maintain that any other of the world's creeds can really dispute with it the world's future. Too wild is the imagination to be gravely entertained, that the progressive races of mankind and the leaders of the rest, should prefer the word of Mohammed, of Zoroaster, of Gautama to the word of Jesus Christ; should turn away from the Bible to the Qu'rân, the Avesta, or the Pitakas. The issue before us is between Christianity and no religion. And the question which I shall proceed to discuss is whether there is anything irrational, and therefore immoral, in accepting The Christian

* J. H. Newman, *Parochial and Plain Sermons*, vol. ii. pp. 74–77.

Synthesis as affording the best answer to The Great Enigma.

Now, what do we mean by Christianity? I suppose we may say with Dr. Johnson that it means the religion of Christians. But there are so many kinds of Christians! Not to speak of the ephemeral sects which every day brings forth in England and America—

"Unfinished things one knows not what to call,
Their generation's so equivocal!"

there are, let us say, Catholic Christians, Greek Christians, Anglican Christians, there are Nestorians and Monophysites, Wesleyan Methodists, and Congregationalists. What have all these in common? They have this, at all events, in common with one another, and with most other varieties of the Christian religion, that they regard baptism as a solemn initiation into Christianity — baptism administered, according to universal practice, in the Name of the Father, and of the Son, and of the Holy Ghost. Christianity is, in its simplest reduction, the doctrine concerning God summed up in the baptismal formula—the most ancient and, in a sense, the most authoritative, of all its formulas—the acceptance of which has, from the first, been required as a condition of admission into the Christian society.

Is this doctrine discredited by the achievements of the modern mind?

First, then, as to belief in an Almighty Father, of whom, and through whom, and to whom, are all things, it may suffice to refer to what I have said in previous chapters of this volume. I very confidently maintain that if the intellect is valid, the true conclusion can never be Atheism or Agnosticism, but must be Theism of some kind. The proposition of St. Paul has not been refuted: "The invisible things of Him from the creation of the world, are clearly seen, being understood by the things that are made, even His eternal power and Godhead." And it is most interesting, and most satisfactory, to find the able and popular writer whom I have selected as the spokesman of Scientific Agnosticism, constrained to employ language which appears to involve a recognition of this great verity. He declares it absolutely certain that we are "ever in presence of an Infinite and Eternal Energy from which all things proceed."[*] I find it difficult to reconcile this declaration with his dictum in *First Principles*, that "the Absolute cannot, in any manner or degree, be known, in the strict sense of knowing." Surely to know with absolute certainty the Being, the Causal Energy, the Omnipotence, the Eternity of the Absolute, is to know, in the strictest sense, a great deal about it. If we add to this, as Mr. Spencer enjoins us

[*] *Nineteenth Century*, Jan., 1884, p. 12.

to do, that the universe is obedient to law and that this law is beneficent, we have a doctrine singularly like that with which the Apostle's Creed opens—"I believe in God the Father Almighty, Maker of Heaven and Earth."

Reason seems a sure thing. Its conclusions are unimpeachable. But they leave us cold. "God as God," Feuerbach has well said, "the infinite, universal, non-anthropomorphic Being of the understanding has no more significance in religion than a fundamental general principle has for a special science; it is merely the ultimate point of support, as it were, the mathematical point of religion."* Objective Reason, Eternal Energy, Supreme Cause, Absolute Being, Perfect Personality—these conceptions, august as they are, by no means suffice for the needs, either of our intellect or of our emotions. We want, in Kant's happy phrase, "a God that can interest us." Our conceptions of Him are, and cannot keep from being, anthropomorphic: † that is to say, they are conditioned by the essential limits of our nature. It may, in a sense, be said, that we incarnate God by a necessity of our intellectual and spiritual existence. "Humanity," observes M. Renan— who irresistibly reminds me, from time to time, of Balaam, the son of Beor—"Humanity will have a

* *Das Wesen des Christenthums*, c. 3.

† As Aristotle points out: Τὰ εἴδη τῶν θεῶν ἀφομοιοῦσιν ἑαυτοῖς οἱ ἄνθρωποι (*Pol.* i. 2).

God at once finite and infinite, real and ideal. It loves the ideal, but it will have that ideal personified. It will have a God-man."* This truth is writ large on every page of the history of religions. Of the endless Oriental avatars I need not speak. But perhaps we seldom realize how familiar the idea of Divine emanations was to the Hellenic mind. Hence it was that philosophers found small difficulty in reconciling the popular polytheism with the conception of the Divine Unity to which many of them had attained. The inferior deity, emanating from the Supreme Principle, made that union between the absolute and the relative, between abstract being and the sensible world, for which there is so unquenchable a longing in the human heart. The claim of Christianity is definitively to satisfy this longing. It presents Christ to the world as "the image of the invisible God," in whom the eternally ideal has become the historically real: the Λόγος Θεῖος, the thought of the Infinite and Eternal, made flesh and dwelling among us: the realization of the Divine Will in the moral and religious order: "the desire of all nations." Will this claim any longer stand? Or is it true that "the good Lord Jesus has had His day"?

Let us consider it. In the first place, what do we really know about Jesus Christ? It is certain that such a Teacher did actually live and die

* *Le Prêtre de Nemi*, act ii. sc. 6.

eighteen hundred years ago, and that the results of His life and death are with us to this day, in the religion which bears His name. Christianity is a fact in the world's history: "ce fait fécond, unique, grandiose," M. Renan calls it: certainly not too strongly. What is the explanation of this fact? Christianity is a comparatively modern word. They spoke originally of "the kingdom of God" or "the Church." What was it that, so to speak, *made* the Christian Church? If I may quote words of my own, "It was assuredly no system or theory, most assuredly no exhibition of thaumaturgic power, which attracted men to Jesus Christ, but the irresistible influence of soul upon soul. To those who forsook all, and took up their cross and followed Him, He exhibited no set of doctrines, no code of laws, but Himself, as being, in very deed, that truth which is the soul's supreme desire. The gospel which St. Paul, in an undoubtedly genuine letter, declares himself to have delivered to the disciples at Corinth, was no catalogue of dogmas, but the manifestation of a Person, who claimed for Himself the heart of man, to reign there as in His proper throne."[*] All this is absolutely beyond question, whatever view we take of the date, authorship, and authority of the documents which make up the New Testa-

---

[*] *Chapters in European History*, i. 55. As to the relative worth of the sources of evidence concerning the teaching of Christ, see p. 52 of the same volume.

ment. "The person of Christ, in whom, as they believed, dwelt all the fulness of the Godhead bodily, was all in all to those early disciples, and was the direct source whence they derived their rule of life, in its highest and lowest details." And as it was in the first age of Christianity, so has it been throughout the ages since. Amid all mutations of the social order, in all diversities of physical environment, through all our political and intellectual revolutions, the life lived " in loveliness of perfect deeds" has been the supreme type and the great exemplar of the foremost races of the world; the imitation of Christ has been a never-failing fount of all that has been noblest in individual action, of all that has been most precious in moral civilization. Of His fulness have eighteen centuries received, each finding in Him the ideal to satisfy their differing aspirations: the character answering to their loftiest conceptions: the perfect and all-sufficient standard of right thought and right doing. What a colossal fact is this, compelling us to exclaim with the Roman soldier, who stood beside Him in His supreme humiliation, "Truly this was the Son of God"! There is that in us—we cannot rid ourselves altogether of it, try how we may—that enforces us to see in great men and great deeds something divine. And what man so great as this? What deeds so great as His? And who, among the world's teachers, makes such transcendent claims? "No man knoweth the

Son, but the Father; neither knoweth any man the Father, save the Son: and he to whomsoever the Son will reveal Him." "The brightness of the Father's glory and the express image of His substance," says the writer of the Epistle to the Hebrews. The revealer of that attribute of the Infinite and Eternal, of which our eyes discern but imperfect evidence in the sensible universe, full of suffering as in the transitory present, so in the boundless past and the boundless future: for by Him "the kindness and love" of the Supreme appeared. I do not say that He has given us a metaphysical solution of that heart-bewildering, soul-subduing problem of evil; but at all events He has mitigated its severity by His manifestation of the infinite compassion of the Divine Father. Christianity has been called "Stoicism plus a legend." But what a legend! The crucifix its symbol, and "Sic Deus dilexit mundum," its interpretation!

> "Conjecture of the worker by the work.
> Is there strength there? Enough. Intelligence?
> Ample. But goodness in a like degree?
> Not to the human eye, in the present state:
> An isosceles deficient in the base.
> What lacks there of perfection fit for God
> But just the instance, which this tale supplies,
> Of love without a limit? So is strength,
> So is intelligence; let love be so,
> Unlimited in its self-sacrifice,
> Then is the tale true, as God stands complete.
> Beyond the tale I reach into the dark,
> Feel what I cannot see, and so faith stands."

"In a world where 'men sit and hear each other groan, where but to think is to be full of sorrow,' it is hard," Mr. John Morley allows, "to imagine a time when we shall be indifferent to that sovereign legend of Pity."* Hard indeed! What is left of Christianity, do you ask? Christ is left. At this moment His will is the strongest spiritual force energizing throughout the world. Now, as for eighteen centuries, the children of men need but touch the hem of His garment to be made whole of whatsoever disease they have. Who can believe that He shall ever be numbered among the dead gods? Nay, He is alive for evermore, "an ideal of humanity now valid for all men, at all times, and throughout all worlds."† "The good Lord Jesus has had His day." "Had?" the sister replies, "Had? has it come? It has only dawned; it will come by-and-by."‡ In the "young child with Mary His mother," mankind will ever more and more discern the noblest, the most elevating of types; will find an inexhaustible fount of tenderness, of purity, the one well of life in the desert of

---

* *Compromise*, p. 156. Mr. Morley adds, "We have but to incorporate it in some wider gospel of Justice and Progress." By all means—if he can find one. I venture to doubt if it has been revealed to him by his "spiritual fathers," as he calls them (*Rousseau*, i. 5), the *philosophes* of the last century.

† Kant, *Religion innerhalb der Grenzen der blossen Vernunft*, p. 76.

‡ See Lord Tennyson's most pathetic poem, *The Children's Hospital*.

VII.] *THE REVELATION OF CONSCIOUSNESS.* 305

existence. The Man of Sorrows will reign from the Tree over an everlasting kingdom, and with a dominion that endureth throughout all ages. We have His own word for it—neither was guile found in His lips—"Heaven and earth shall pass away, but My word shall not pass away."

But external nature and human history are not our only sources of knowledge. The first fact about me is that I—the thinking being—exist.* That is the most certain of all my certitudes, the one reality of which it is impossible for me to doubt: and it is the true starting-point of all philosophy. The fleeting phenomena of consciousness are bound together and made intelligible by the *ego*, which, manifesting itself in and through them, declares that it abides among all changes, and does not change with them. By the same intellectual power we affirm the reality of the *non-ego*, of a world of sense and matter which is something more permanent than the phenomena dealt with by physical science. This process of objective affirmation is a primary fact of our intellectual life, revealing to us the *ego* and the *non-ego* as things in themselves. A permanent self and the unity of self-consciousness are the essential foundations of all philosophy, properly so called: of every rational account of man. Now one of the primary facts of consciousness is the feeling of ethical obligation. It is a fact abundantly verifi-

* See what I have written on this subject at p. 239.

able, its simplest expression being "Thou oughtest;" and it is the starting-point of morality. It is as real, as undeniable, unless we choose to close the eyes of our understanding (than which nothing is easier) as is the fact of sense-perception. As surely as consciousness reveals to me, in the ordinary exercise of my faculties, myself, and an objective world not myself, so surely does it reveal to me, through the feeling of moral obligation, a Higher than I, to whom that obligation binds me. This Kant deemed the surest revelation of the Divine. "Ethic," he writes, "issues inevitably in religion, by extending itself to the idea of a sovereign moral Lawgiver, in whose will *that* is the end of creation, which at the same time can be, and ought to be, man's chief end."* And here the great philosopher of these latter days does but express, in his own language, what has been delivered, in divers manners, by the world's spiritual teachers, of all creeds, in all ages. Here, too, I find, as it seems to me, the answer to Kant's own doctrine that the nature of God is not the object of experience. I venture to say that he takes experience in too narrow a sense. We must take it in its totality. We must accept the testimony of our whole being. And surely we have experience of God through our moral nature. Consider the emotional element in

---

* *Religion innerhalb der Grenzen der blossen Vernunft.* Vorrede zur ersten Auflage.

ethics. "The wicked flee when no man pursueth." No *man* pursueth. From whom, then, do they flee? Why do they feel that they violate the moral law at their peril? It is because "in the ultimate penetralia of the conscience, the Living Spirit of God himself is met, it may be unconsciously, it may be consciously." * And "the moral law first reaches its integral meaning when seen as *impersonated* in a Perfect Mind, which communicates it to us, and lends it power over our affections, sufficient to draw us into Divine communion." † Consonant with this is the teaching of Plato in the *Meno*, that even ordinary virtue, which has the praise of men, is of Divine inspiration. Every impulse after good, every thought in which we forget ourselves, every action in which we sacrifice ourselves, is an influx of the Divine Spirit into our spirits. The direct revelation of the personal God is that which is made to the personality of man. "Spiritus Domini replevit orbem." This is that Wisdom—Sancta Sophia—whereof the son of Sirach speaks, that "in all ages, entering into holy souls, maketh them friends of God and prophets." "I believe in the Holy Ghost." Surely this stands as firmly now as it did eighteen hundred years ago. How

---

* Martineau's *Address to the Students of Manchester New College at the opening of the Session* 1881–2, p. 17.

† Martineau's *A Study of Religion*, vol. ii. p. 29. The italics are mine.

can it pass away? We have "the witness in ourselves." "Prope Deus est," says Seneca, "tecum est, intus est; Sacer intra nos Spiritus sedet, bonorum malorumque observator et custos; hic prout a nobis tractatur, ita nos tractat; bonus vero vir sine Deo nemo est." "So long as there is in the human heart one fibre to vibrate to the sound of what is true, pure, and honest, so long as the instinctively pure soul prefers purity to life, so long as there are found friends of truth to sacrifice their repose to science, friends of goodness to devote themselves to useful and holy works of mercy, woman-hearts to love whatever is worthy, beautiful, and pure, artists to render it by sound and colour and inspired accents—so long God will live in us. Est Deus in nobis." [*]

It appears to me, then, that external nature, human history, and our own consciousness, harmonize clearly with the conception concerning the Infinite and Eternal which is of the essence of Christianity. The genesis of that conception, although, no doubt, an interesting topic of historical inquiry, is of no moral or religious importance whatever. It is enough that Christianity possesses the conception, and that it is true.[†] It

[*] Renan, *Nouvelles Études d'Histoire Religieuse*, p. 531.
[†] It must not be supposed that I am endeavouring to *prove*

will, however, be said: That is all very well; but Christianity, as it comes before us, means a great deal more than that: it is not merely a religion: it has become a theology: there is our difficulty. Well, the difficulty is by no means a new one.

"Formerly," says St. Hilary, "the word of the Lord, 'Go and teach all nations, baptizing them in the name of the Father, the Son, and the Holy Ghost,' was enough for the faithful. . . . But now, through the faults of heretics and blasphemers, we are compelled to do what is not permitted: to scale the lofty peaks: to express the inexpressible: to presume beyond what is given to us. Instead of accomplishing by faith alone what had been commanded us—to adore the Father, to venerate with Him the Son, to be filled with the Holy Ghost—we are compelled to elevate our humble speech to the point of making it tell forth the ineffable, and are enforced to fault by the fault of others: and thus what should have remained shrouded in the religion of souls, is exposed to the peril of human language." *

So this champion of orthodoxy—the author, as seems most probable, of the Athanasian Creed—a witness beyond suspicion. I can well believe that his words, coming to us across fifteen centuries, will awaken an echo in many ingenuous minds. "We have no sort of objection," I fancy I hear

the Christian doctrine of the Trinity by appealing to the facts of physical nature, history, and consciousness. I am merely contending, for the purposes of this *argumentum ad hominem*, that there is nothing in those facts inconsistent with the theistic conception of Christianity, but that, on the contrary, they harmonize with it.

* *De Trinitate*, l. ii. c. 1.

them say, "to adore the Father, to venerate the Son, and to be filled with the Holy Ghost. But theological determinations, ecclesiastical theses, in a word, the whole vast accretion of dogma! That is precisely our real difficulty. And if we excise all that from Christianity, should we not perform a mortal operation upon the religion itself?"

Yes, undoubtedly, I think you would. I think, moreover, you would be a fool for your pains. Nothing is so stupid as an anachronism. Christianity comes before us "rich with the spoils of time." We may take it or leave it. But if we cannot take it as it is, with its doctrines and its traditions, we had better leave it. It is hard to imagine anything less satisfactory than the results attained by the method called rationalistic. Why so called? "Well, I suppose God knows, I don't." For it seems to me extremely irrational. Consider, for example, the *New Life of Jesus*, with which Herr Strauss some time ago favoured the world. His object there is to disengage what he calls the "legendary" from the historic Christ. And what an astral phantom is the result! What a thing of shreds and patches! What an incoherent mixture of dubiety and dogmatism! Primitive Christianity in this nineteenth century? You might as well try to return to the primitive fig-leaf. Better to make the best of Catholic fulness and of modern sartorial art. I do not, of course, deny—what intelligent man candidly can?

—that we may sometimes find difficulties in reconciling the positions of dogmatic theology with the exigencies of criticism. But it seems to me that those difficulties are such as we may rightly discount—if I may be allowed the word—when we are unable fully to solve them. For what is a dogma *philosophically* considered? It is the result of several factors. There is the original idea, there is the concrete image, and there is the logical deduction. Ideas have a life of their own: they germinate in the human mind: they assimilate nutriment from all sides. They are like the language in which they find expression: so long as they are living they change. They, in fact, obey the great law of evolution. The view of religious dogma maintained by Luther, which represents the doctrines of Christianity to have sprung fully formed from its Divine Founder, like Pallas from the head of Zeus, is as philosophically absurd as it is historically false.* The metaphysical formulas in which faith embodies its ideals, must have antecedents; they require preparation in time. The facts of the Divine Life, with their redemptive and recreative energy, are not the subject of evolution. The Confessions, in which we sum up our appreciation and interpretation of those facts, are slowly elaborated by

* The learned Cardinal Laurentius Brancata writes: "Multæ veritates initio ecclesiæ aut obscuræ erant, aut penitus ignotæ."
—*De Predestin*, No. 34.

the human intellect. It is impossible to deny this without shutting our eyes to the plainest lessons of ecclesiastical history. But it cannot, for one moment, be allowed that the historical truth of the gradual growth of the Christian creed—"occulto velut arbor ævo"—supplies a valid argument against it, any more than it can be allowed that facts established by modern exegesis regarding the date, authorship, scientific language, or quasi-historical statements of the Christian Sacred Books, affect their commanding claims upon our religious reverence. A very early Christian writer, St. Hippolytus, in his curious work, *De Antichristo*, has a passage which may be fitly referred to in this connection. He is commenting upon the "great wonder in heaven," spoken of in the Apocalypse: a woman clothed with the sun, and the moon under her feet, and upon her head a crown of twelve stars; who brought forth a male child. The woman, he says, is the Church, always giving birth to Christ, the male and perfect offspring of God, who is styled both God and Man: and thus acting as the teacher of all nations. The Church, in every age, seems to be bringing forth the Eternal Word, formulating it in such shape as each age requires. Creeds, Confessions, of Faith, Definitions of Doctrines, are as essential to religion as words are to thought. There is something in us which compels us to reduce to system the various aspects of truth. But our

synthesis must necessarily be imperfect. "Verba sequuntur non modum essendi qui est in rebus," says Aquinas, "sed modum essendi secundum quod in nostra cogitatione sunt." To which we must add that human language has an essentially physical, sensual, materialistic character. This is apparent from comparative philology. What, indeed, if we weigh the matter well, is a word but a phonetic notation of the psychological state in which we are placed by phenomena affecting our organism? Words now most abstract had originally a concrete signification. And so our philosophical and theological theories, expressed in words, what are they but imitations of the inimitable? Those bold and large formulas which we call dogmas are indispensable to any teaching which has to act upon the masses of men. Doctrine is the vertebration of religion. Still it must be ever remembered that "Christian teaching professes to be symbolical and an economy of divine things. Every article of faith must be construed according to the sense of Goethe's line: 'Alles Vergängliche ist nur ein' Gleichniss.'"*
"The best in this kind are but shadows." The symbolized is greater, and deeper, and older, than the symbol. Considerations of this sort may be of a twofold use. They may serve to curb the "licence of affirmation" about divine things in which some of us are too prone to indulge: to

* *Ancient Religion and Modern Thought*, p. 235.

check us when we are tempted to speak of the Infinite and Eternal as if He were a deeply read theologian, an infallible inquisitor, an inerrant casuist, a "magnified non-natural" Pope, and not so very non-natural after all. They may help others to transcend difficulties which they cannot solve—possibly from deficiency of knowledge or of dialectical skill—and to use as " human nature's daily food" the great spiritual verities presented in the formulas of inherited Christianity. It has been strikingly observed by a powerful French writer—no divine, but a man of the world, well known as a novelist and a critic—

"C'était la paix, cependant, ce dogme, et la communion avec les grands génies qui ont cru. Un philosophe sincère avoue son impuissance à répondre autrement que par des hypothèses aux questions d'origine et de finalité. La religion est une hypothèse entre vingt autres. Elle a suffi à un Pascal, et à un Malebranche .... S'ils ne s'étaient pas trompés, cependant?"*

Of course I do not admit that Christianity is a mere hypothesis. It is *credibile et credendum*. Its credentials are sufficient for "men of good will." To such alone is its peace offered; "pax hominibus bonæ voluntatis." Aristotle truly teaches that, in the moral order, truth is apprehended not only by the intelligence, but by the whole soul, σὺν ὅλῃ τῇ ψυχῇ. As a matter of

* Paul Bourget, *Essais de Psychologie contemporaine*, p. 83.

fact, there is only one way in which Christianity ever has made, or ever will make, proselytes in the world. Its victories have been won not by mere argument—arguments have been well called the symbols of something deeper—not by mere eloquence, not by the wisdom of this world, but by an appeal to those fundamental spiritual instincts of men, whereunto it supremely corresponds. "Non in dialectica complacuit Deo salvum facere populum suum." "The Christian evidences," Dr. Liddon has excellently observed, "presuppose a certain moral sympathy in an inquirer. They are, in fact, moral and not mathematical or experimental. They are not of so imperative a character as to impose themselves, as the sensible experience of an earthquake or of an eclipse imposes itself, upon reluctant wills. . . . Christianity expects to be met—if not half way, yet to a certain point—by desire based upon a clear discernment of its need of knowledge, and of its need of strength. If the evidences of Christianity were of such a character that no honest and educated man could possibly reject them without intellectual folly, whatever his moral condition or history might be, the Christian belief would be, like a university degree, a certificate of a certain sort of mental capacity, but it would be no criterion whatever of a man's past or present relation to God. St. Paul makes faith such a criterion; because faith is a moral as much as an intellectual act; because it combines our sense of moral want with our perception of the bearings of moral evidence. Thus a margin of deficiency, mathematically speaking, is even necessary in the Christian evidences, as a whole, in order to leave room for the exercise of faith; that vital, emphatic act of the whole soul, by which the soul throws itself upon the invisible, and thus secures the proper moral objects of Christianity itself." *

So much is certain. But, further, we must always remember that "quidquid recipitur secundum modum recipientis recipitur." Christianity is one thing. Popular conceptions of it are another. As I have insisted, all our conceptions of spiritual truth are based on data supplied by our mode of existence, by our internal perceptions. That is to say, they are more or less anthropomorphic. It is a question of *more* or *less*. We all start, as children, with most human views of divine things. And the vast multitude of men remain all their lives children, in this respect: children in understanding, although in virtue they may attain "unto a perfect man, unto the measure of the stature of the fulness of Christ." Fetishes,

* *Sermons preached before the University of Oxford*, Second series, p. 216.

of one kind or another, these must have. Why should they not? "Omnis cognitio est secundum modum cognoscentis," observes Aquinas. The wildest legend of the saints current among Spanish or Neapolitan peasants is but the vesture in which the popular imagination has clothed some spiritual truth, has, so to speak, dramatized it and put it on the stage. The most revolting form of the "blood and fire" gospel yelled forth by British Salvationists may serve to render deepest verities concerning human sin and divine compassion apprehensible by gross and vulgar minds. Professor Tyndall stands aghast at "the more grotesque forms of the theological." I dare say he has cause. But why trouble one's self about them? "The most superficial grocer's back-parlour view of Calvinistic Christianity" was George Eliot's account of the late Mr. Spurgeon's preaching. The sufficient answer is that the congregation of that excellent man was composed, for the most part, of people who were intellectually grocers, and who, probably, would have been unable to rise to the height of a greater argument than that which he ministered to them, even if he had been in a position to offer it. But to seek in such homiletics the measure of the Christian faith, is as unwarrantable as it would be to seek the measure of Christian charity in what Robertson of Brighton called "the snarling gossip of the religious newspapers." My contention is that there is no more reason in the nineteenth century than there was in the first, why the message of Christianity should not be received by cultivated and intelligent men, who feel their need of it, and who will carefully and candidly examine its claims for themselves. That it affords us a complete explanation of the scheme of things, who pretends? We know in part and we prophesy in part; we see through a glass darkly: per speculum et in ænigmate. Mystery encompasses us everywhere. "Lost in the infinite immensity of space, of which I know nothing and you know nothing, I am in a terrible ignorance of all things." Yes, of the least things as of the greatest; of the latest and most ephemeral, as of the oldest and most enduring. The mystery which a single anthill contains is as insoluble as the mystery of the solar system. Add to this that, if we escape from the prison of the senses, if we penetrate to the noumenal, great and small, past and present, are words devoid of meaning. What are space and time but mere forms of sensibility? "Qui démêlera cet embrouillement? Humiliez-vous, raison impuissante: taisez-vous, nature imbécile: apprenez votre condition véritable, que vous ignorez. Écoutez Dieu!" Call Christianity a chapel in the infinite, if you will. Still it is a sacred shrine where life and death are transfigured for us, where we may gaze into the eternal realms of Spirit and Deity, where wise and learned, foolish and ignorant, alike, may handle everlasting realities, and realize, in their deepest experience, the powers of the world to come. "Quam terribilis est locus iste! non est hic aliud nisi domus Dei, et porta cœli."

INDEX.

PAGE

Absolute, the
    Mr. Spencer's conception of . . 149–151, 214–220
    presupposed by the Relative 222
    contradictories in 244
    our human and relative notions not the measure
    of 244, 245
Actus Purus 203
Agnostic,
    the term invented by Professor Huxley . . . 29
Agnosticism,
    two varieties of 29, 71
    Critical 72–116
    Scientific 117–119
d'Alembert,
    his "terrible question" 198
Attributes, the Divine,
    what they are 218, 244, 245
Animals, the lower,
    possess an analogon of the moral sense . . 235, 236
    terrible problem offered by 251–253
Anthropomorphism 246, 299, 300, 316
Aristotle,
    on the moral eye of the sage 20
    on the idea of a thing 142
    on "energy" 203, 227
    his definition of will 232
    on cognition 233
Arnold, Dr.,
    on the brute creation 252

INDEX.

	PAGE
Aquinas, St. Thomas,	
on the intellectual light within us	3
on the perfection of man	33
on the object of the intellect	144
on words and symbols	313
Atheism,	
different senses of the word	28
how employed in the present volume	29, 34
argument on which it is based	37
practical importance of	38
in Germany	38
in England	39
in France and the Latin races generally	41–66
how recommended *ad populum*	67
and elementary education	68, 69
Athenagoras,	
his vindication of the primitive Christians from the charge of Atheism	28
Augustine, St.,	
on the Bible	108
on sensation and abstract thoughts	132
on the incomprehensibility of God	226, 276
on the transcendental	279
Baptism	297
Bain, Professor,	
on mind and matter	135
on the one ultimate premiss of all induction	153, 154
Being,	
the category of	145
Bentham,	
his method in ethics	184
on obligation and duty	194
Bernard, Claude,	
on a creative and directive idea	136
Bernard, St.,	
on the inner revelation of the Divine	266, 267

INDEX.

Bible, the,
    doctrine of the plenary inspiration of   30, 88, 105–110, 312

Bonaventura, St.,
    on silence 268

Boscovitch,
    on space 231

Bourget, Paul,
    on dogma 314

Brancata, Cardinal Laurentius,
    on the ignorance of the primitive Church . . 311

Buddhism,
    not atheistic 33
    the supreme power recognized by 234
    on the indestructibility of our doing . . . 253

Candolle, M. de,
    on finality 210

Carlyle, Mr.,
    his "Pig Propositions" 53
    on the Bible 110
    on the allurements to heroic action . . . 188

Catechism, the,
    of the Council of Trent. 41
    of the Established Church 41

Catéchisme du Libre-Penseur, Le 42–46

Causation,
    Mr. Herbert Spencer's doctrine of . . . 129–138
    true doctrine of 203
    Kantian view of 223–225

Cause,
    a first 211–213, 227–232, 298

Christianity,
    and ethics 18–25, 160
    M. Monteil's account of 54–61
    M. Renan's reasons for rejecting . . . 87–90
    those reasons examined 105–115
    Mr. Herbert Spencer's view of 160
    Mysticism in 265–268

Christianity—*continued*.
    and history 293
    what it means 297
    is it discredited by the achievements of the modern
        mind? 298–314
    expects to be met to a certain point . . . 315
    and popular conceptions of it . . . 317–319
Church, Dean,
    on the sternness of the New Testament . . . 34
Cicero,
    his definition of philosophy 2
    his question as to the origin of the mind . . 232
Cognition 140–142, 233
Coleridge,
    his definition of a miracle 111
    his definition of metaphysics 144
    on the sum total of moral philosophy . . . 161
Concupiscence,
    proper meaning of the word 63
Conscience,
    what it is 22, 195, 237, 306
    Mr. Spencer's account of . . 170–174, 235–237
    analogon of in lower animals 236
Criticism,
    the "higher" 7–10, 88, 106, 312
Critique of Practical Reason, the 277–279
Critique of Pure Reason, the 273–276

Darwin, Mr.,
    on Mr. Herbert Spencer 117
    evidence in his books of purpose in nature . . 211
    on the evolution of the moral sense . . . 237
Deity. *See* God.
Dionysius, the Carthusian,
    his definition of mysticism 267
Doubt,
    prevalence of, in this age 15–18

Downes, Mr.,	
on Pantheism	29
Dubois-Reymond,	
on Force	129
Ego, the,	145, 239, 305
Eliot, George,	
on Mr. Spurgeon's preaching	317
Emerson,	
on the revelations of the Soul	254, 255
Ethics	
and Christianity	18–25, 159
of Atheism	62–70
true foundations of	98
of Critical Agnosticism	98–105
of Scientific Agnosticism	158–197
two great Schools in	161
the two great problems in	190
a revelation of the Ultimate Reality	234, 235, 278, 279, 306, 307
Evolution	126, 163, 165, 166, 174, 177, 190, 192, 194, 196, 212, 311
Exeter Hall and "the Open Bible"	40
Failure,	
the argument from	209–212
Fénelon,	
on the Ultimate Reality	228
Feuerbach,	
on non-anthropomorphic Deity	297
Flourens, M. Gustave,	
on Atheism	68
Force,	
the doctrine of the Persistence of, in Mr. Spencer's philosophy	125, 130–136, 148, 162–166, 198
what we know of	231
Franzelin, Cardinal,	
on the source and measure of metaphysical truth	155

Gerson,
    on ecstasy 268
GOD,
    speculations concerning 16
    what is meant by the word in the present volume . 35
    growth of the conception of 35–36
    dogmatic denial of 37, 45–48, 52
    M. Renan on 96–97
    Mr. Spencer on 122, 146–152
    and absolute laws 154, 159
    Sir Robert Peel on belief in 201
    reasons why men ought not to believe in, examined 207–225
    grounds for belief in 220–244
    antinomies involved in conception of . . . 244
    Spinoza's conception of 246
    mystical doctrine concerning . . . 254–289
    Christian conception of 297–308
    licence of affirmation concerning 314
Good,
    Reynaud on 64
    Laromiguière on . . . . *ibid.*
    Mr. Herbert Spencer on 167–170
    the Schoolmen on 185
Green, Professor T. H.,
    on Mr. Spencer's vivid aggregate 130
    on Mr. Spencer's doctrine of the generation of
        thought 131, 180
    on necessary truths 283

Hartmann, E. von,
    on Kant's defective insight into *a priori* forms of
        intuition 280
    on non-sensuous perceptive power . . 282–283
Hegel,
    on Being and Nothing 219
    on the laws of nature 228
    on personality 241

INDEX.

Heine,
    on German Atheism 38
    on the Kantian philosophy 277, 278
Helmholtz,
    on great physical discoveries 156
Herodotus,
    his question to the priestesses at Dodona . . 5
Hilary, St.,
    on the growth of dogma 309
Hippolytus, St.,
    on the "great wonder in heaven" . . . 312
Hugo, Victor,
    on the prevalence of doubt 17
Huxley, Professor,
    on astronomy and religious beliefs . . . 14
    invents the term Agnostic 29
    his eulogy of Mr. Darwin 117
    on the growth of "science" 205
    on certain theistic philosophers . . . 245
    on God 246

Individuation,
    the problem of 198
Intellect,
    the essential nature of 219
    and sense 233
    self-affirmations of 241

Jelâlu-d'-Din,
    on ignorant devotion 248
    on the world of unity 263
Joubert,
    his definition of philosophy 1
    on the authors who have most influence : . 71

Kant,
    on the moral law 21, 23, 24
    on religion and morality 24

INDEX.

Kant—*continued*.
 his definition of the word "God" 25
 on miracles 111, 115
 on the three steps in our knowledge . . . 143
 on purpose 211
 on the Theistic postulate 223
 his doctrine of causality 223–225
 on matter 231
 on space 231
 his *Critique of Pure Reason* . . . 273–276
 his *Critique of Practical Reason* . . . 277–280
 on Christ as an ideal of humanity . . . 304
 on the surest revelation of the Divine . . 306

Katha Upanishad, the 256–259

Knowledge,
 three steps in 143
 the condition of 145
 what it is 241

Kosmos 228

Law,
 the Divine 63
 the moral. *See* Ethics.
 physical 202
 of evolution, the 212, 311
 of righteousness, the 234
 revealed by external and internal phenomena . 237

Laws,
 of consciousness 214–220
 of nature 228

Lecky, Mr.,
 on an important achievement of Christianity . 45

Leibnitz,
 on the source of knowledge 143
 on necessary truths 154, 155
 on sense and intellect 233
 on the concepts of being and cause . . . 242

INDEX.

	PAGE
Liddon, Dr.,	
on Pantheism	30
on the moral element in faith	315
Littré	
his definition of Atheist	28
Lotze,	
on the unity of the *ego*	239
Luther,	
at the Diet of Worms	195
his view of Christian dogma	311
Matter,	
what we know of it	231
Mansel, Dean,	
on absolute morality	159
Martineau, Dr.,	
on retributory happiness and suffering	24
on the meaning of the word "God"	35
on Mr. Spencer's explanation of the notion of moral obligation	173
on cause	203, 224
on the constitution of our moral nature	234
on the condition of knowledge	240
on conscience	307
on the attainment of its integral meaning by the moral law	*ibid.*
Materialism,	
properly means absolute Atheism	31
Mazzini,	
on Theism and morals	67
Metaphysics,	
definition of	144
Mr. Spencer's ignorance of	154, 198, 240
the ultimate basis of	155
the only possible foundation of morality	197
the province of, invaded by physicists	204–206
Mill, Mr. John Stuart,	
on miracles	115
on mysticism	284

330   INDEX.

	PAGE
Monteil, M.,	
his *Catéchisme du Libre-Penseur*	42–66
Morison, Mr. Cotter,	
his *Service of Man*	207–220
Morley, Mr. John,	
on popular Atheism	40
on the " sovereign legend of Pity"	304
Müller, Professor Max,	
on the growth of the Theistic idea	35, 36
on common-sense philosophy	118
Nantes,	
Resolution of the Conseil d'Arrondissement of, on Atheistic education	69, 70
Natural Selection	229
Neo-Platonists, the	261, 262
Newman, Cardinal,	
on the inspiration of Scripture	108, 109
on the spectacle of brute nature	251
Nihilism,	
and the Kantian philosophy	225
and mysticism	271
Nirvâna	262
Optimism,	
unchristian	34
Palmer, Professor,	
his view of Sûfism	263, 264
Pantheism	29–31, 49, 244, 265
Personality	129, 145, 232, 241, 242, 305
Pessimism,	
varieties of	32
Philosophy,	
Cicero's definition of	2
the great problem of	2
Atheistic	62–65
M. Renan's	102, 104

Philosophy—*continued.*

    Mr. Herbert Spencer's 121–199
    two indispensable postulates of 202
    physiological 205, 206
    the Kantian 223–225, 273–280
    of the Upanishads 256–259
    Neo-Platonic 259–262
    Sûfite 262–264
    of the Christian Mystics 265–268
    of Nihilistic Pessimism 271
    essential foundations of 305

Plato,
    on the source of the moral law 20
    his view of ideas 238
    his attitude to popular superstition . . . 247
    on ordinary virtue 307

Plotinus 261, 262
    his influence on Christian Mysticism . . . 265

Positivism,
    a variety of Agnosticism 31

Public Worship,
    the rationale of 294, 295

Reason,
    and the moral law 20
    held by a certain physiologist to be phosphorus . 66
    and miracles 115
    manifested by the relations of things . . . 152
    outraged by Mr. Herbert Spencer 153
    supplies the key to the problem of existence . 199, 202
    is the constituent element of reality . . . 228
    and natural selection 229
    inseparably connected with Will 232
    the speculative 274, 275
    the practical 277–280
    immoral to act against 296

Relativity of knowledge,
    Mr. Spencer's doctrine of 138–145

332   INDEX.

                                                                   PAGE

Religion,
    what it proposes to do 2
    is behind all religions 4
Religiosity 291, 292
Renan, M.,
    a type of Critical Agnosticism 71
    causes of his vast influence 71–80
    his life as a seminarist 80–88
    renounces Christianity 88–91
    engrafts modern criticism on a religious temperament 92
    regarded the being of God as a question beyond us 96, 97
    his critical method fatal to ethics . . . 98–100
    was another and a better Voltaire 103
    in unlearning Christianity unlearned Theism . . 105
    his reasons for renouncing Christianity examined 108–116
    on the desire of humanity for a God-man . . 229
    on the Deity within 308
Richerer, the Rev. Mr.,
    on South African bushmen 235
Robert Elsmere,
    profession of faith in 291, 292
Romanes, Mr.,
    on a mechanical equivalent of thought . . . 137

St. Hilaire, Geoffroy,
    on the succession of species 229
Schopenhauer,
    on man as a metaphysical animal 2
    on Pantheism 30
    character of his Pessimism 32
    on the sufferings of the animal world . . . 252
    on the Neo-Platonists 261
Science,
    the, of religion 6–10
    effects of conquests of physical, on old religious conceptions 10–15
    ethical 20, 183
    the word used as a synonym for physics 50, 205, 208

INDEX.

Science—*continued*.
 Mr. Spencer's definition of 120
 physical, dwells in the sphere of the relative . . 201
 antitheistic objections from physical . . 208–214
 theological, proper starting-point in . . . 217

Secularism,
 a variety of Agnosticism 32

Seeley, Professor,
 on contemporary want of fixed moral principles 17, 18

Seneca,
 on the Deity within 308

Spencer, Mr. Herbert,
 on transcendental moralists 18, 159
 the most influential teacher of Scientific Agnosticism 118
 his account of philosophy 120
 the foundation of his philosophy 121
 reproduces the theory of Democritus . . . 128
 his doctrine of Causation 129–138
 his doctrine of Relativity of Knowledge . 138–145
 his doctrine of The Unknowable . . . 145–155
 his ignorance of metaphysics . . 154, 198, 240
 his system based upon assumptions . . 155–157
 his moral philosophy 158–197
 his Scientific Agnosticism inadequate to life . . 199
 on necessity. 204
 his antitheistic argument from the laws of consciousness 214–220
 his logical puzzles 220, 240
 his positive teaching concerning the Ultimate Reality
         226, 227, 232, 298
 his view of consciousness and thought . . . 233
 his account of the concept of duty . . . 235
 his notion of personality 241
 his philosophy mechanical 243
 on popular beliefs 247

Spinoza,
 on the Divine attributes 218
 on Divine and human intelligence 241

INDEX.

	PAGE
Spinoza—*continued.*	
his conception of God	246
Spurgeon, Mr.,	
his preaching	317
Stephen, Mr. Leslie,	
on transcendental moralists	18
Strauss, Herr,	
his *New Life of Jesus*	310
Suarez,	
on the moral law	19, 20
Teresa, St.,	
on ecstasy	287
Trinity,	
the Christian doctrine of	217, 297–309
Tyndall, Professor,	
on cause and physical science	214
on Atheists and certain Theists	245
on popular theology	246
on "the error of the priests"	291
Ultimate Reality, the,	
see Chapters IV. and V., *passim*	
Unknowable, The,	
Mr. Herbert Spencer's doctrine of	145–155
Voltaire,	
on dogmatic Atheism	37
his life philosophy	104
on final causes	210
on a certain cowherd	220
Will,	
the only known primary cause of force	231
and Reason	232
World, the,	
what it means in the New Testament	33